Rubens to Sickert: The Study of Drawing

Rubens to Sickert: The Study of Drawing

24 April – 7 August 2021

Edited by Naomi Lebens

Published for the exhibition held from 24 April – 7 August 2021
at Reading Museum, Blagrave Street, Reading, RG1 1QH.

IBSN 978–0–902702–03–5

Catalogue edited by Naomi Lebens.

Catalogue designed and typeset by Charlotte Prince, student in the Department of Typography & Graphic Communication, University of Reading.

Front cover designed by Studio Noon.

Cover image: John Thomas Young Gilroy (1898–1985), James Anthony Betts as Art Editor from *The Royal College of Art Student Magazine*, Vol.2 No. 7 (December 1923), p.19. © Estate of John Thomas Young Gilroy, courtesy of The Royal College of Art Archive

Printed and bound by Gomer Press.

University of Reading
Art Fund_
Garfield Weston Foundation
Supported using public funding by ARTS COUNCIL ENGLAND
MUSEUMS PARTNERSHIP READING

Contents

Acknowledgements

This exhibition project and catalogue has been the work of several people. Gracie Maddison, my Undergraduate Research Opportunity Placement student was the most capable assistant I could have asked for. The dossier and chronology she compiled made writing this catalogue a much smoother process than it might otherwise have been. My thanks also go to Charlotte Prince from the Department of Typography & Graphic Communication's Real Jobs Scheme, who designed this catalogue. I am grateful to Martin Andrews, Rob Banham and Paul Davies who have kindly offered help and advice to myself and the students throughout this process. Rick Scorza, Elizabeth Sobczynski, Hannah Higham, Anna Gruetzner Robins, Catherine Whistler, Colin Harrison, Caroline Palmer, Angelamaria Aceto, Hugo Chapman and Martin Clayton have provided invaluable support as I have navigated the eclectic Betts Collection. Special thanks also go to Nigel Pilkington, University of Reading alumnus and long-time supporter of the collection, for his generous assistance with conservation. Sue Hourigan, paper conservator and trouble-shooter extraordinaire, has made it possible to get the work on the walls, and has patiently provided me with every detail I have, belatedly, remembered to ask for. Laura Bennetto is responsible for the photography, and Clare Plascow for almost every other detail. Elaine Blake has managed everything equally wonderfully on the Reading Museum side.

Bringing together the University and Reading Museum Collection with loans from national collections was made possible with a grant from the Weston Loan Programme with Art Fund. We are also grateful for funding from Arts Council England via their National Portfolio

Organisation programme and the University of Reading Visual Arts Strategy. I would like to thank Sophie Szynaka, Beth Hughes, Laura Peterle, Theodora Georgiou and Neil Parkinson for their assistance in arranging key loans. I have also been fortunate to meet several private collectors who have lent their support and works from their collections to the exhibition. It would not be possible to name every former student of Betts, but I was overwhelmed by their generosity in sharing their recollections and surviving work. Anthony Harris, Michael Twyman and Clive Ashwin have all contributed works to the exhibition, and Clive Ashwin has also generously contributed to this catalogue.

Finally, thank you Dan, for being my editor-in-chief and supporting me in all things.

Foreword

When I came to the University of Reading in the early 1980s, the very fine University Drawings Collection, which had been largely formed by Anthony Betts, Professor of Fine Art, was stored in a basement on the London Road campus. After the History of Art Department moved to Whiteknights campus, the collection was easily available for teaching and study. With the closure of the Department, it moved again to the Museum of English Rural Life. I have missed the pleasure of looking at these wonderful drawings with students, and the interested public, and it is gratifying to know that provision has been made in the collection's new home for a designated study room.

With the help of donations from former students, Betts' own collection was acquired from his son in 1994. It was clear that the collection as a whole needed the serious attention of a conservator. Thanks to a generous donation from Patricia Cornwall, the Sickert drawings were sent to conservation in 2002 while Nigel Pilkington provided the means to conserve another three drawings in 2014. When further research proved that one of them was a Rubens, the discovery received national coverage.

Dr Naomi Lebens points out in her excellent essay that Betts was heavily influenced in his teaching by Walter Richard Sickert, particularly after the University awarded one of Britain's most distinguished artists an honorary doctorate in 1938. The Betts Collection also shows a debt to Sickert, not only because it includes one of the most important Sickert drawing collections in a British institution but because Betts acquired modern drawings together with Old Master drawings. Sickert depicted modern subjects and used modern techniques but he believed that artists should use the art of the past as a touchstone, not because he thought they should copy this art, but because they should be "the interpreters of the Old Masters".[1]

Betts' admiration for Degas and Sickert, and the collection of drawings that he formed, reflects a wider belief that can be traced back to Sickert, about the making of art, which a host of major artists including Frank Auerbach, Francis Bacon, and Lucian Freud, shared. It is gratifying to know that Betts' place within this British tradition has been recognised.

Anna Gruetzner Robins
Professor Emerita in History of Art

1 Walter Sickert, "The Polish Rider", *New Age*; cited in Anna Gruetzner Robins, *Walter Sickert: The Complete Writings on Art,* (Oxford, 2000), p.249

Introduction: James Anthony Betts and the Study of Drawing

Naomi Lebens

James Anthony Betts (1897–1980) oversaw the School of Art at the University of Reading for 30 years from 1933–1963. Amongst the most important legacies of his tenure is the collection of drawings he amassed in the 1950s.[1] These drawings illuminate Betts' approach as an artist and educator and highlight the value he placed on drawing as the cornerstone of pedagogic practice.

Betts' approach to drawing over the course of his career, and in relation to wider trends in modern British art schools, is the subject of this exhibition. Showcasing a little-known University collection and the career of its collector-professor, it offers a window into the teaching and appreciation of drawing during a period of significant change.[2]

This introduction provides a brief overview of the Betts Collection (a) before looking at the beginning of Betts' career and his postgraduate studies at the Royal College of Art (b). The novel drawing practices he was introduced to at Underwood's Brook Green School are the subject of (c), whilst (d) considers how he put these into practice during his first teaching appointments in Sheffield and Kingston. Betts' move to Reading, and his wholesale reform of the School of Art, are discussed in (e). The central role of drawing, and the commanding influence of Sickert's methods in Reading, are introduced in (f). Finally, (g) shows how drastically things changed after Betts retired in the early 1960s.

(a) The Betts Collection: Old Masters, Modern Masters and the Body

The Betts Collection is eclectic, biographical, and intimately related to the social and educational aspirations of its collector. There is no record of the decision to purchase drawings for the University. However, Betts allocated departmental budgets to this purpose from 1953–1961. The available funds were insufficient to acquire a comprehensive teaching collection of the most celebrated masters, yet Betts regularly frequented up-market London dealerships and carefully selected drawings from their wider stock. His purpose is evident in the first group of seven works he acquired from H.M. Calmann in June 1953 **(cats.1–7)**. These include a highly finished pen and ink *Lucretia* by Jost Amman (1539–1591) **(cat.1) (fig.1)**; a *St Catherine and the Philosophers* then attributed to Jacopo Salimbeni, (1324–1420), now given to Flaminio (1587–1683) or Francesco Allegrini (1615/20–after 1679) **(cat.4) (fig.2)**; and a black chalk sketchbook study attributed to Eugène Delacroix (1798–1863) **(cat.6) (fig.3)**. The range of styles, media and types of drawing indicate that Betts was looking to demonstrate the different forms and functions of drawing; from independent works of art, to experimental sketchbook sheets, to complex compositional studies. He was also selecting works that could serve as representatives of the key qualities associated with important schools and movements. It is likely that Betts intended the collection to support the History of Art courses he had introduced as part of the degree and diploma courses at Reading, which at the time were taught by the celebrated Warburg Renaissance scholar Leopold D. Ettlinger (1913–1989).

The most notable Old Master represented in the Betts Collection is Peter Paul Rubens (1577–1640). The celebrated Flemish artist-cum-diplomat worked for the greatest courts of Europe, where his art served

Fig.1 Jost Amman (1539–1591), *Lucretia*, ink, UAC/10548.
Fig.2 attributed to Flaminio Allegrini (1587–1683) or Francesco Allegrini (1615/20 –after 1679), *St Catherine and the Philosophers,* ink and wash, UAC/10540.
Fig.3 c19th French School, formerly attributed to Eugène Delacroix (1798–1863), *Study of a Head and Bandaged Arm*, chalk and pencil, UAC/10543.

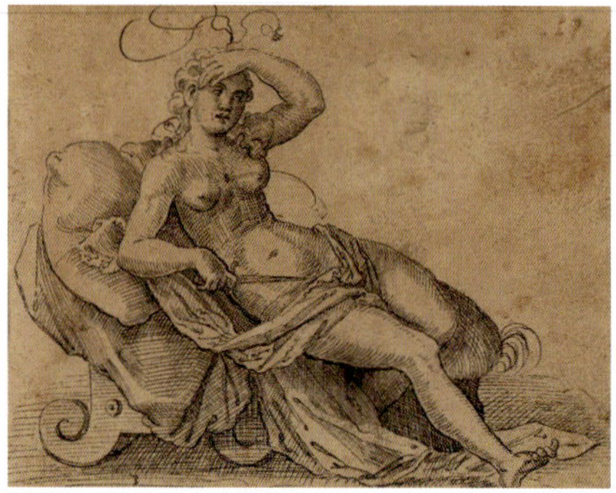

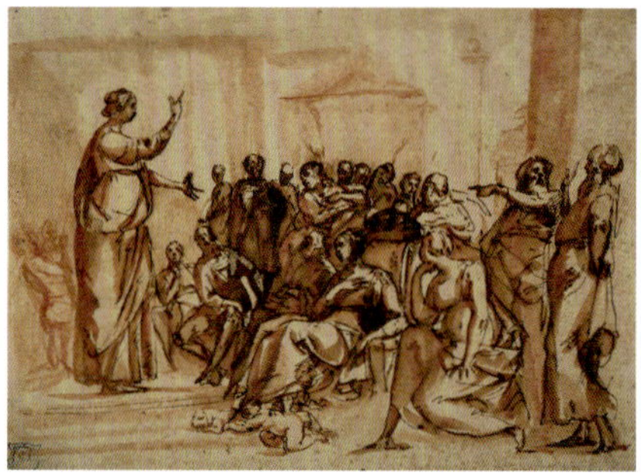

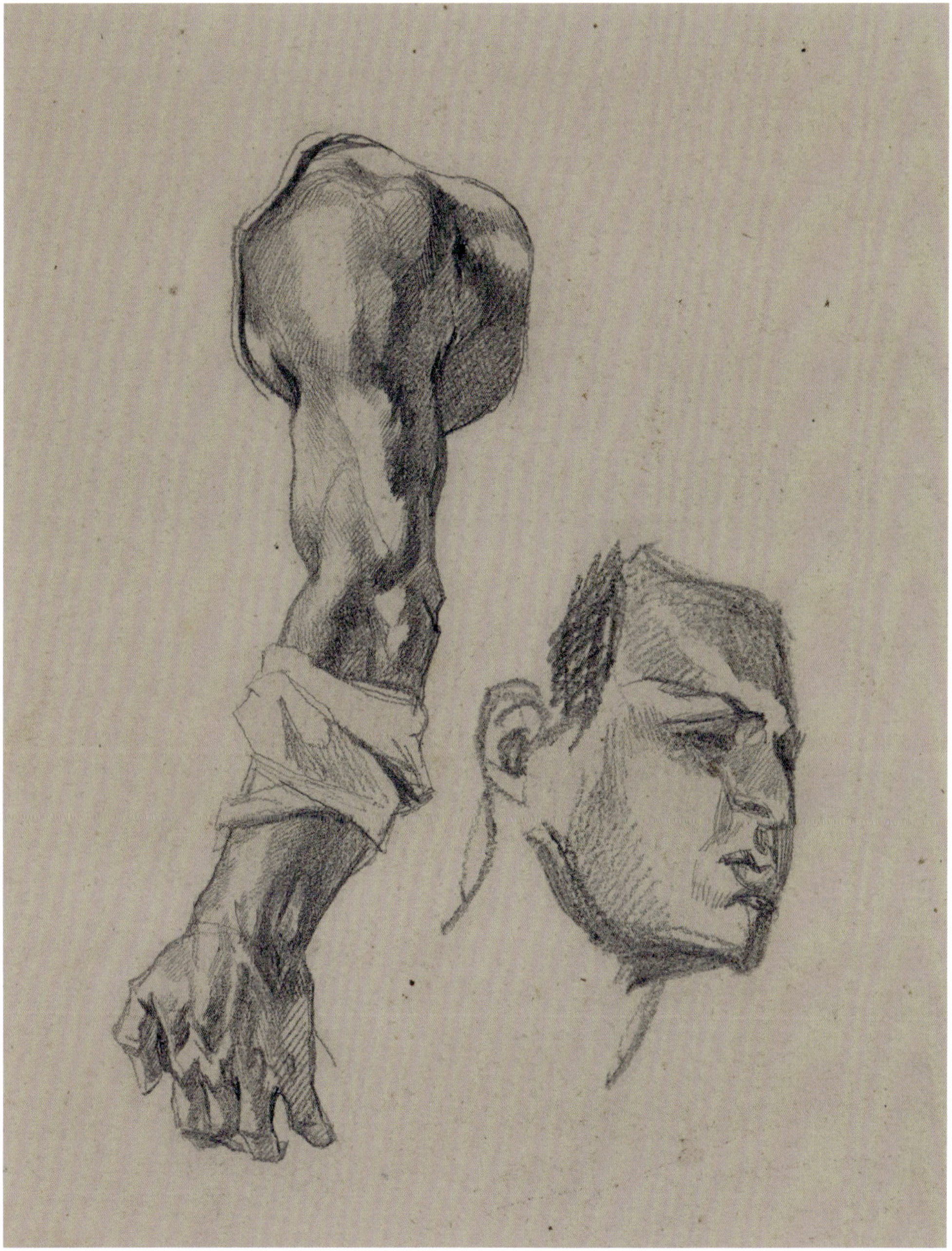

the most powerful rulers. In 1621, the French Queen Marie de' Medici commissioned Rubens to paint a cycle of monumental paintings that would re-cast her turbulent regency and difficult relationship with her son in a more positive light. It is to this series that the University's small *Portrait sketch of Marie de' Medici* is connected **(cat.14) (fig.4)**. A subtle drawing which appears to be a work from life, it captures the Queen with a soft expression with detail focused around the eyes and mouth. It is more intimate and informal than the few other surviving drawn portraits connected to the series.[3] Certainly it is less flattering, which further suggests it was intended for Rubens' personal use. The same expression and pose is used in the finished painting *The Meeting of Marie de' Medici and Henri IV at Lyon* (1621–1625), where Marie is cast as the modest new wife, head demurely bowed in the presence of her husband.[4] Recorded as an anonymous gift to the University in 1954, donated via a friend of Betts, the drawing was conserved in 2013.[5] This revealed the stamp of renowned eighteenth-century collector, Jonathan Richardson (1667–1745).

When faced with budgetary constraints, Betts expressed the belief that one should acquire "the old masters of the future".[6] The Betts Collection is, therefore, strongest in modern, and especially modern British, drawing.[7] He purchased works by more established artists when he could, for instance James Abbott McNeil Whistler's (1834–1903) late pen and ink sketch of his brother-in-law *The Fellow Traveller (Portrait of Ronald Philip)* **(cat.28) (fig.5)**. However, among the interesting prospects he identified for the Reading collection was the Welsh-born nobleman Count Albert de Belleroche (1864–1944). Belleroche grew up in impressionist circles in Paris and was a friend and contemporary of Henri Toulouse-Lautrec (1864–1901). A portrait study of Lautrec comprises one of five sketchbook pages documenting regular visits to the Moulin Rouge that Betts acquired from the artist's son in 1956

Fig.4 Peter Paul Rubens (1577–1640), *Portrait sketch of Marie de' Medici*, *c.*1622, chalk, UAC/10539.
Fig.5 James Abbott McNeill Whistler (1834–1903), *The Fellow Traveller (Study of Ronald Murray Phillip)*, 1900–1901, ink, UAC/10519.

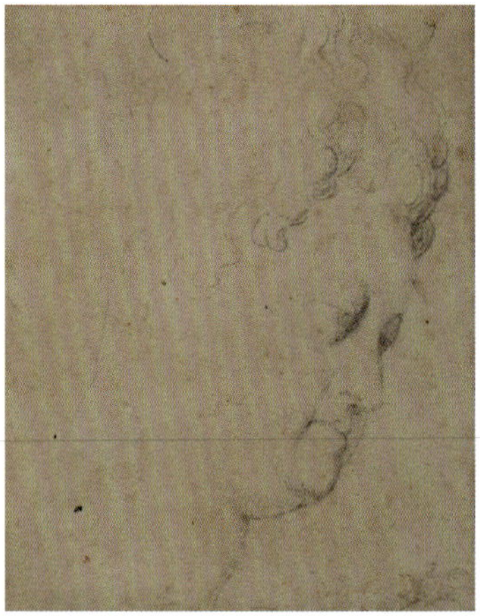

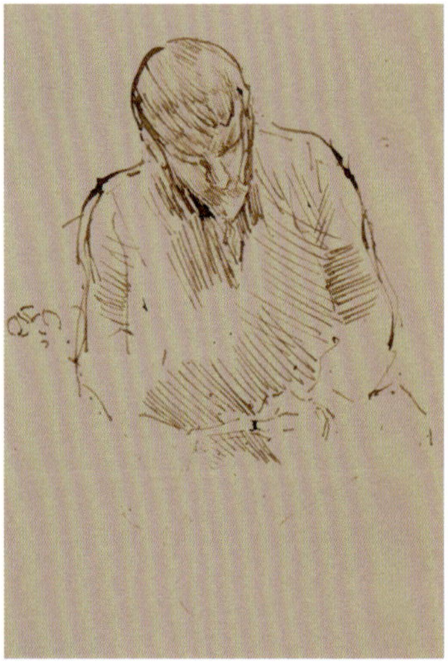

(**cats.21–25**) (**fig.6**). Jean-Louis Forain (1852–1931), an artist of a similar pedigree, is represented in the Betts Collection by two satirical drawings of a military officer and a man in formal attire (**cats.26–27**) (**fig.7**). Both evidence Forains' celebrated ability to capture characteristic social types, achieving maximum expressive effect with an economy of line, but their appeal to Betts was probably also connected to their provenance. The drawings had belonged to the collection of Ambroise Vollard (1866–1939), Paris' foremost dealer of twentieth-century French art, who had been a mentor and patron of Forain along with Paul Cézanne (1839–1906), Pablo Picasso (1881–1973) and many other notable artists.

Other works in the collection had a more personal appeal to Betts, like the *Nude Study* by Barnett Freedman (1901–1958) (**cat.33**) (**fig.8**), which he acquired directly from the artist. The drawing shows a shift away from the idealized body types, clean contours and careful shading of traditional academic studies of the nude, but its inclusion in the collection is almost certainly due to the personal relationship between the artists. Freedman had studied alongside Betts at the Royal College of Art (RCA) in the 1920s. Whilst not illustrated here, the only prints in the Betts Collection were also by Betts' fellow RCA student, Edward Bawden (1903–1989), and Edwin La Dell (1914–1970). La Dell studied at Sheffield College of Art under Betts before going on to the RCA. Both went on to build reputations as celebrated artists and designers.[8]

Landscape subjects are lacking in the Betts Collection. There are seven and, as a group, they again demonstrate great variety. The most modern and strikingly different is *Suburban Gardens* by Victor Pasmore (1908–1998) (**cat.18**) (**fig.9**), a preparatory pen and ink study for a painting.[9] Beyond the solid contour of the horizon line, the composition is almost entirely made up of dots and dashes in a pointillist style, marking the beginnings of Pasmore's experimentation with

Fig.6 Albert de Belleroche (1864–1944), *Study from the Montparnasse Sketchbook: Portrait of Henri de Toulouse-Lautrec*, chalk, UAC/10550.

Fig.7 Jean-Louis Forain (1852–1931), *Military Officer*, ink, UAC/10581.

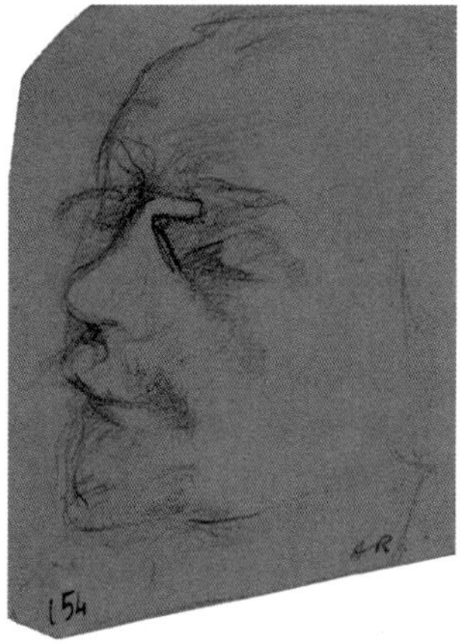

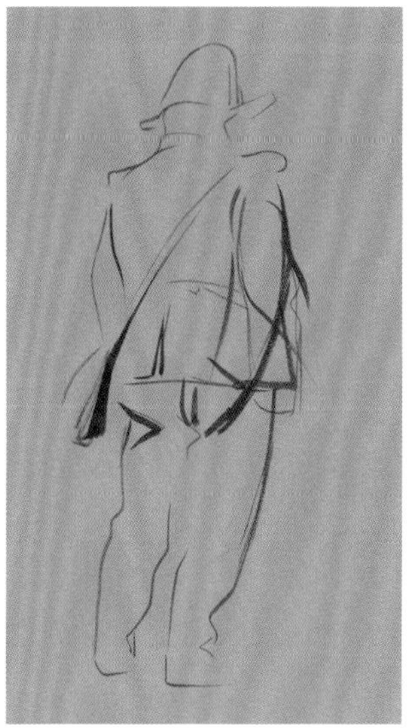

Fig.8 Barnett Freedman (1901–1958), *Standing Female Nude*, 1929, ink and wash over pencil, UAC/10546 © Estate of Barnett Freedman.
Fig.9 Edwin John Victor Pasmore (1908–1998), *River Landscape (Drawing for 'Suburban Gardens')*, *c.*1947, ink, UAC/10571 © Estate of Victor Pasmore. All Rights Reserved, DACS 2020.
Fig.10 Edwin John Victor Pasmore (1908–1998), *Portrait of William Coldstream*, charcoal, UAC/10570 © Estate of Victor Pasmore. All Rights Reserved, DACS 2020.

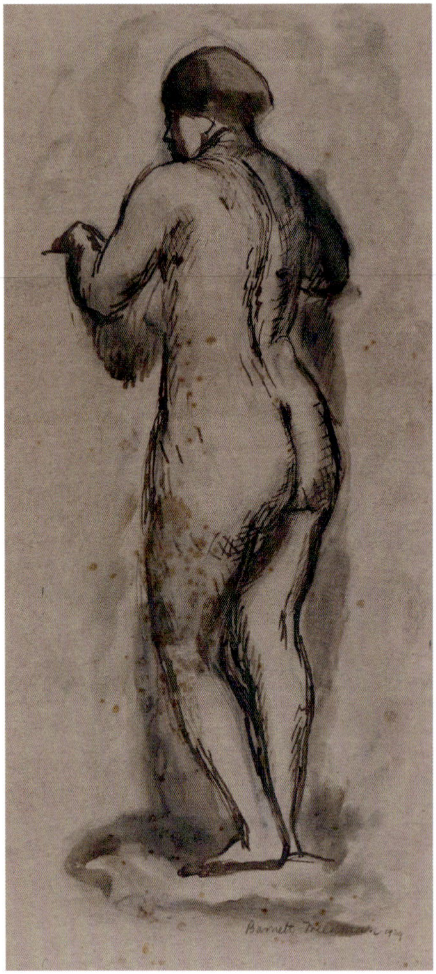

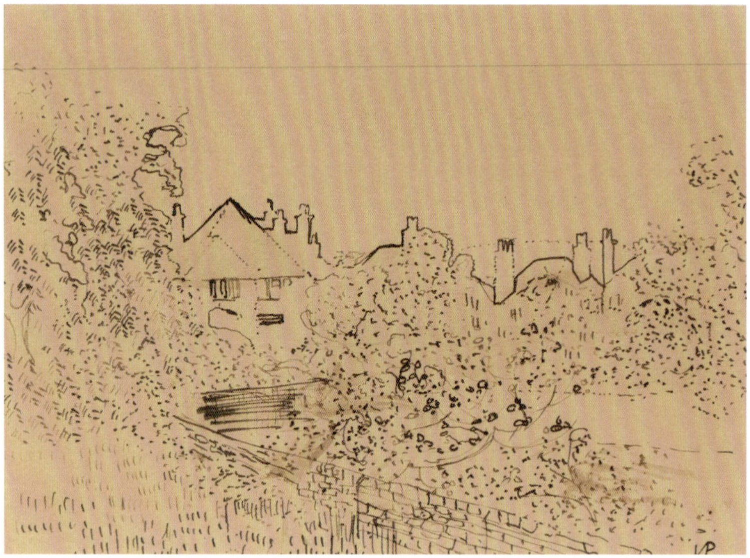

abstraction.[10] Previously, his work had been purely figurative with a strong emphasis on observation. Together with William Coldstream (1908–1987) and Claude Rogers (1907–1979), he had founded a school in opposition to the trend for avant-garde abstraction, known as the Euston Road School.[11] It promoted accessible subjects drawn accurately from everyday life and taught a system of drawing based on careful measurement. This element of Pasmore's practice is also evidenced in the Betts Collection. Appropriately, his *Portrait of William Coldstream* (**cat.31**) (**fig.10**) shows the sitter engrossed in the act of drawing. Dots and intersecting planes, used for points of reference, are visible throughout the study, including along Coldstream's lapels and through the top of his head.

Betts never relinquished his attachment to observational drawing, nor to the human body as the principal training ground for artists. This explains the emphasis placed on the figure in the Betts Collection. Together with its collector, the focus on the human body is its single most unifying characteristic. The specific approach Betts took at Reading to teaching *how* the body should be drawn is also reflected in the work of Walter Richard Sickert (1860–1942) (**cats.56–59, 65–69**) and, to a lesser extent, the wider Camden Town Group. The Betts Collection comprises 18 Sickert drawings, all except one figurative, together with drawings by Walter Bayes (1869–1956) (**cats.54–55**), Frederick Spencer Gore (1878–1914) (**cats.63–64**) (**fig.11**) and, their collective source of inspiration, the prolific *Punch* illustrator Charles Keene (1823–1891) (**cats.60–62**). *Marie Seated on a Bed* (**cat.58**) (**fig.12**) was the very first drawing that Betts purchased for the University after the group of Old Masters from Calmann, demonstrating the commanding influence Sickert was to assume in relation to the wider collection.

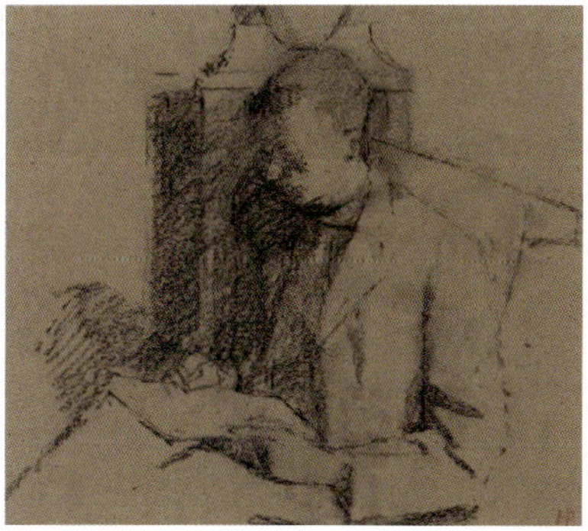

Sickert was a well-respected artist who had been at the centre of debates about art and education for decades prior to his death in 1942.

Fig.11 Spencer Frederick Gore (1878–1914), *Ballet at the Alhambra*, pastel, UAC/10566.

Fig.12 Walter Richard Sickert (1860–1942), *Marie Seated on a Bed*, 1911–1912, pencil, chalk and white heightening on grey paper, UAC/10536.

Fig.13 James Anthony Betts at Bradford School of Art, Photo courtesy of Betts' Family Archive.

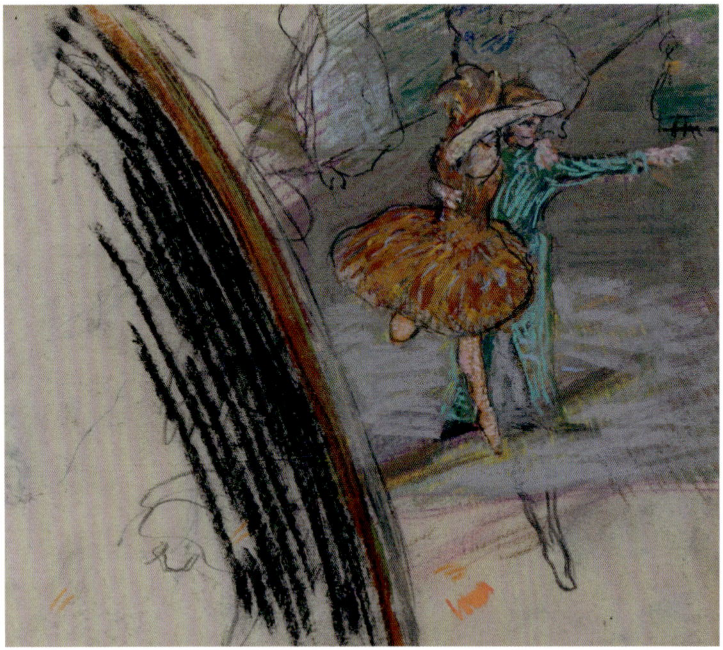

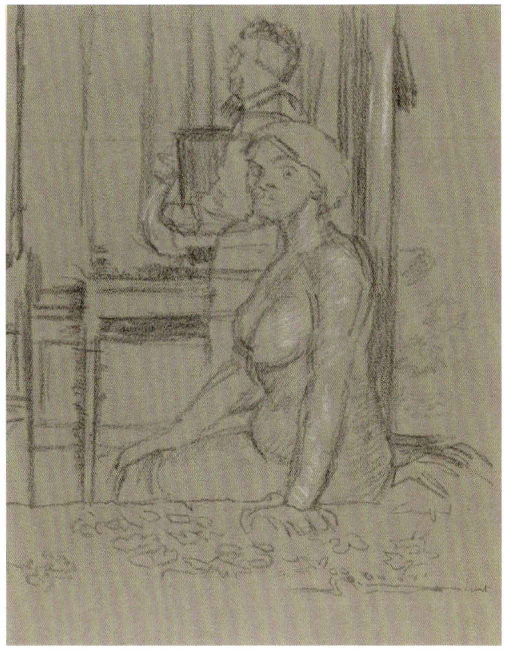

Betts' admiration of his work was not just a matter of personal taste – it was a statement of allegiance to a kind of pedagogy. As Pasmore's example shows, observational drawing was rapidly being abandoned in favour of abstraction by the 1950s. How Betts navigated this trend, amidst the competing influences that buffeted modern British art schools over the course of his career, will now be explored.

(b) The Professor as Student

Born in Skipton, Yorkshire on 28 December 1897, Betts came of age during the First World War. The details of his early life are sparse. After attending St Stephen's School in Skipton it appears he joined is railway foreman father, James Betts (b.1867), working as a goods clerk on the Midland Railway during the war. Meeting Eleanor (Nellie) Flexen (1887–1967), who taught art at Skipton High School from 1917, was key to his future career.[12] A talented artist, who graduated from Bath School of Art before attending the RCA in London from 1913–1917, Flexen had a significant impact on Betts both personally and professionally. He attended her evening classes at Skipton, and she encouraged him to attend Bradford School of Art. On a personal level, they fell in love and were married in 1923.

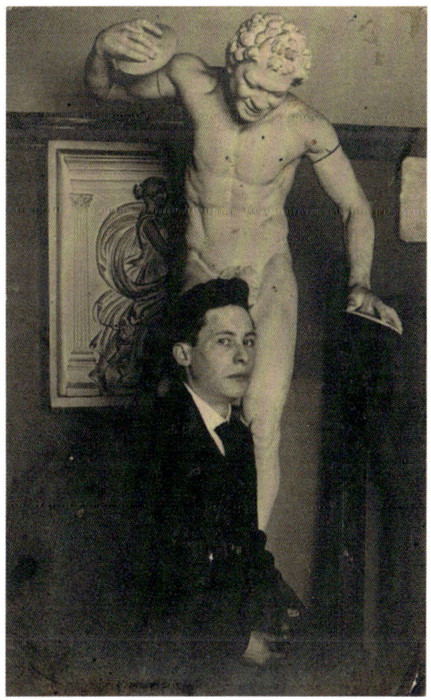

A photograph of Betts at Bradford School of Art shows him in front of a classical relief and an antique sculpture known as the Dancing Faun (**fig.13**). Drawing "from the antique" was still, as it had been for centuries, a key foundation of the typical British art school curriculum and Betts would have spent hours producing studies after casts like these. Such drawings formed part of a portfolio of work which qualified the best students to apply to the prestigious postgraduate fine art schools in London. Betts went on to attend the RCA, where he won a place on a special scholarship in 1921. As was increasingly the trend, the RCA placed a growing emphasis on its students working directly from life. Those wanting to be considered for acceptance to the School of Drawing and Painting were required to submit three drawings of the nude from life in addition to six "careful" drawings demonstrating their wider practice. They would be tested further on their life drawing skills at interview, when they would be asked to draw a head and a nude from a model.[13]

The Principal William Rothenstein (1872–1945), a successful professional painter, arrived at the RCA the year before Betts in 1920. He disagreed with the prevailing system at the College where would be art teachers were trained in the theory of teaching. Rather, he thought that teaching should be done by "distinguished young artists, designers and craftsmen" and transformed the RCA into an "active school for artists", in particular by developing the School of Drawing and Painting.[14] The central role of the figure, drawn from life, within this programme is evident in the 1925/26 school prospectus:

> The aim of this School is to develop in the student, *through the study of the human figure*, a sense of design, and form; to this end all students of the School are expected to devote a considerable part of their time to Drawing from the Life, and any student, if the Professor thinks fit, may be required to postpone or interrupt his study of Painting in order to concentrate upon attaining the necessary standard of draughtsmanship.[15]

At the RCA, Betts studied alongside ambitious young artists across different years and schools.[16] He was an active presence in the Student Common Room, where he made a name through his contributions to the Student Magazine. He acted as the Art Editor under Douglas Percy Bliss (1900–1984) for the editions published in December 1923 and June 1924.[17] In the December edition, he is caricatured twice. First, by Bawden, in the editorial, where Betts' approach on "the copy hunt" is described by Bliss as that of "an Empson and a Dudley in one" (**fig.14**).[18] Second, a stand-alone caricature by John Thomas Young Gilroy (1898–1985) on page 19 (**fig.15**). A comic response to his determined zeal, Betts stands astride the rim of a broad-brimmed black hat (which would remain one of the defining features of his appearance for decades to come), his cigarette drooping from his mouth below a handle-bar moustache, as he points his finger into the air and admonishes his fellow students: "Don't forget the Drawings for the next issue". A well-known character, Betts' affectations were again the source of gentle ribbing in the June issue. Imagining a future Royal Academy exhibition in 1950 entitled "When the Fauves Grow Old", this included a piece by one "Sir J.A. Betts PRA" (President of the Royal Academy) of a "Femme nue tricotant une Camisole" (Female nude knitting a vest).[19] He responded in kind in the student magazine *The Mandrake* (1926), edited by Cecilia Dunbar Kilburn (1903–1984), in which he submitted his own caricature of a formidable-looking Dunbar Kilburn, hands on hips, a disembodied eye by her waist and a modernist, featureless sculpture at her feet (**fig.16**).[20]

The July 1926 RCA graduation photo shows Betts standing in the back row, towards the middle of the right side, directly behind Randolph Schwabe (1885–1948) (**fig.17**). Betts had worked as an assistant instructor in life drawing for Schwabe since 1924. Schwabe would go on to be a professor, then Principal, at the Slade and was renowned as a meticulous, academic draughtsman. The students imagined an advert for him in their June 1924 magazine, which described him as "Le Boucher de Notre Temps – has never been out of a life class since early youth – literally lives in 'Life'".[21] As Schwabe's chosen assistant, Betts' approach must have been compatible.[22] A few seats to the left of Schwabe, sits Henry

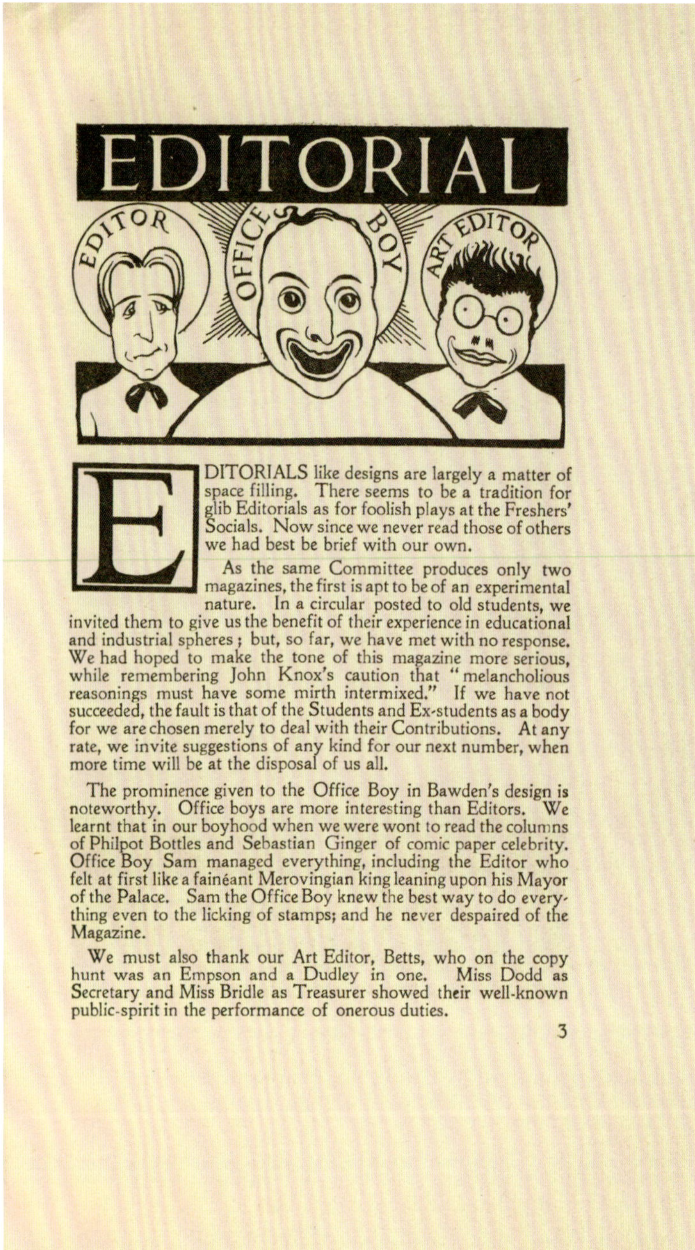

EDITORIAL

EDITORIALS like designs are largely a matter of space filling. There seems to be a tradition for glib Editorials as for foolish plays at the Freshers' Socials. Now since we never read those of others we had best be brief with our own.

As the same Committee produces only two magazines, the first is apt to be of an experimental nature. In a circular posted to old students, we invited them to give us the benefit of their experience in educational and industrial spheres; but, so far, we have met with no response. We had hoped to make the tone of this magazine more serious, while remembering John Knox's caution that "melancholious reasonings must have some mirth intermixed." If we have not succeeded, the fault is that of the Students and Ex-students as a body for we are chosen merely to deal with their Contributions. At any rate, we invite suggestions of any kind for our next number, when more time will be at the disposal of us all.

The prominence given to the Office Boy in Bawden's design is noteworthy. Office boys are more interesting than Editors. We learnt that in our boyhood when we were wont to read the columns of Philpot Bottles and Sebastian Ginger of comic paper celebrity. Office Boy Sam managed everything, including the Editor who felt at first like a fainéant Merovingian king leaning upon his Mayor of the Palace. Sam the Office Boy knew the best way to do everything even to the licking of stamps; and he never despaired of the Magazine.

We must also thank our Art Editor, Betts, who on the copy hunt was an Empson and a Dudley in one. Miss Dodd as Secretary and Miss Bridle as Treasurer showed their well-known public-spirit in the performance of onerous duties.

3

Fig.14 Edward Bawden (1903–1989), *The Editorial Board* from *The Royal College of Art Student Magazine*, Vol.2 No. 7 (December 1923), p.1 © Estate of Edward Bawden, courtesy of The Royal College of Art Archive

Fig.15 John Thomas Young Gilroy (1898–1985), *Betts as Art Editor* from *The Royal College of Art Student Magazine*, Vol.2 No. 7 (December 1923), p.19. © Estate of John Thomas Young Gilroy, courtesy of The Royal College of Art Archive

Fig.16 James Anthony Betts (1897–1980), *The Editor* (Cecilia Dunbar Kilburn) from *The Mandrake* (May 1926), p.30. © Estate of J. Anthony Betts, courtesy of The Royal College of Art Archive

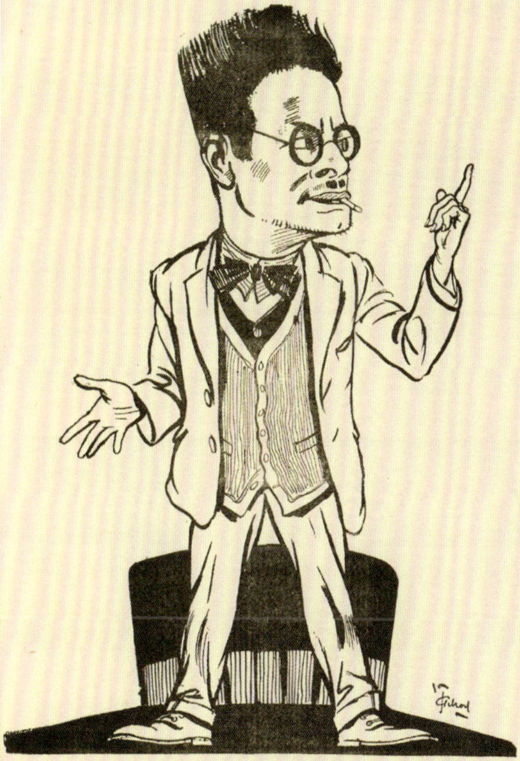

Don't forget the Drawings for the next issue. 19

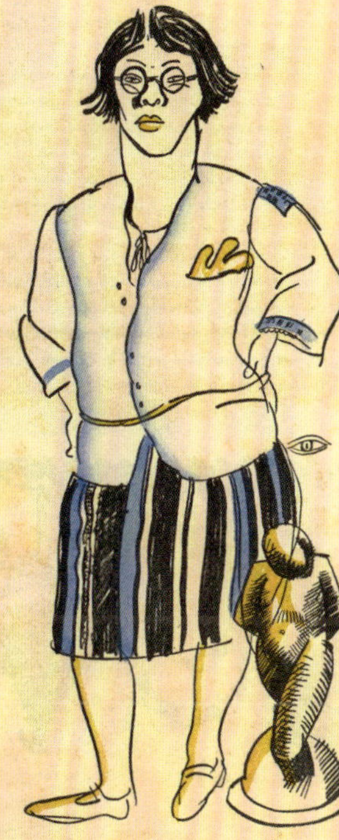

THE EDITOR BY BETTS

30

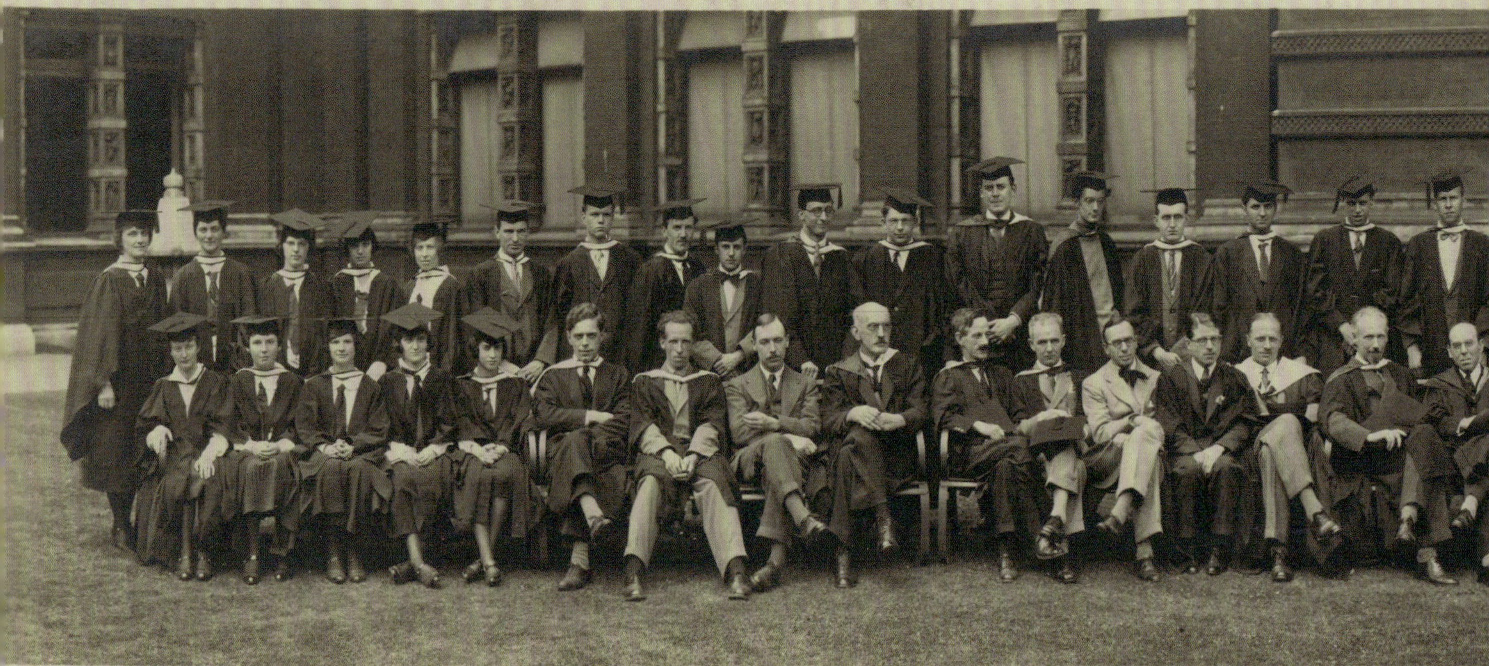

ROYAL COLLEGE OF ART, SO

JULY, 1926.

A.Marsh. A.McAdoo. E.Turner. G.Graham. K.Soane. D.McIntyre. R.Keevil. H.Dow. H.Parker. J.Tucker. F.Spear. J.Hunt. D.Towner. O.Camp. J.Ososky. J.Fairhurst. B.Twinn.
E.Morris. P.Ellingford. V.Wheeler. M.Perris. L.Parker. E.Dinkel. R.Capey. A.Gwynne-Jones. E.Alston. Prof. E.Tristram. F.Richards. W.Murray. H.Harding. Prof. J.Worthington. Prof. W.Rothe
H.L.Wellington.

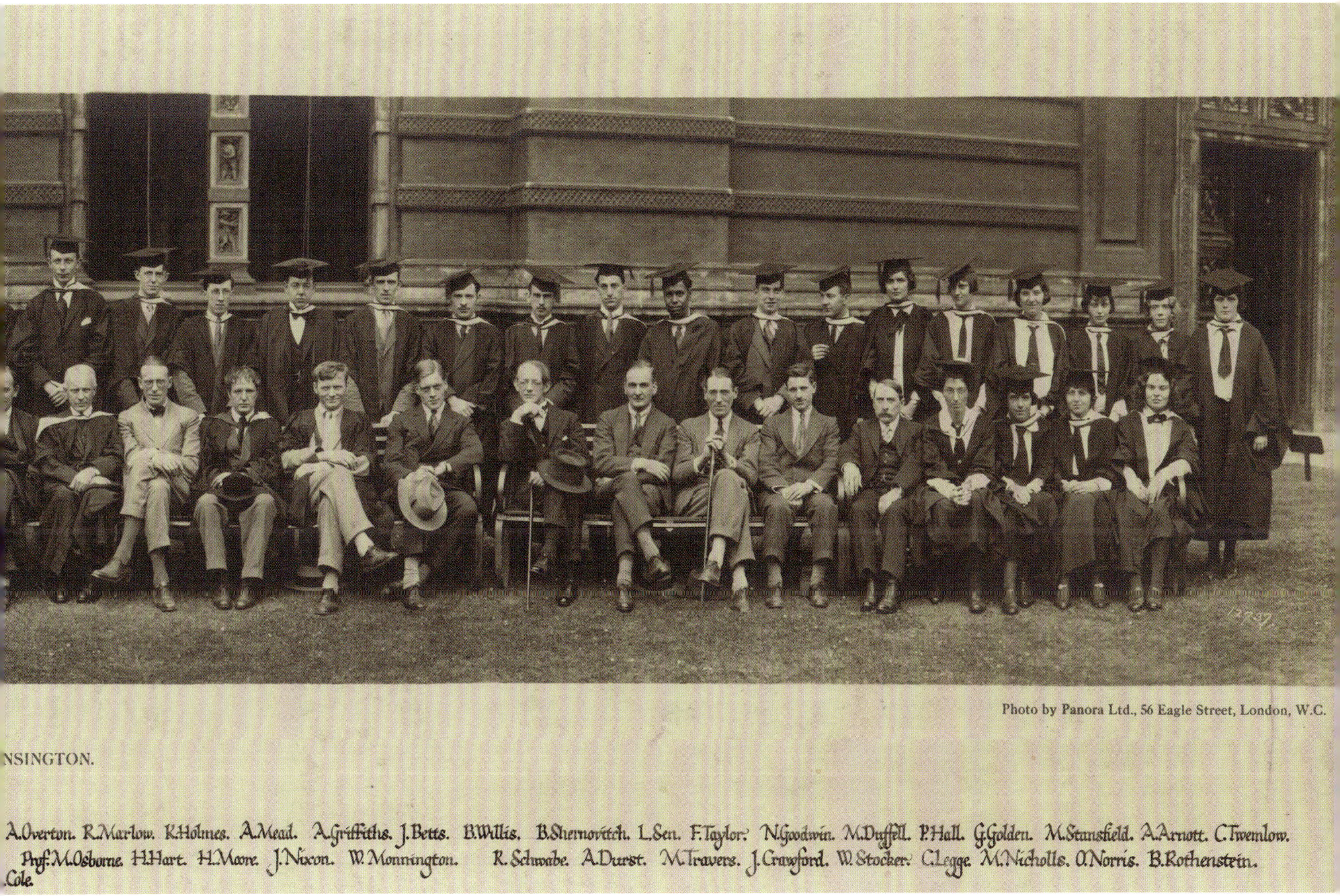

Fig.17 RCA Convocation Ceremony Photograph, June 1926, Courtesy of The Royal College of Art Archive.

Moore (1898–1986). A contemporary of Betts at the RCA, Moore had followed the three-year sculpture course from 1921–1924 before returning to take up a position as a part-time sculpture tutor at the College in 1925.

Drawing was equally important to sculpture students and Moore's sketching practice is evident in his *Drawing of Anthony Betts at the R.C.A.* (1924) **(cat.49)** **(fig.18)**. He captures Betts sitting hunched over in an expression of intense, inward concentration in which you can see the serious, driven character caricatured in the Student Magazine. An abbreviated outline of the same figure, upside down, its shapes and features simplified and exaggerated, gives a nod to the more experimental forms of the sculpture Moore was already exhibiting. However, this is still very much a realistic study. With areas of shade and graduating tones used to build depth and volume, it displays a fairly traditional approach to drawing the figure.

Fig.18 Henry Moore (1898-1986), *Anthony Betts at the R.C.A*, 1924, pencil and chalk, The Henry Moore Foundation. Reproduced by permission of The Henry Moore Foundation. Photo: Nigel Moore

Fig.19 Leon Underwood in his Studio, Private Collection © Estate of Leon Underwood.

Fig.20 Leon Underwood (1890–1975), *Standing Nude*, 1924, conté crayon with white heightening, Private Collection © Estate of Leon Underwood.

(c) Modern Form: Drawing from the RCA to the Brook Green School

The RCA was not dominated by a single manner of drawing during Betts' and Moore's studies. Whereas Schwabe was characterised as the French eighteenth-century Rococo artist François Boucher (1703–1770), in a nod to his prolific draughtsmanship, academicism and the elegant use of red chalk, Rothenstein was deemed the "Holbein of today".[23] Like the sixteenth-century German Renaissance portraitist Hans Holbein the Younger (1497–1543), he emphasized accuracy, clean lines and contour, admiring the work of the French Neoclassical artist Jean-Auguste-Dominique Ingres (1780–1867).

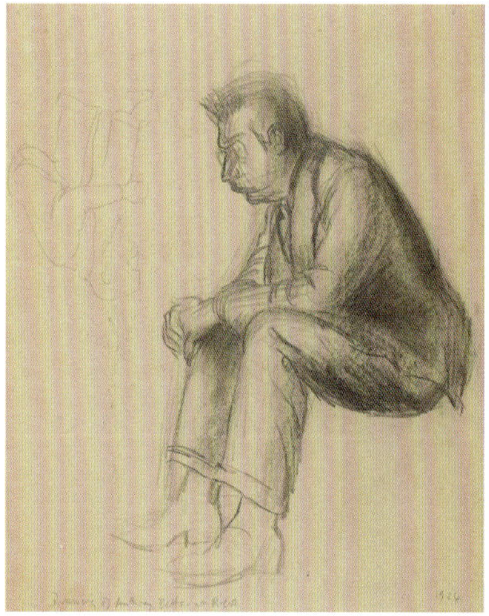

Both approaches were antithetical to the other noteworthy RCA tutor at the time, Leon Underwood (1890–1975) **(fig.19)**. In the Student

Magazine, Underwood was "advertised" as: "The modern Michelangelo – expert in Solid Form – special tuition in cylinders – no Japaneries – occidental solidity insisted upon".[24] Underwood encouraged an experimental approach to drawing, "Form" was his motto and students were directed to think about volume, mass and movement, and to abandon the laborious practice of laying down careful contours and building solidity through meticulous shading.[25] Instead, they were encouraged to work quickly and expressively, building the up the figure from its constituent parts. An illustrative example of Underwood's own life drawing, showing how he expressed weight and motion by drawing contours within the body's outline, is *Standing Nude* (1924) (**cat.42**) (**fig.20**). Unsurprisingly, this divergence caused tensions among the tutors, especially as Rothenstein had the habit of intervening in Underwood's classes. Ultimately, it led to Underwood's resignation (written on a piece of toilet paper) following a final interruption in 1923 when Rothenstein directed students to draw a bundle of foliage he had found.[26]

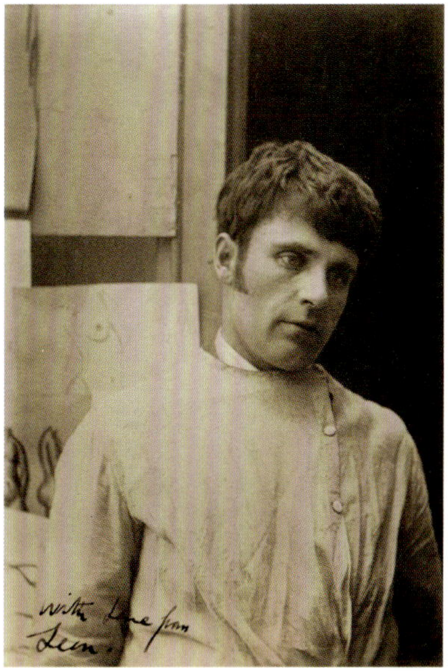

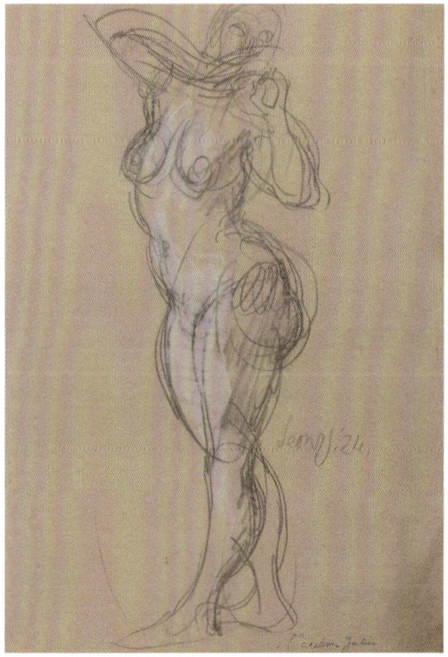

Betts was no pure disciple of Schwabe or Rothenstein. In fact, he numbered among a select group of RCA painting and sculpture students who lobbied Underwood to continue teaching them in evening classes at the Brook Green School of Drawing.[27] The School had been established in Underwood's home and studio in Girdlers Road, Hammersmith in 1921 and was attended by notable students including Blair Hughes-Stanton (1902–1981), Gertrude Hermes (1901–1983) and Eileen Agar (1899–1991) (**fig.21**). Among those from the RCA who joined in 1923 were Betts, Moore, Raymond Coxon (1896–1997), Barbara Hepworth (1903–1975) and Enid Marx (1902–1998).[28] Underwood had agreed to continue teaching the RCA students in exchange for their best drawings and two-and-sixpence per week.[29] Life drawing was the only subject strictly on the syllabus. However, as Betts' early efforts show, they also collectively experimented with printmaking, and especially wood

Fig.21 Leon Underwood (1890–1975), *Students at the Brook Green School* (Reproduction), 1923, Private Collection © Estate of Leon Underwood.
Fig.22 Life Model at the Brook Green School, Private Collection © Estate of Leon Underwood.

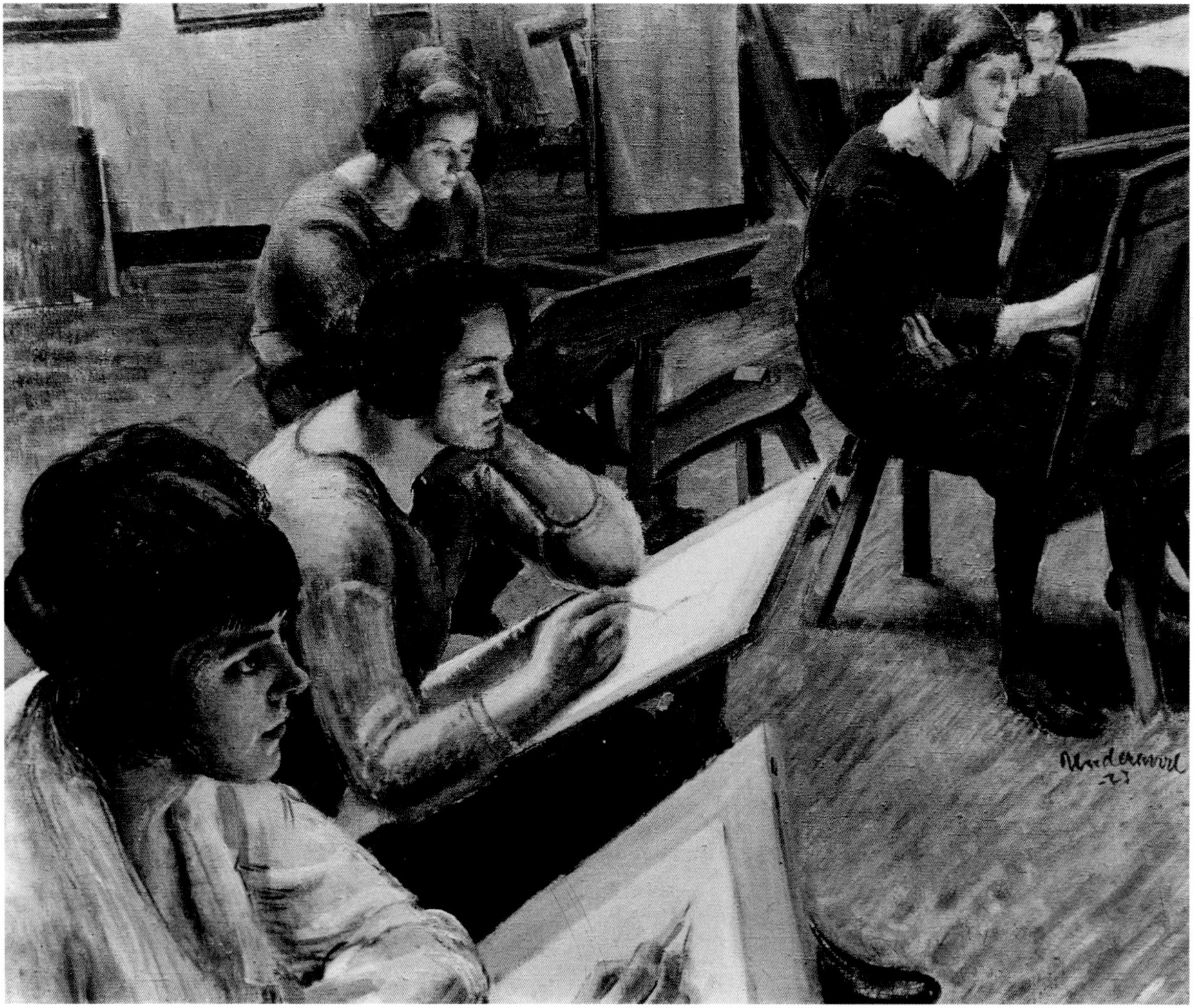

engraving, for which many of the Brook Green alumni became well recognised (**cat.51**).[30]

Underwood had an unorthodox teaching style, rarely speaking, but rather scrawling phrases on the wall, drawing on the edges of students' work, and even drawing directly onto models' bodies with lipstick, to divide them into sections (**fig.22**).[31] The group would sketch quickly, sometimes trying to capture the body in motion. Underwood destroyed most of the student work he was given. However, Betts was an exception, having been singled out amongst the Brook Green students along with Hughes-Stanton for his draughtsmanship by the then Keeper of Prints and Drawings at the British Museum, Campbell Dodgson (1867–1948).[32] Betts' *Reclining Figure* (**cat.47**) (**fig.23**) was swiftly donated to the British Museum by Underwood, via Dodgson and the Contemporary Art Society, in 1927. Dodgson later donated Hughes-Stanton's *Standing Female Nude* (*c.*1924) (**cat.46**) (**fig.24**) to the British Museum in 1940, noting that it was drawn at Brook Green. The drawing shows the influence of Underwood's collection of African sculpture, which was the other defining feature of the Girdlers Road studio.[33] With its broad, flat features and the spherical, weighted quality of its torso and thighs, Moore's *Reclining Figure* (1924) (**cat. 48**) (**fig. 25**) is another study that shows the clear influence of Underwood's teaching. Moore later remarked that Underwood "was the only teacher I ever learned anything from in a useful way".[34]

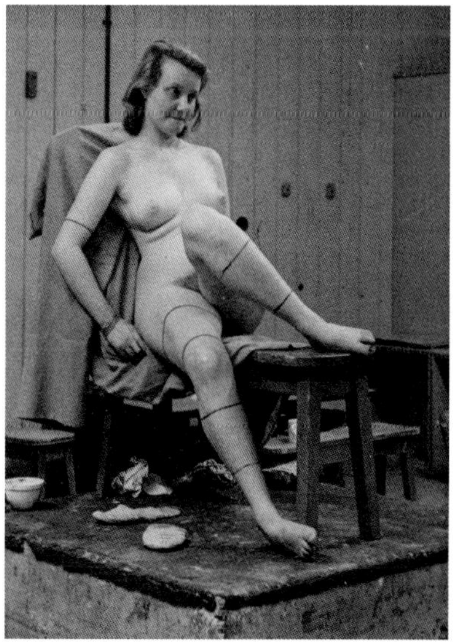

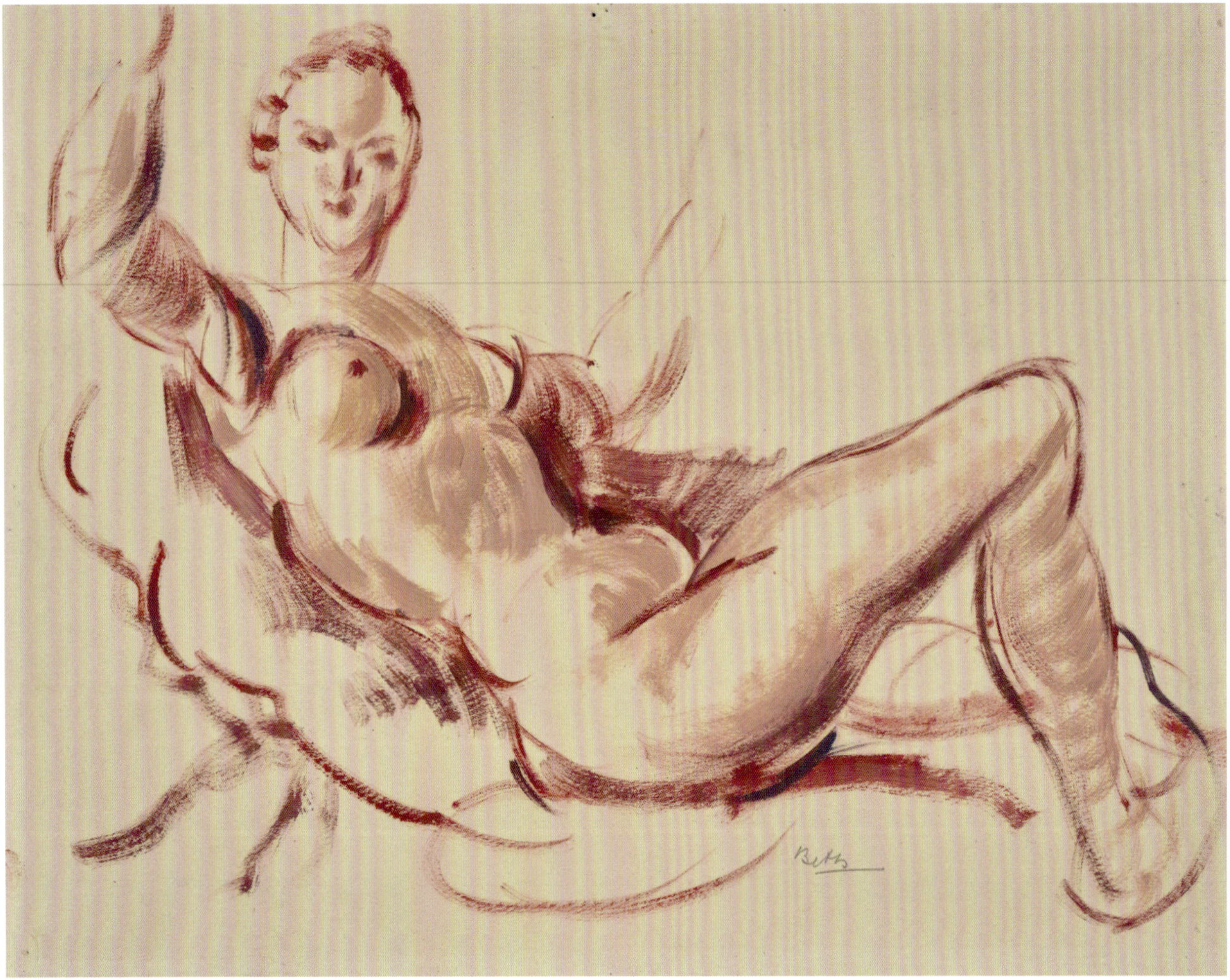

Fig.23 James Anthony Betts (1897–1980), *Reclining Nude*, bodycolour, British Museum © Estate of J. Anthony Betts ©The Trustees of the British Museum.

Fig.24 Blair Hughes-Stanton (1902–1981), *Standing Female Nude*, *c.*1924, chalk, British Museum © Estate of Blair Hughes-Stanton. ©The Trustees of the British Museum.

Fig.25 Henry Moore (1898–1986), *Reclining Nude*, 1924, pencil, gouache and wash, British Museum. Reproduced by permission of the Henry Moore Foundation ©The Trustees of the British Museum.

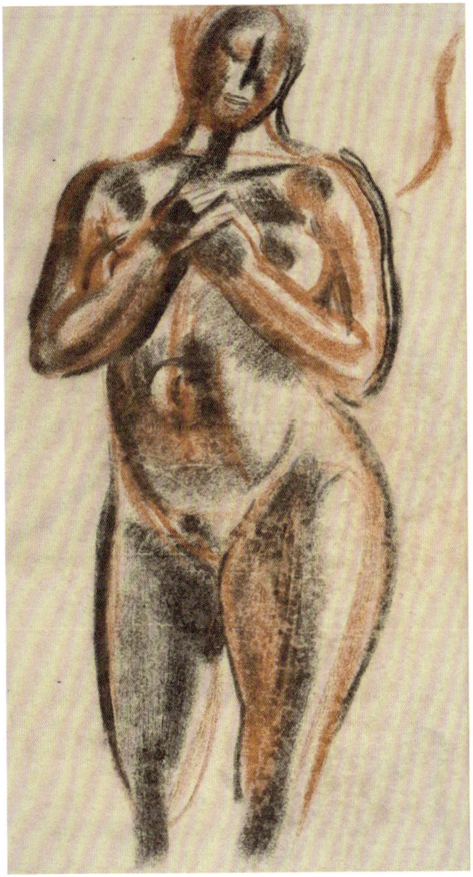

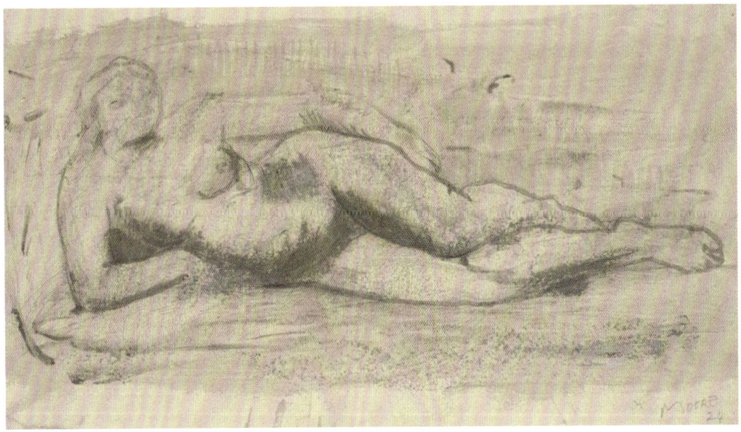

(d) Sheffield and Kingston

At the RCA, Betts had been exposed to shifting attitudes towards life drawing. Whilst still at the centre of British art education in the 1920s, tensions around the role and way in which life drawing should be taught continued to rise over the following decades. A combination of Underwood's experimental teaching and Rothenstein's ambitions for his students meant that Betts emerged from his RCA Diploma as a contemporary artist who wanted to be part of this process of change (**fig.26**). This became evident when he was appointed to his first teaching position in June 1926, as Assistant Teacher of Painting at the City of Sheffield Technical School of Art (renamed The Sheffield College of Arts and Crafts in November 1926).

Joining the Drawing and Painting Department alongside the notable Sheffield artist Henry George Hoyland (1895–1947), Betts took on most of the teaching in the life room as well as instruction in lithography and etching (the two most draughtsman-like printmaking techniques). By June the following year, he was given a rise of £24 and made responsible for all the advanced students in draughtsmanship with painting. His classes were so oversubscribed, he was given an assistant.[35]
The College appointed a new principal in October 1928, another RCA graduate, John E. Sunderland (1895–1956), who was previously Head of Rochester School of Art. Sunderland proposed a broad re-organization of the College aimed at improving the skills of students undertaking courses in the industrial arts, such as painting and decorating.
In contrast, the instruction on the fine art side was praised for the high standard of drawing, painting and general draughtsmanship. Betts was commended to the Education Committee for having "proved his worth" and promoted to Head of the Drawing and Painting Department.[36]

Taking to heart Rothenstein's message that professional artists made the best teachers, Betts also began exhibiting his work, focusing mainly on drawing. Continuing in the mould-breaking model of Underwood and the "London Group", drawings like *Study for the Head of a Soldier* (*c.*1929) **(cat.39)** **(fig.27)**, exhibited at the Mappin Gallery in 1929, and *Baby Betts* (*c.*1929–1930) **(cat.36)** eschew contour and use sparing areas of shade to build geometric form.[37] With stylized, angular shapes echoing the modernist portrait drawings of Wyndham Lewis (1882–1957), *Head of a Solider* was deemed like a "male robot" by one local critic.[38] Another was slightly more generous, given that:

> [Betts] favours a convention of rectangular forms, which he handles with unmistakable power, and though one may take leave to doubt whether he gains anything by his purposeful distortions of nature, his right to be a law unto himself cannot be denied.[39]

Betts was roundly criticized for "exclud[ing] beauty from his work", doing his utmost "to bring out the ugly side of art".[40] He regularly invited locals in from the streets in order to draw them **(cat.37)** **(fig.28)**, but his compositions, such as those featuring local steel grinders' families, were condemned as bearing little relation to Sheffield life.[41] His nudes, which were exhibited in Sheffield before being shown at the Cooling Galleries in London in 1933, were particularly controversial **(cat.40)** **(fig.29)**.[42] Repeatedly described as resembling "figures hewn out of blocks of wood",[43] Betts defended his work as "creative art" and the nude as "the basis of all good drawing".[44] He was likely recalling Underwood's instruction in solidity and form. In 1931, after leaving Sheffield, Betts was interviewed for the Sheffield Daily Independent in his office in Kingston. The reporter found him surrounded by nudes, and he declared: "I believe in drawing the nude because that is the real training ground for the artist. In the human figure you get more

Fig.26 James Anthony Betts *c.*1925–1930, Photo courtesy of Betts' Family Archive.

Fig.27 James Anthony Betts (1897–1980), *Study for the Head of a Soldier*, *c.*1929, pencil, UAC/10852 © Estate of J. Anthony Betts.

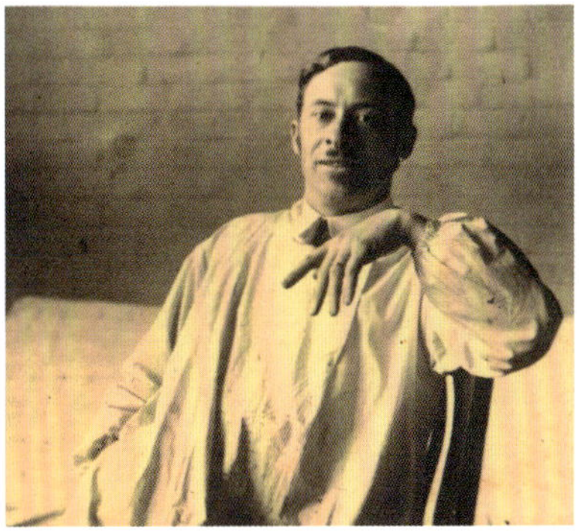

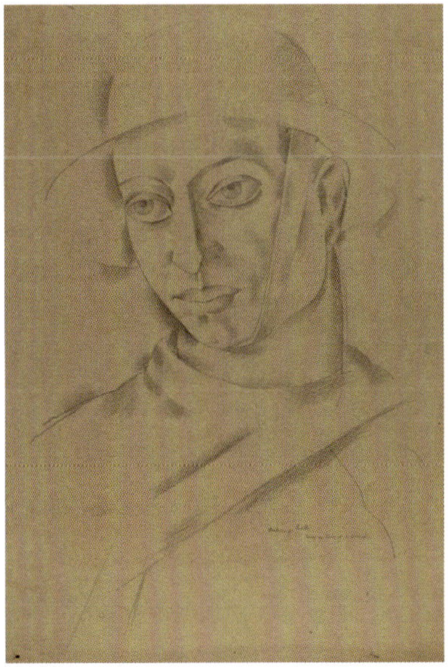

Fig.28 James Anthony Betts (1897–1980), *Man Sitting on a Bar Stool*, 1927, ink, Reading Museum © Estate of J. Anthony Betts.

Fig.29 James Anthony Betts (1897–1980), *Standing Female Nude*, *c.*1928, watercolour, bodycolour, ink, charcoal, UAC/10853 © Estate of J. Anthony Betts.

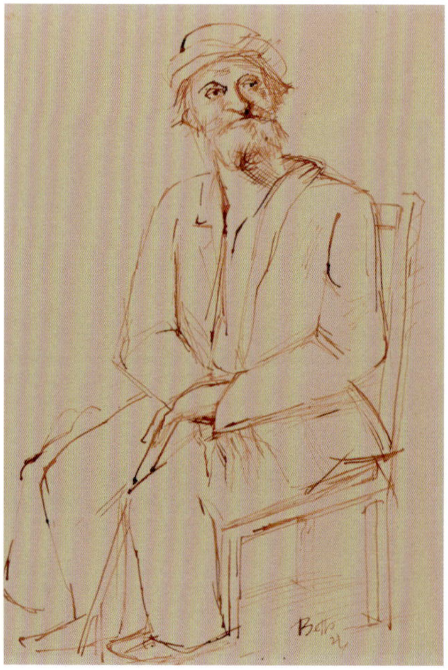

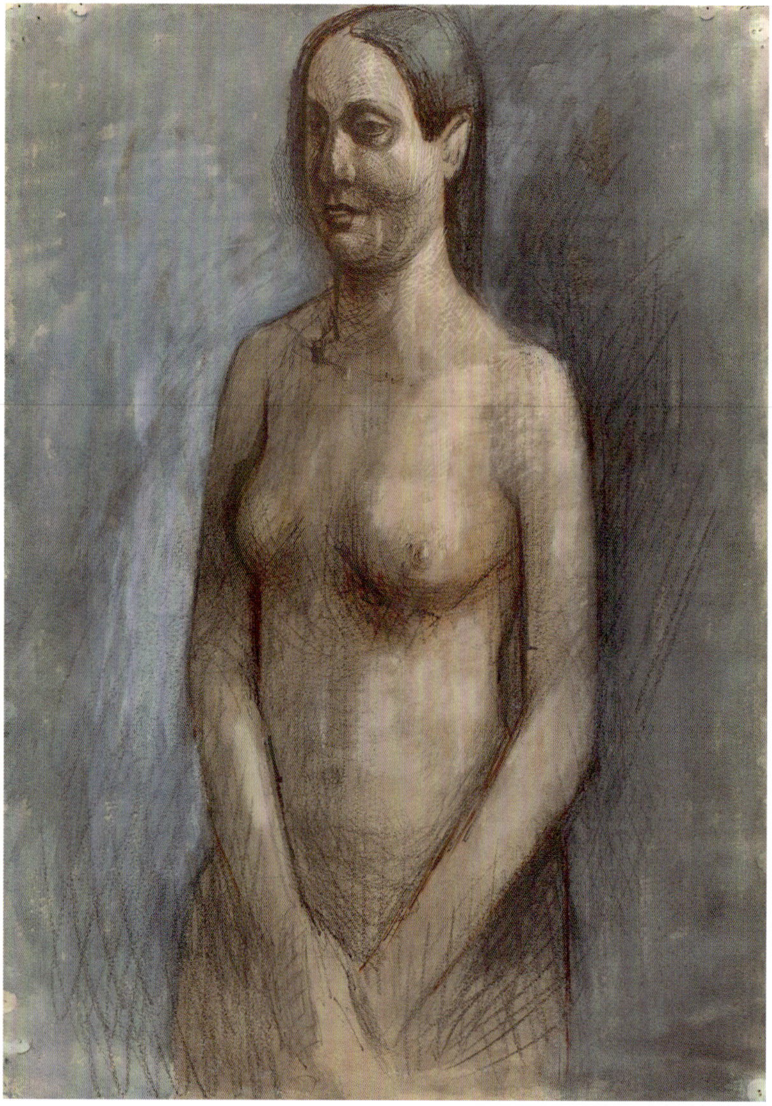

subtleties of line and figure than in anything else".[45] Showing the reporter a large drawing of a nude woman and child, he asked "What would Sheffield say to that?"[46]

Sheffield galleries, and their approach to their collections, was another source of tension between Betts and the local art establishment. He accused the Mappin Gallery of "absurd Victorianism" made worse by the fact that it lacked work by any eminent English artists of the period. In lieu of the money to invest in Old Masters, he lobbied for them to acquire works by contemporary artists, and suggested that drawings should be purchased if paintings were too expensive.[47] Reflecting with indignation in 1931 that a drawing by contemporary English sculptor Eric Gill (1882–1940) was rejected by the Mappin committee, he remarked that there were "no morals in art".[48] Betts maintained an unwavering belief in the power of art and believed that municipal galleries had a duty to educate and foster an aesthetic culture. He was somewhat mollified when John Rothenstein, William's son, assumed the role of director of Sheffield Galleries in 1934.[49] However, by that point, Betts had left the city.

Not a great deal can be uncovered about Betts' short tenure at Kingston School of Art, where he assumed the role of Headteacher of the College of Art in October 1930. This is likely due to a comparative lack of public controversy. In the Sheffield Daily Independent article of 1931, Betts' residual bad feeling towards the city was clear. Kingston was declared his "spiritual home" characterised by "freedom and life" whereas in Sheffield there was only "death and despair".[50] Betts' inspirational leadership at Kingston was remarked upon in The Surrey Comet where he was commended for introducing a "new and virile policy" and "quite modern" teaching techniques.[51]

(e) Reading School of Art (1933–1963)

"I do not want Reading to be just another art school" Betts is quoted as saying in "Fine Arts from the Evening Standard" in 1955.[52] He sat in his office surrounded by paintings by Degas as he explained how he looked for "intelligence plus skill" in his students, wanting them to turn out as "educated artists who can do a real job".[53] Accounting for the presence of works by the impressionist artist Edgar Degas (1834–1917) in his office, and demonstrating his commitment to ensuring the department stood out, Betts had organized an exhibition of twentieth-century French drawings in the School of Art the same year, opened by the French Ambassador. Deemed "one of the most important ever held in the town", it included works by "Degas, Picasso, Matisse, Derain, Despiau, Forain, Maillol, Renoir, Toulouse-Lautrec, and many others".[54]

A lot had changed since Betts first arrived in Reading in 1933, to a studio apparently furnished with a single kitchen chair.[55] Only seven years out of the RCA, with an intention to make a name for himself on the contemporary art scene with his "controversial" nudes, he was aware (as he later reflected) that he had arrived somewhere that his friends looked upon as an "artistic backwater".[56]

> I was very conscious of an air of leisurely inactivity in the School; the tempo (as one of my new colleagues informed me) was distinctly and happily *andante*. There was a prevailing sense of an arty-crafty attitude...The so-called Fine Arts were distinctly limited. I could not accept any of these activities being work of the kind one should expect from a University School of Fine Art and I knew that if the school were to survive, I had to change it.[57]

Eager to elevate the "enclosed community" of Reading to the status of a London Art School, Betts took a dual approach. First, he began hiring staff directly from London. This included Walter Bayes, who had previously lectured at the Royal Academy and Westminster School, and Allan Gwynne Jones (1892–1982), Betts' old RCA tutor in painting. Frank Ormrod (1896–1988), the painter, printmaker and illustrator from the Slade School of Art was employed to teach a new course in Design. This was part of Betts' second key endeavour: a mass reorganization of the syllabus. He introduced strict academic discipline – requiring fine art students to take additional courses in subjects like philosophy, languages, classics and music on top of a broad general course in sculpture, lithography, composition, painting and life drawing before specializing. Another important component was the introduction of art history, which Ettlinger was engaged to teach from 1950. Even prior to this, a series of talks and "autumn" lectures were offered by star speakers including Roger Fry (1866–1934), Anthony Blunt (1907–1983) and Ernest Gombrich (1909–2001). By 1937, the University's Faculty of Letters had recommended the introduction of a Fine Art Honours Degree, the first of its kind in the country. Betts also re-organized the Diploma course in Fine Art, intended for training art teachers, and did not neglect the so-called "industrial" arts and crafts. Together with his new appointment Robert Gibbings (1889–1958), the celebrated artist, book designer and printmaker of the Golden Cockerel Press, he introduced apprenticeships and courses in typography.[58] These were later taken over by William McCance (1894-1970) of the Gregynog Press.

Big names were also brought in via honorary doctorates. Henry Moore, who according to students Betts continued to refer to as his "friend Harry", was awarded the degree of Doctor of Letters on 10 May 1959.[59] Betts introduced him as "without doubt one of the most distinguished of living sculptors", referenced their shared youth and praised Moore's "scholarly and sensitive understanding of the great art of the past".[60] But the first honorary doctorate that Betts was involved with awarding at Reading was that of Walter Sickert in June 1938 (**fig.30**). Described as looking like a "Highland Chieftain" in the Reading Chronicle, Betts painted the 78-year-old Sickert's portrait outside the Senior Common Room on the occasion of the degree ceremony.[61] He was reported to have developed a close relationship with the artist before his death in 1942.[62] Betts spoke of the friendship frequently, as is widely recalled by his students. It had a defining influence on his teaching at Reading over the next 25 years.

(f) Reading Drawing

A dedicated teacher, Sickert both taught at and set up several art schools, and was always looking for avenues (such as published lectures, criticism and correspondence) to explain the principles behind his drawing, which he saw as fundamental to his art.[63] His primary lessons included drawing to "visual" size, meaning that you should be a sufficient distance from your subject so when you hold up your sketchbook the image on the page should cover it exactly. He taught students to sketch lines in rapidly (thus avoiding the mistakes that come from over labouring); to always see the subject and its background as part of the same design (never to sketch them separately); and to finish by adding in shadows and going over the drawing with a pencil to pick out essential parts. Crucially, nothing should ever be rubbed out.[64]

In terms of subject-matter, Sickert advocated for "truthful" images of subjects observed in everyday life. Following his friend and mentor, Degas, he was fascinated by documenting popular, urban scenes such as interiors and performers in music halls, and favoured partially obscured or back views (**cats.65–69**) (**fig.31**).[65] It was for this reason that Sickert admired the *Punch* illustrator Keene who was celebrated for his indiscriminate

Fig.30 James Anthony Betts with Walter Sickert at the University of Reading in 1938. Photo courtesy of the Betts' Family Archive.

Fig.31 Walter Richard Sickert (1860–1942), *The New Oxford Music Hall (The New Bedford)*, c.1907-1908, pencil, UAC/10522.

Fig.32 Walter Richard Sickert (1860–1942), *The Little Bed*, 1902, pencil and chalk, UAC/10520.

Fig.33 Anthony Harris (b.1931), *Man Sitting on a Bed (University of Reading School of Art)*, 1952, conté crayon on grey paper, Collection of the Artist © The Artist.

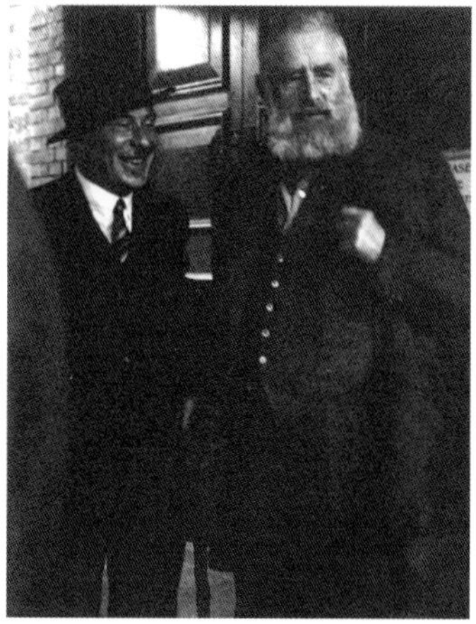

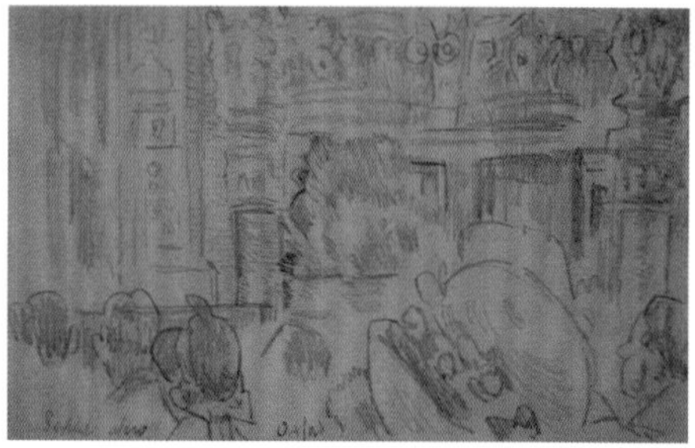

documentation of London life and its human dramas (**cats.60–62**). By 1900, Sickert had alighted on his second great subject: the female nude.[66] Typically drawn as part of a domestic environment, soft flesh is juxtaposed against hard iron bedsteads (**cat.56**) (**fig.32**), poses are natural and, often, unflattering (**cat.57**), and psychological drama is heightened, for instance, by the introduction of clothed, male models (**cat.58**) (**fig.12**).

The introduction of an iron bedstead into the life drawing classroom at Reading, illustrated in the work of Anthony Harris (b.1931), a student under Betts from 1948–1952, is a telling reference to Sickertian practices at the School (**cat.76**) (**fig.33**).[67] Back, and partially obscured, views are common among student work from this period, with attention given to the intersections of the figure and its surroundings (**cats.75–79**).

Unlike the highly finished, experimental drawings he exhibited and promoted in the 1920s and early 1930s, in Reading Betts seems to have adopted Sickert's approach entirely. Drawing became a more firmly preparatory and working practice, evidenced by the huge archive of drawings and sketchbooks he left behind from this period.

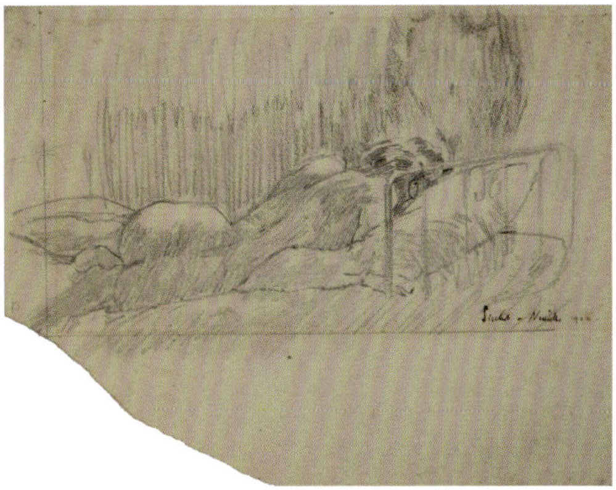

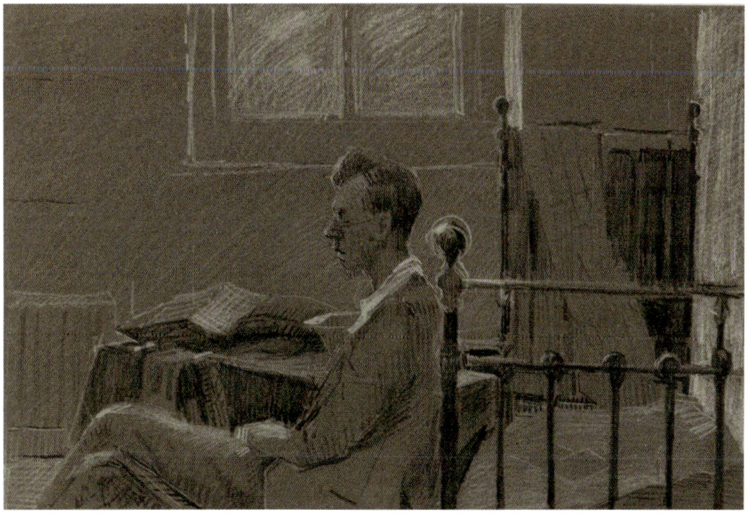

These frequently repeat the same motifs and, in another Sickertian parallel, often feature colour notes for paintings written on the page (**fig.34**). He further echoes the unfinished, sketch-like quality of much of Sickert's drawing, such as in *Standing Female Nude* (**cat.70**) (**fig.35**) where the figure seems to emerge from the scribbled walls. His intimate drawn portrait of his wife, *Nellie Flexen* (*c*.1966–1967) (**fig.36**) is among the motifs Betts repeated several times during this period. Again, it has the angular downward viewpoint, dark atmosphere and blurred boundaries between figure and background typical of Sickert's work.

In 1952, Betts engaged Harry Redman (1920–1994), a former pupil of Sickert's, as tutor in the department (**cat.72**) (**fig.37**). Redman was a disciple of Betts' and students recall similarities between their approaches in the life room. These included admonitions to look and draw what was seen, including the spaces between objects, and a pointed emphasis on the position of intersecting planes (based on Sickert's idea that all observed lines and edges had direction, like the hands of a clock).[68] Both Betts and Redman demonstrated corrections directly on the edges of students' drawings (**cats.78–79**), but Betts was notoriously protective of his work, including such corrections, and always scrupulously rubbed them out. Students reported rumours that this was to prevent their hoarding and sale in the strong market for Betts' work in Europe and the USA. However, by this stage, it seems that his exhibiting practices were far more modest, mainly consisting of pieces shown in the local guild and university exhibitions.

However, there was not complete harmony among drawing instructors at Reading. After the war, in 1946, Betts engaged Hubert Arthur Finney (1905–1991) (**cats.73–74**) (**fig.38**) as a sessional, then full-time, tutor at the School. A fellow RCA alumnus, Finney took on much of the teaching in the life room alongside Redman. Renowned for his stern critiques, but still highly respected, Finney (in echoes of Rothenstein)

Fig.34 James Anthony Betts (1897–1980), *Country Landscape,* chalk, UAC/10789 © Estate of J. Anthony Betts.

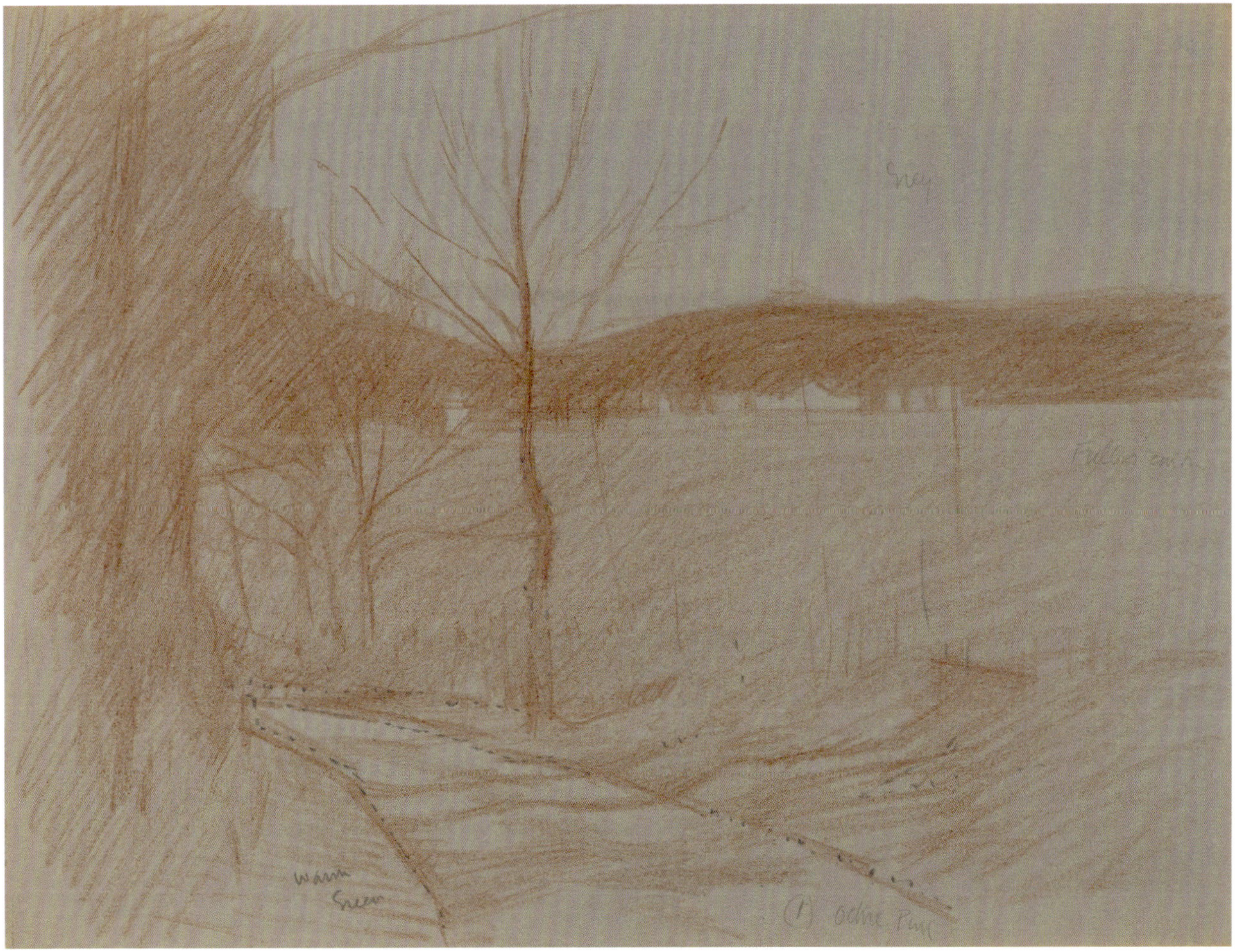

Fig.35 James Anthony Betts (1897–1980), *Standing Female Nude,* conté crayon, UAC/10779 © Estate of J. Anthony Betts.

Fig.36 James Anthony Betts (1897–1980), *Nellie Flexen*, chalk, UAC/10779 © Estate of J. Anthony Betts.

Fig.37 Harry Redman (1920–1994), *Man Sitting on a Stool*, charcoal and ink, Private Collection © Estate of Harry Redman.

Fig.38 Hugh Finney (1905–1991), *Reclining Female Nude*, conté crayon on Japanese paper, Private Collection © The Artist's Estate, Courtesy of Liss Llewellyn.

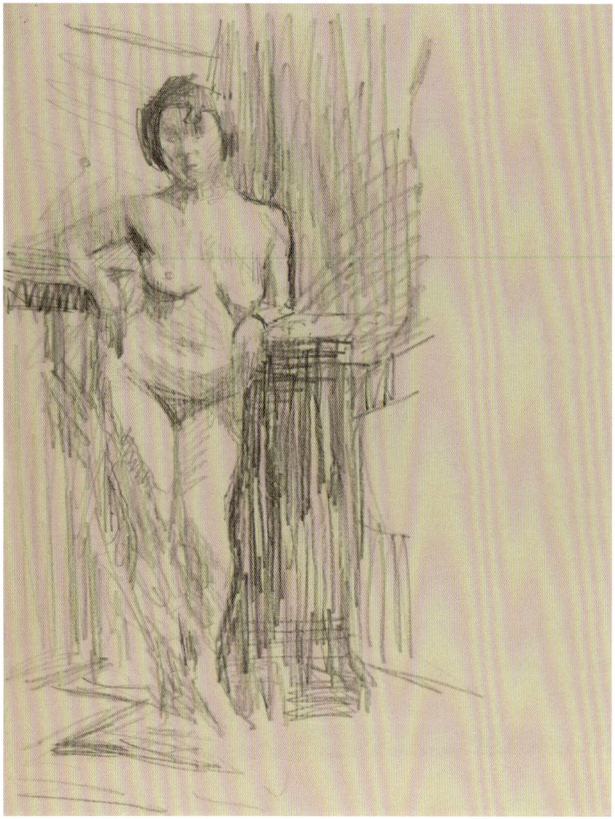

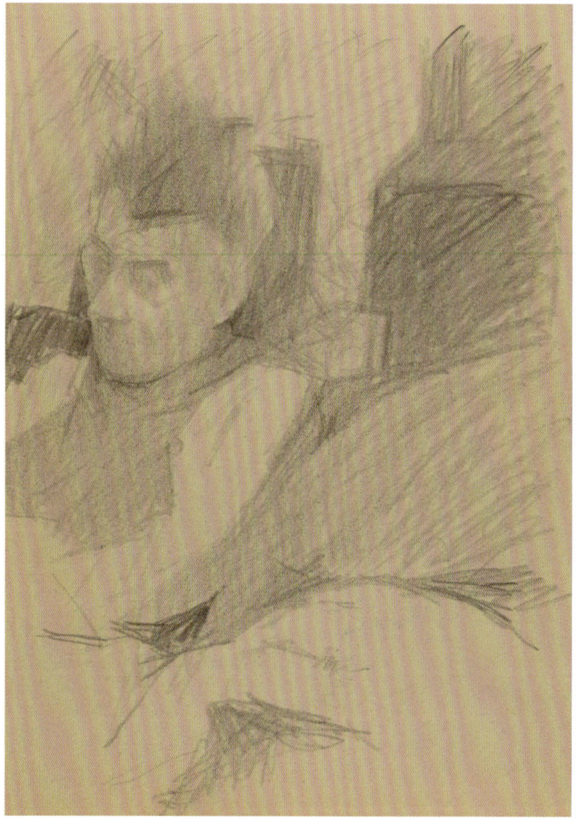

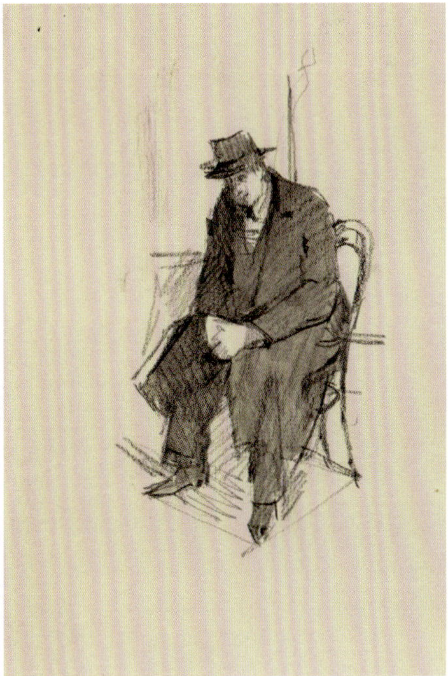

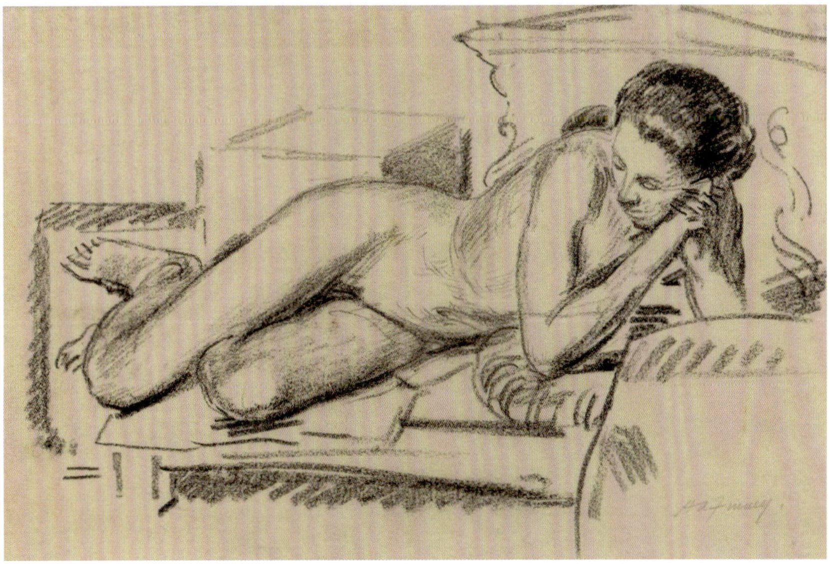

focused on the accurate study and rendering of the human body, unadorned and uncomplicated by its surroundings. One former student described him as a "draughtsman of the old school". Another reflected on a telling occasion in which Finney singled out a member of the class as being the only one capable of drawing an ear "correctly". Such ideas had far more in common with Renaissance practices in which the student learned to draw the body through the building blocks of idealized parts, than with the Sickert-inspired realism of Betts and Redman.[69]

(g) Drawing after Betts

Claude Rogers, who took over the running of the Department from Betts in 1963, had this cutting summary for the school in which he arrived:

> The teaching is limited (only last year has any abstract painting been done) – Sickerty. The syllabus and examination requirements are odd, besides being old-fashioned.[70]

Abstraction had been a growing influence in British art education for some time and elsewhere students were increasingly encouraged to experiment with line, form and colour.[71] To address this perceived gap at Reading, Rogers appointed Tom Cross (1931–2009), Roger Cook (b.1940), Rita Donagh (b.1939), and Terry Frost (1915–2003) among others, who introduced different ideas about drawing to the curriculum.

Donagh's *Life Size* (**cat.80**) (**fig.39**) is evidence of the new direction. A study for the central figure in the Tate's R*eflection on Three Weeks in May 1970* (1971), it is directly related to a period of teaching at Reading in which Donagh and her students were allocated a room and a model.[72] Instead of setting up a life-studio in the traditional manner, they decided to devise a

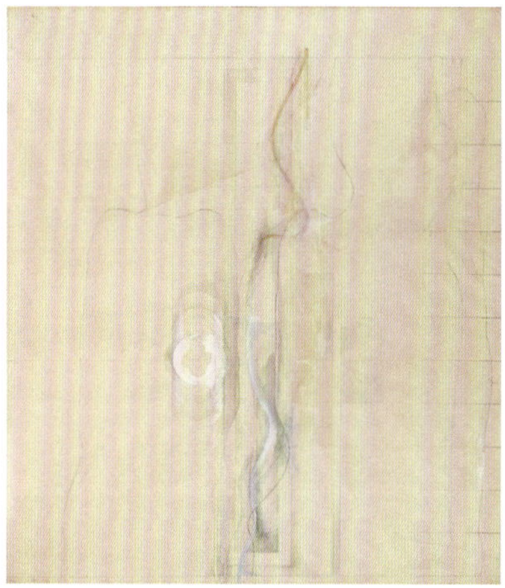

Fig.39 Rita Donagh (b. 1939), *Life Size*, 1971, pencil and watercolour, Arts Council Collection, Southbank Centre, London © Rita Donagh. All Rights Reserved, DACS 2020.

group performance as a response to the student demonstrations of 1968. They painted every surface of the studio white and drew a grid structure across the room. Crosses were marked in spaces where travel was prohibited, as a means of regulating movement within the space.[73] The following year, Donagh took nearly a year off teaching in which she worked on *Three Weeks in May* and investigated "the extent to which a painting could encompass ... multidimensional events and relationships".[74]

Conclusion

The idea that Betts was ever on the "modern" side of drawing practices in Reading was, of course, highly relative. This is apparent even when compared with the more experimental, collegiate approach of Underwood he encountered in his own education, and the "ultra-modern" work that he began exhibiting in Sheffield as a response. As the decades passed, however, Betts' vehement attachment to the Sickertian teaching model became increasingly unusual. And, whilst the reframing of drawing as an entirely autonomous and independent practice was not universally popular, it is ironic that Betts may be viewed by some as having returned Reading to the status of a "backwater" among many forward-thinking schools.

Rogers, who had been a primarily figurative artist and a keen follower of Sickert for much of his prior career, reset the course of the School in an environment where life drawing had widely lost its prominence. Another result was that responsibility for the Betts Collection, which had been so central to Betts' vision of the connection between historic and contemporary practice, passed to the History of Art department before becoming part of the main University Art Collection in 2015.

Notes

1 The surviving departmental ledger lists 24 purchases and 4 donations of 54 drawings and 3 prints which form the core of the Betts Collection. This was augmented in 1994 by the University's purchase, from the family, of 14 drawings from Betts' private collection.

2 For a comprehensive survey of changing attitudes and approaches to drawing across education and artists' practice, see Deanna Petherbridge, *The Primacy of Drawing: Histories and Theories of Practice*, (New Haven and London, 2010).

3 See examples in the Victoria and Albert Museum (D.906–1900) and the Louvre (Inv. 20224).

4 Louvre, Paris. Inv 1775.

5 After conservation, the drawing was the subject of a symposium "Rubens in Reading" held on 8 May 2013, with invited speakers Jeremy Wood and Paul Joannides.

6 "Art Critic's Choice – Suggestions for New City Gallery", *The Sheffield Daily Independent*, 10 December 1929.

7 Whilst "modern" is used here, to avoid confusion, Betts preferred the term "contemporary" for artists who lived within his own lifetime. He believed that the term "modern" (which was frequently applied to his own work) bred prejudice. See "Mr Betts on the Mappin Gallery Collection", *The Sheffield Daily Telegraph*, 17 December 1929.

8 On Bawden, see Brian Webb and Peyton Skipwith, *Edward Bawden: Design*, (London, 2016). For Bawden in the University Art Collection, see UAC/10015, UAC/10357, UAC/10855, UAC/10856. Two of these prints were purchased by Betts, though it is unclear which. The La Dell print listed in the Betts Collection ledger has never been located.

9 *Suburban Gardens*, 1947, oil on canvas, 59.7 × 81.3 cm. British Council Collection, P16.

10 Neil Walker (ed.), *Victor Pasmore: Towards a New Reality*, exh. cat., British Council, (London, 2016).

11 See Bruce Laughton, *The Euston Road School: A Study in Objective Painting*, (Aldershot, 1986).

12 Little is known about Flexen's career, though it is apparent from a few surviving pieces in the family, and photographs in the family archives, that she continued to practise as an artist and worked with embroidery and textiles in a modern style.

13 Royal College of Art Prospectus 1925–1926, p.12.

14 Cited in Theophilus P. Cowdell, "The Role of the Royal Academy in English Art, 1918–1930", Unpublished PhD Thesis, Sheffield Hallam University (1980), p.67.

15 Royal College of Art Prospectus 1925–1926, p.18. Emphasis added.

16 On the RCA during this period, see Neil Sharp, "Rothenstein's Success? The Royal College of Art in the Inter-War Years", in Christopher Frayling and Claire Catterall (eds.), *Design of the Times: One Hundred Years of the Royal College of Art*, (Somerset, 1996). The "outbreak of talent" among the RCA students of the 1920s and 30s, including Edward Burra, Edward Bawden, Barnett Freedman, Eric Ravilious, Enid Marx, Norah Bradon, William Chappel and Barbara Ker-Seymer, has also been the subject of exhibitions at the Fry Art Gallery (31 March – 30 June 2013) and at Pallant House Gallery (14 March – 14 June 2020).

17 Prudence Bliss, the daughter of Douglas Percy Bliss, recalls that her father shared lodgings with Betts and other RCA students during their early years at the college. A photograph showing Betts together with Bliss, George Branson and "Goodwin" is reproduced in Malcolm Yorke, *The Lives of Douglas Percy Bliss & Phyliss Dodd*, (Huddersfield, 2017), p.24.

18 *The Royal College of Art Student Magazine*, Vol.2 No.7 (December 1923), p.1.

19 *The Royal College of Art Student Magazine*, Vol.2 No.8 (June 1924), p.36.

20 A photograph of Betts in the Common Room together with Cecilia Dunbar Kilburn and Eric Ravilious is reproduced in Helen Binyon, *Eric Ravilious: Memoir of an Artist*, (Guildford and London, 1983), p.26.

21 *Ibid.*, p.50.

22 An anecdote related to Betts' skill as a student draughtsman is that he used to make copies of Old Master drawings, which he is variously recalled to have tea-stained and shown to dealers for their opinions and, much to the annoyance of his RCA fellows, submitted as his own work.

23 *The Royal College of Art Student Magazine*, Vol.2 No.8 (June 1924), p.50.

24 *Ibid.*

25 On Underwood's teaching see Christopher Neve, *Leon Underwood*, (Bradford, 1974), esp. pp. 44–49, 75–77; Charlotte Stokes, "The Brook Green School", in Simon Martin (ed.), *Leon Underwood: Figure and Rhythm*, exh. cat., (Chichester, 2015), pp.41–47; Ben Whitworth, *The Sculpture of Leon Underwood*, (Aldershot, 2000), pp.12–14.

26 Neve, *Underwood*, p.76.

27 *Ibid.*

28 See "Checklist of Students at the Brook Green School of Drawing" in Whitworth, *Sculpture of Leon Underwood*, p.145.

29 Neve, *Underwood*, p.76.

30 Stokes, "The Brook Green School", p.42; Simon Martin, "Making an Impression: Underwood the Print-maker" in Martin (ed.), *Underwood: Figure and Rhythm*, pp.59–62.

31 Stokes, "The Brook Green School", p.42.

32 Campbell Dodgson, "The Etchings of Leon Underwood", *Artwork*, (May – August 1925): 212–219, p.216.

33 Celina Jeffrey, "Leon Underwood: An Artist Collector", in Anthony Shelton (ed.), *Collectors: Expressions of Self and Other*, (London, 2001), pp.33–54.

34 Cited in Roger Berthoud, *The Life of Henry Moore*, (London, 1987), p.57.

35 Sheffield City Council, Education Committee minutes, 10 June 1927.

36 Sheffield City Council, Education Committee minutes, 12 April 1929.

37 The subject of *Baby Betts* is Betts' son, Paul Betts (b.1929).

38 "Art Extremes in City Exhibition, Few Provocative Works", *The Sheffield Independent*, 11 April 1929.

39 "Gifted Amateur Artists", *The Yorkshire Post*, 15 April 1929.

40 "Art Extremes in City Exhibition, Few Provocative Works", *The Sheffield Independent*, 11 April 1929.

41 Two such compositions include *Arabesque Grinders Harmony* (sold Criterion Auctioneers, 3 June 2017, Lot 288) and *Grinders' Saturday Night, Sheffield*. The latter, shown at an exhibition of the British Independent Society of Artists at the Redfern Galleries in 1928, was described as "a big drawing in pen and coloured wash" in "A Forceful Picture That is Not Typical", *The Sheffield Daily Independent*, 12 June 1928.

42 It is not clear if any of the exhibited nude drawings survive. Those illustrated here are thought to date from the same period and are included to give a sense of the work being discussed.

43 "Ghosts of Saint Anthony", *The Sheffield Daily Independent*, 29 September 1933.

44 "The Artist who Shocked Sheffield – Bold Mr Betts Finds His Spiritual Home", *The Sheffield Daily Independent*, 23 November 1931.

45 *Ibid.*

46 *Ibid.*

47 "Letters to the Editor – Mr Betts on the Mappin Gallery Collection", *The Sheffield Daily Telegraph*, 17 December 1929; "Art Critic's Choice – Suggestions for New City Gallery", *The Sheffield Daily Independent*, 12 December 1929.

48 "The Artist who Shocked Sheffield – Bold Mr Betts Finds His Spiritual Home", *The Sheffield Daily Independent*, 23 November 1931.

49 Rothenstein served as director from 1934–1938, before he moved on to the Tate. At Sheffield he oversaw the major redevelopment of the Sheffield City Museum and Mappin Art Gallery.

50 "The Artist who Shocked Sheffield – Bold Mr Betts Finds His Spiritual Home", *The Sheffield Daily Independent*, 23 November 1931.

51 *The Surrey Comet*, 7 November 1931, cited in Michael R. Gibson, *A History of Kingston University*, (Kingston, 2001), p.31.

52 University of Reading Newspaper Cuttings 1946–1966, "Fine Arts from the Evening Standard", 1955.

53 *Ibid.*

54 University of Reading Newspaper Cuttings 1946–1966, "Ambassador Will Inaugurate French Week in Reading", 1955.

55 J. C. Holt, *The University of Reading: The First Fifty Years*, (Reading, 1977), p.17.

56 *Ibid.*, p.32.

57 *Ibid.*

58 Typography was later established as an independent department, unique in English universities, in 1974. On Gibbings, see Martin J. Andrews, *The Life and Work of Robert Gibbings*, (London, 2003).

59 A letter in the Henry Moore Foundation archives, sent by Betts on Moore's 80th birthday, further attests to their life-long connection.

60 University of Reading Newspaper Cuttings 1946–1966, "Conferment of Six Honorary Degrees" from *The Reading Standard*, 1959.

61 *The Reading Chronicle*, 24 June 1938. Betts' portrait of Sickert is still in the possession of the family.

62 Richard Seddon, "Technical Page: The Studio Methods of Walter Richard Sickert", *The Artist Magazine*, v.97 (March 1982), p.10. Seddon was a former pupil of Betts.

63 See essays by Anna Gruetzner Robins, Wendy Baron, Nicola Moorby and Alistair Smith in *Walter Sickert: "Drawing is the Thing"*, exh. cat., Whitworth Art Gallery, (Manchester, 2004). This exhibition featured several Sickert drawings from the Betts Collection.

64 For more information on Sickert' s drawing techniques see Alistair Smith, "Walter Sickert's Drawing Practice and the Camden Town Ethos": https://www.tate.org.uk/art/research-publications/camden-town-group/alistair-smith-walter-sickerts-drawing-practice-and-the-camden-town-ethos-r1104369#fn_1_11. (Accessed 11 February 2020).

65 For a detailed discussion of the themes in Sickert's drawings, especially in relation to the University of Reading Art Collection, see Anna Gruetzner Robins, *Walter Sickert: Drawings. Theory and Practice: Word and Image*, (Cambridge, 1996).

66 *Ibid.*, pp.25–37.

67 Harris went on to study at the Courtauld Institute of Art, before taking up positions as Principal of St Albans School of Art (1967–1975), Vice Principal of Chelsea School of Art (1975–1986), and Head of Camberwell School of Art & Crafts (1986–1989).

68 Tom Barrett, "Tribute to JAB", 1980.

69 On the ABC drawing method, based on Renaissance models, see Adriano Aymonino, Anne Varick Lauder and Eloisa Dodero (eds.), *Drawn from the Antique: Artists & the Classical Ideal*, exh. cat., Sir John Soane's Museum, (London, 2015).

70 Jenny Pery, *The Affectionate Eye: The life of Claude Rogers*, (Warwick, 1995), p.178.

71 See Elena Crippa and Beth Williamson (eds.), *Basic Design*, (London, 2013).

72 *Reflection on Three Weeks in May 1970*, 1971, oil and graphite on canvas, 1524 × 1524 mm, Tate, London, T01687.

73 https://www.tate.org.uk/art/artworks/donagh-reflection-on-three-weeks-in-may-1970-t01687 (Accessed 11 February 2020).

74 Donagh's Artists' Statement, 1972, cited in *Ibid.*

A Student's View

Clive Ashwin

I was a student of the Fine Art Department at the University of Reading from 1957 to 1961, towards the end of the period that Professor James Anthony Betts (1897–1980) taught at the University (1933–1963). I am probably one of a dwindling number of people who remember his teaching at first hand (**cat.77**) (**fig.1**). In this memoir I shall try to describe what it was like to study under Betts' tuition and also to identify the aesthetic and philosophical foundations of his approach to drawing instruction. This experience led me to make the teaching of drawing one of the central interests of my future research, resulting in several publications and a doctoral thesis.

When I applied for a place in 1957 there were only two universities in the United Kingdom that offered degrees in art as a studio pursuit, Newcastle and Reading. All other post-school art education took place in colleges of art, many of them in provincial towns, offering courses up to diploma level in the form of the National Diploma in Design. The location of the Reading course within a fully-fledged university had numerous benefits for its students, giving them access to a subject and cultural range of great richness, including the arts, sciences, philosophy and humanities.

I came for interview in July 1957, after my National Service with the Royal Air Force. I remember coming to the Department on a beautiful sunny day carrying a portfolio of work I had done at school and during my time in the RAF. I was ushered through one room, which was occupied by Betts' secretary Joyce Cullum, and into the Professor's office, which was full of drawings and paintings propped and heaped

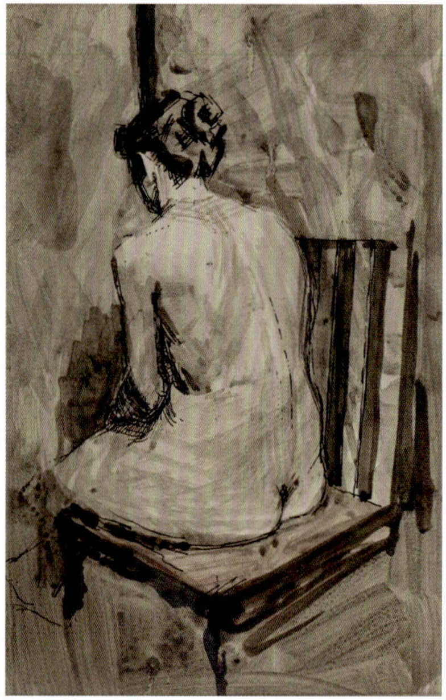

Fig.1 Clive Ashwin (b.1937), *Woman Seated on Chair*, 1960, pen, ink and wash, Collection of the Artist © The Artist.

around the room. Betts leafed through my work and asked me a few questions. Knowing that I came from Cornwall he inquired whether I knew anything about local Cornish painters. I mentioned Henry Scott Tuke (1858–1929), who had lived in Falmouth, my home town. After a few days I received a letter telling me that I had been offered a place commencing that October, which I accepted.

For a Fine Art student, contact with Betts tended to be limited in the first year or two but if you specialised in painting and drawing, as I did, this increased in the final two years up to graduation. He was fairly short, probably about 5' 6" and rather stocky. He always wore a grey pin-stripe suit and tie. He came to work in what was called a pork pie hat and carried a cane which he sometimes twirled as he walked. He sported a small moustache, just under his nose, and a miniature imperial beard on his chin. He smoked more or less continuously, including in the teaching studios. When teaching in a life class, he would approach a student and start drawing with a soft pencil on the margin of their paper. He rarely if ever studied the student's drawing before he started drawing. As he drew, he talked continuously, explaining what he was doing.

Betts' emphasis was always on the unique character and configuration of the subject and he injected a feeling of discovery and surprise into the process. He would say things like, "My God! Look at the way the plane of the jacket falls away!" He had favourite words, like "dichotomy" to denote an intersection between planes. His vocabulary was complemented by a repertoire of noises, such as a clucking sound produced by drawing his tongue away from his palate. He would say things like, "Now look at the way the arm intersects with the bed! Cluck, cluck, cluck!" Students used to enjoy doing impersonations of his little mannerisms. When a fellow student and I did impersonations of all the staff, including Betts, at a departmental party he seemed to enjoy it immensely.

The driving motivation behind Betts' drawings and his teaching of drawing was first-hand observation and the direct recording of visual experience. This might sound self-evident, but in fact a great deal of drawing then, and perhaps always, can be deeply influenced by other motives and aesthetic principles. One of these is the notion of "style". I was taught at school by a graduate of the Slade School of Art, and the Slade ethos during his period as a student between the wars was much preoccupied with the quest for a distinctive drawing style. The drawings of Augustus John (1878–1961), who was a very significant painter between the wars, are characterised by this sense of style, manifesting itself in elegant sweeping lines of almost calligraphic quality. At its best it produced drawing of great beauty and character; at its worst it degenerated into elegant curlicues.

Betts was totally opposed to the notion of a quest for a "style". Trying to draw in a preconceived style meant that you were making compromises with the recording of observed form. He tried to eradicate the idea that there was a mystique about drawing. I once said that something he pointed out was "subtle". He immediately rebuked me, saying it was not subtle, but plain as a pikestaff to anyone prepared to look. "Subtle" was a word he disliked.

Betts' approach to drawing can be characterised in philosophical terms as empirical, which is to say based entirely upon the observation of visual reality. This may be contrasted with the variants of idealism which were current in drawing before and at that time. Idealism can take several forms, such as the quest for the perfect human form, improving upon the model if necessary by correcting perceived defects.

Closely allied to the notion of style in drawing is the practice of drawing from memory. In practical terms, this implies that there is a "way" of drawing any object, from an ear to an aeroplane. My own training at school provided me with a repertoire of memorised forms which I could produce at will. There was a popular series of instructional books called *How to Draw [Dogs/Cats/Ships/Aeroplanes etc]* which I studied avidly, committing a repertoire of forms to memory for future use and reference.[1] Drawing from a memorised stock of graphic formulae can then come into conflict with real observation, a situation which Betts wished to avoid at all costs.

Betts described himself as a pupil of the Camden Town Group artist, Walter Richard Sickert (1860–1942). This may be true. Sickert was a prolific teacher during Betts' student days and worked at several art schools, even setting up short-lived schools of his own. He appears to have enjoyed teaching greatly. However, it is irrelevant to estimate just how extensive his contact with Sickert would have been; Betts was also a pupil of Sickert vicariously as a keen student of Sickert's drawings and paintings.

In some respects, the Sickertian approach to drawing was the antithesis of the kind of "stylish" drawing, which I have described, with its elegant lines and curlicues. Sickert, as both a painter and a draughtsman, was completely obedient to the eccentricities of nature, an aesthetic which can be traced in a direct line from his association with the French impressionist artist, Edgar Degas (1834–1917), early in his career. It is not surprising that Degas was, with Sickert, one of Betts' most admired artists.

In addition to the nature of execution – how a drawing is created – Betts' philosophy of drawing informed by Sickert and Degas also had important implications for subject matter. A great deal of drawing at all times has been motivated by the notion of the inherent value of certain subjects as appropriate for art. The plastic arts of the nineteenth century were, accordingly, dominated by subjects derived from myth, allegory, history, morality and the quest for the perfect human form. The Realist tradition of the mid-nineteenth century rejected the notion of classical idealism but maintained the principle of subject significance by shifting its subject focus to the new area of moral value, such as the dignity of the labouring poor. In the twentieth century, the quest for subject matter with inherent artistic value continued in, for example, Augustus John's romanticised depictions of Romany life.

In his extensive and brilliant published output, Sickert completely repudiated this approach to subject matter.[2] For Sickert, the only claim a subject had to attention was its intrinsic visual excitement, and that applied to the grandeur of St Marks in Venice or a squalid back bedroom in Camden Town. In fact, Sickert sought out subjects which he knew would challenge the spectator's expectations and lead them to ask why he thought it was worth recording at all. Subjects could be ordinary, dull, ugly even boring. Significantly, one of his most iconic images, repeated as a painter, draughtsman and printmaker, is called *Ennui (Boredom)* **(cat.59)** **(fig.2)**.

Far from searching for the perfect human form, Sickert preferred models with fallen breasts and big backsides floundering around on grubby linen on a creaking bedstead, often viewed from the most unflattering perspective **(cat.57)** **(fig.3)**. His human subjects are 'seized' rather than 'posed', often in postures and situations which they would not wish to be recorded. Sickert had a mischievous sense of humour, and often his titles provide a red herring which he knew some viewers would find irresistible.

Betts maintained the same indifference to subject matter. Most teaching was done in the life room, and there was no attempt to search for elegant poses or evocative props. If there was any value to be found in the model it was in the excitement of discovery and visual surprise. One day I arrived for the life class to find he had set up a middle-aged man in a grey suit sitting on a brass bedstead. I did not realise that this subject had a deep resonance within the Sickertian

Fig.2 Walter Richard Sickert (1860–1942), *Woman Lying on a Couch (Study for Ennui)*, *c*.1912, chalk and ink, UAC/10524.

Fig.3 Walter Richard Sickert (1860–1942), *Practice*, *c*.1909, pencil and chalk, UAC/10538.

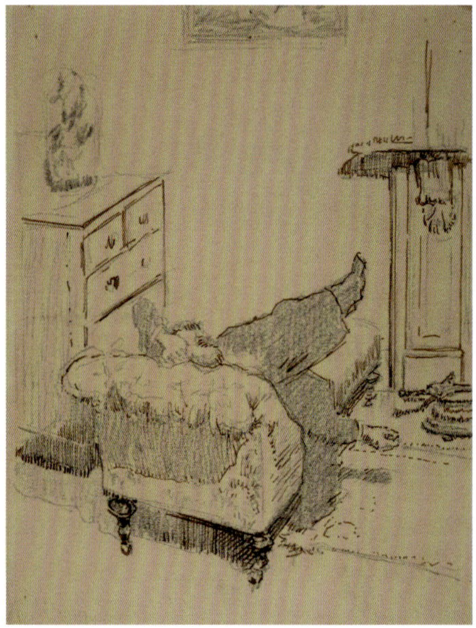

tradition. After struggling with the drawing for some time I had the temerity to suggest that I found it difficult to draw because it was so boring. He rounded on me and said, "If you think like that you'll end up like Lord Leighton!" The art of Lord Frederic Leighton RA (1830–1896) was, of course, the epitome of everything that Betts rejected in the art of his parents' generation, with its classical allusions and quest for perfect form.

Like Sickert, Betts was always alert to the oddities and idiosyncrasies of life. There was a theatricality in daily life there to be discovered. We should remember that Sickert's first career was as an actor, and he remained a keen observer and mimic of those around him. One morning Betts came into the studio, and the first thing he wanted to tell us was to relate a pithy exchange he had just overheard between two ragamuffins in the street, which he acted out with appropriate comic voices.

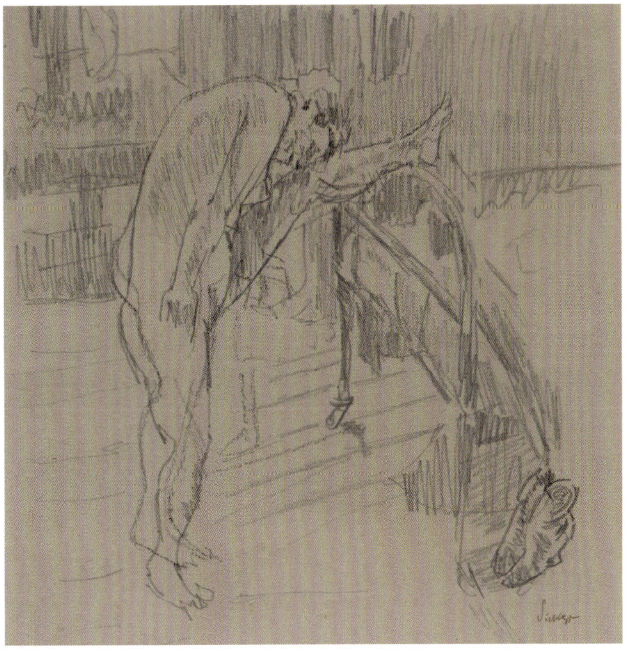

He relished showing us drawings from his collection or in books which he carried with him. His principal enthusiasms were Sickert and Degas, but they extended widely to artists such as Charles Keene, the great *Punch* magazine illustrator who was also admired by Degas (**cats.60–62**) (**figs.4–5**), and to good master drawings of all periods. Under Betts, the life room became a workshop or laboratory of vision, an in-depth attempt to see the world as it really is, and not as we might imagine it or have been taught to see it or represent it.

As students in the late' fifties, we were aware of the rise of continental modernism since the beginning of the twentieth century in the varying forms of abstraction, Cubism, Surrealism and Expressionism, but it had strangely little impact on the way we thought or worked. When a loan exhibition of prints of Paul Klee (1879–1940) was mounted in the corridor of the Fine Art Department, they were viewed with amused interest. A member of staff observed to me that he thought Klee was "a good designer", but was clearly not to be taken seriously as an artist.

The irresistible watershed of modernism came to a head during the closing years of Betts' tenure. A critical event fell in 1959, in the middle of my time at Reading. This was the exhibition "The Developing Process", held at London's Institute of Contemporary Arts which presented and promoted the radical educational theories of figures like Victor Pasmore (1908–1998), Richard Hamilton (1922–2011), Tom Hudson (1922–1997) and Harry Thubron (1915–1985). The new impulse in art education they represented originated in numerous centres, notably the Central School in London, King's College Newcastle and Leeds College of Art. Its watchword was "basic design" and it claimed its origins in the pedagogical work of the Bauhaus, in particular in the theories of Paul Klee, Wassily Kandinsky (1866–1944) and Johannes Itten (1888–1967). Such artists attempted to close a perceived gap between fine and applied art by providing a common foundation of abstract exercises

Fig.4 Charles Keene (1823–1891), *Number One,* 1888, chalk and heightening on paper prepared with a white ground, UAC/10557.

Fig.5 Charles Keene (1823–1891), *Robert, at Cook's Little Swarry,* 1886, ink and white heightening, UAC/10575.

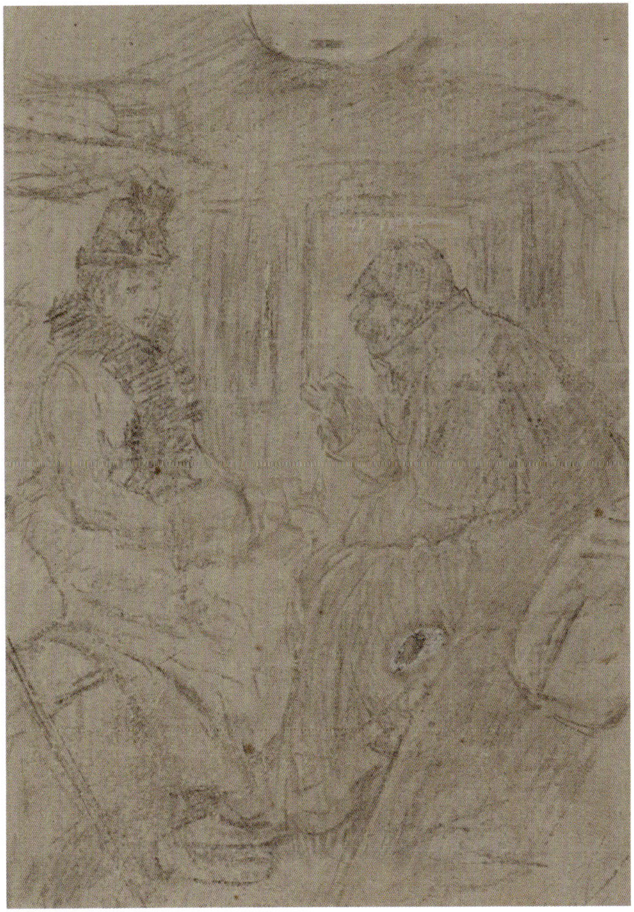

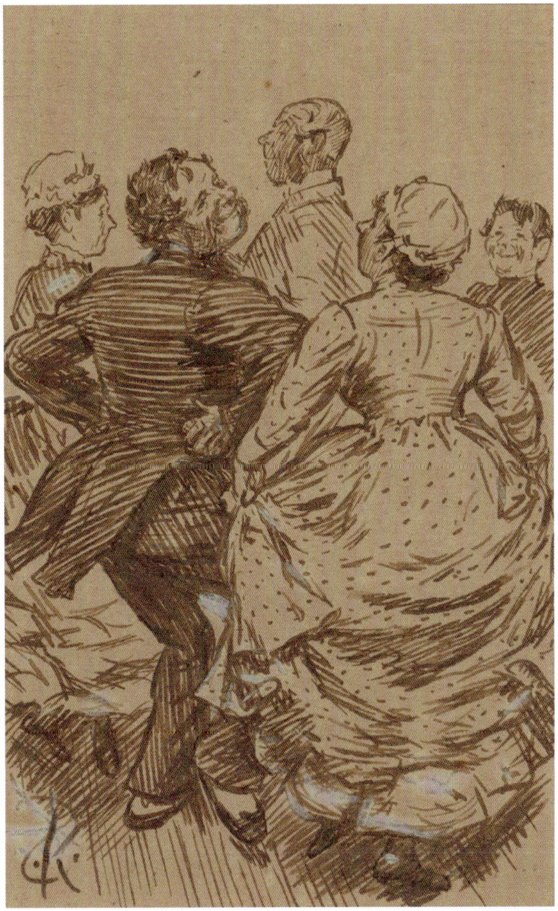

in line, tone, shape and form, and was highly influential in the concept of the so-called "foundation courses" established at many colleges as a route into more specialised studies.

In addition to such initiatives arising within British art schools, a growing awareness of American art had an enormous influence on British art practice and art education. This created an appetite for a wide range of abstract and semi-abstract ways of making art, such as abstract expressionism, hard-edge abstraction and colour field painting. The journal *Studio International*, with its vivid colour illustrations, was avidly studied in college libraries throughout the UK. The traditional practice of drawing for long periods in the life studio and the production of closely observed drawings no longer seemed tenable.

By the time I began teaching in a college of art, in 1966, the concept and practice of the life room as a laboratory of vision had been largely abandoned. The college whose staff I joined had only one Fine Art student who continued to wish to draw and paint from life. He was treated as a harmless eccentric and given a room in an annex remote from the main college so that he did not infect or disturb the more serious work being done there.

The time has come to reconsider whether the Betts' approach to drawing and teaching had some elemental value which has been lost to successive generations. In this connection, it is instructive to observe that David Hockney (b.1937), who is arguably one of the most significant living British artists of the present time, received his artistic formation in a regime very similar to that favoured by Betts.[3] Similarly, the art of the late Lucien Freud (1922–2011) owes much more to the British tradition of closely-observed realism than it does to the many waves of modernist experimentation which swept across Western art during his creative life. For several decades, Freud's work fell below the critical radar, hardly appearing in major surveys of current British art.

When he re-emerged into public prominence in the 1990s, and until his death in 2011, his work bore little evidence of the modernist tides which had swept across European art culture in the meantime, and which had led to the abandonment of the life studio tradition of teaching drawing. Perhaps this is an opportune moment for a reappraisal of the value of closely observed depictive drawing as Betts promoted and taught it.

Biography

Clive Ashwin's first degree was in Fine Art (Painting and Drawing) at the University of Reading. His postgraduate qualifications include an MA in Philosophy (University of London), a PhD in Education (University of London) and he is an Associate of the Royal College of Music (Clarinet Performance). He has held several senior posts in higher education. His publications include two books on drawing, *Drawing and Education in German Speaking Europe* (1981), *Encyclopaedia of Drawing* (1982) and several journal articles. He has written for *Studio International* for many years. He is a Professor Emeritus of Middlesex University and Life Fellow of the Royal Society of Arts.

Notes

1 These included Peter F. Anson, *How to Draw Ships*, (London, 1941). Other titles in the series included trees, birds, dogs, locomotives, portraits, etc.

2 See Anna Gruetzner Robins, *Walter Sickert: The Complete Writings on Art*, (Oxford, 2000).

3 Hockney studied at Bradford College of Art between 1953–1957 before attending the Royal College of Art. His early student drawings and paintings reflect an ethos very similar to that of Reading during the same period. See Peter Webb, *Portrait of David Hockney*, (London, 1988).

Chronology

Gracie Maddison

1897 James Anthony Betts, eldest child of James (b.1867), a Railway Foreman, and Ellen Betts (b. 1869), born in Skipton, North Yorkshire, 28 December. He has two younger siblings, George and Kathleen. Attends St. Stephen's School, Skipton.

***c.* 1914** Works as a goods clerk on the Midland Railway at Skipton. Attends night school at Skipton High School, followed by Bradford College of Art.

1921 Secures a special talent scholarship to study at the Royal College of Art (RCA) in London.

1923 Marries Nellie Flexen on 23 July in Bath, Somerset. Works as the Art Editor for the RCA student magazine. Leon Underwood (1890–1975) resigns from the RCA. Betts is among a select number of students who attend evening classes at his Brook Green School.

1924 Henry Moore sketches Betts' portrait at the RCA. Betts works as an Assistant Instructor in Life Drawing for Professor Randolph Schwabe (1885–1948). Works as the Art Editor of the RCA Student Magazine for a second time.

1926 Contributes caricature of Cecilia Dunbar-Kilburn (1903–1984) to student magazine, *The Mandrake*. Leaves RCA and moves to Sheffield. Begins new role as the Head of the Drawing and Painting Department at the City of Sheffield Technical School of Art. Becomes involved in the wider Sheffield art scene and joins several local art groups. Gives public lectures on artists including Ingres, Picasso and Rembrandt at the Fargate YMCA and the RotherhamMuseum and Art Gallery.

1927 Betts' drawing *Nude Woman Reclining* is acquired from Underwood by the British Museum through the Contemporary Arts Society.

1928 Designs a set for Elmer Rice's expressionist play *The Adding Machine* at the Sheffield Repertory Theatre. Exhibits six works, both paintings and drawings, representing contemporary life among the working-class of Sheffield in the Annual Hallamshire Sketch Club Exhibition. Exhibits with the British Independent Society of Artists at the Redfern Galleries, London and the Sheffield Society of Artists Annual Exhibition at the Mappin Gallery, Sheffield.

1929 Birth of son, Paul Betts (1929–2007) in Ecclesall, South Yorkshire. Writes scathing criticism of the Mappin Gallery in the Sheffield Daily Telegraph condemning its lack of contemporary art. Exhibits black and white drawings at the Sheffield Society of Artists and the Hallamshire Sketch Club's Annual Exhibition.

1930 Establishes and edits the inaugural edition of the Sheffield College of Art Magazine. The College mounts an exhibition of drawings loaned from the renowned collection of Charles Rutherston (1866–1927). A record number of students from Betts' department exhibit at the College's annual art exhibition. Moves to Kingston and becomes Head of Kingston School of Art.

1933 Succeeds Allen Seaby (1867–1953) as Lecturer in Charge of the School of Art at the University of Reading. Made an *ex officio* member of the Council of the Reading Guild of Artists. Exhibits at the Cooling Galleries, New Bond Street.

1934 Begins an extensive reorganization of Reading School of Art. Employs Walter Bayes (1868–1856) as External Examiner and Visiting Lecturer as well as Frank Ormrod (1897–1988), Geoffrey Jellicoe (1900–1996) and Valerie Bayford (1910–1958) as Sessional Lecturers. Encourages handicraft teachers to take retirement. Exhibits with the "New Kingston Group", of which he is president, at the Kingston Public Library.

1935 Participates in informal seminar meetings with lecturers from other departments, including Herbert Hodges (1905–1976) from Philosophy. They discuss topics of common interest with a student audience which contributes to the development of combined-subject degrees. This continues until the outbreak of WWII.

1936 Appoints former owner of the Golden Cockerel Press and Penguin Book illustrator Robert Gibbings (1889–1958) as a Departmental Lecturer and together they develop an advanced course in "Design applied to Typography and Book Production". Betts acknowledges the need for commerce in art and encourages teaching processes such as printing for advertising. Ormrod, acting as the Critic of the Reading Guild of Artists' Annual Exhibition, picks out Betts' oil painting *Study of a Dancer* as the outstanding entry.

1937 The Faculty of Letters at the University of Reading recommends the introduction of an Honours Degree in Fine Art, the first B.A. degree course in the subject in England.

1938 Sickert is awarded an Honorary Degree by the University of Reading. Betts is amongst several eminent artists chosen to illustrate a new series of Penguin illustrated classics and he produces a suite of wood engravings to illustrate Milton's Paradise Lost. The series is later abandoned. Engages Eric Kennington (1888–1960) to paint the portrait of Dr William Childs (1869–1939), the first Vice-Chancellor of the University.

1939 Appoints Allan Gwynne-Jones (1892–1982) as Sessional Lecturer in Drawing and Painting. Joins a group of Reading lecturers who write to the Air Ministry, pleading for the Berkshire Downs to be protected from use as a possible bombing range.

1940 Teaches "Advanced Figure Composition" and "Drawing Life" with Harold Yates (1916–2001), and "Advanced Drawing and Painting Life" with Gwynne-Jones.

1941 Exhibits two wash drawings in the Reading Guild of Artists Eleventh Annual Exhibition. Anthony Eyton (b.1923) studies at Reading for one term.

1943 Awarded the chair of the School of Art, assumes title of Professor. Appoints William McCance (1894–1980) as Sessional Tutor in Book Production. McCance contributes linocut prints to the student magazine, *Tamesis.*

1946 Appoints Hugh Finney (1905–1991) as Sessional Lecturer in Drawing and Painting. University seeks to acquire Whiteknights Park for the establishment of a new campus.

1948 Involved in the architectural planning of the Whiteknights Campus and is part of a small directing group which advises architects on the University's requirements.

1950 Becomes a member of the Guild of St George educational charity for art, craft and the rural environment, founded in 1871 by John Ruskin (1819–1900), alongside Hodges (Master of the Guild of St George from 1950–1972).

1952 Involved in discussions regarding moving the Ruskin Collection (an important teaching collection amassed by Ruskin for Sheffield's metal workers), from Sheffield to Reading following the closure of the Meersbrook Park Museum.

1953 Begins to collect drawings for the University from a variety of Bond Street galleries. Purchases works throughout the 1950s by artists including Sickert, Jost Amman (1539–1581), Ambrose McEvoy (1878–1927), Victor Pasmore (1908–1998) and Edwin La Dell (1914–1970). Betts is also gifted drawings for the University Collection by Spencer Frederick Gore (1878–1914) and David Villiers (1906–1985).

1954 Acquires drawings for the University Collection by Albert de Belleroche (1864–1944), Jean-Louis Forain (1852–1931) and Theodule-Augustin Ribot (1839–1916). Receives a gift of a drawing of Marie de' Medici by Sir Peter Paul Rubens (1577–1640).

1955 Acquires two landscape drawings by Gwynne-Jones for the University Collection, directly from the artist. Advises on space needed to house the Ruskin Collection at the University.

1956 Acquires two prints for the University Collection by Bawden, two drawings attributed to Jacopo Tintoretto (1518–1594), drawings by James Abbott McNeill Whistler (1804–1903), Gwen John (1876–1939) and Daniel Maclise RA (1806–1870), and two drawings directly from fellow RCA student, John Piper (1903–1992).

1959 Moore is awarded an Honorary Degree by the University of Reading.

1960 University Exhibition of Sickert drawings is staged in the Faculty of Letters to celebrate the centenary of the artist's birth. Betts receives funding from the Andrew Carnegie Foundation to run drawing classes for the Reading Guild of Artists.

1963 The Ruskin Library is transferred to the University of Reading. Betts exhibits alongside Ormrod, Finney, Michael Twyman (b.1934) and Harry Redman (1920–1944) at a University exhibition showcasing a variety of staff members' work as part of the Students' Union "Week of Art and Culture". Retires from the University of Reading. Moves away from figure drawing and turns his hand to landscape painting. Work stems from his time spent on holiday in Wales and the Dordogne. Continues to paint and teach with the Caversham and Bussock Mayne Art Groups.

1964 The remainder of the Ruskin Collection is transferred to the University of Reading, where it is stored in the cellars of the Old Library under the care of the Art Department and University Library.

1970 An exhibition room is provided for the Ruskin Collection in the Old Library on the London Road Campus.

1978 Writes a letter to Moore wishing him a happy 80th birthday.

1980 Dies on 27 September, aged 83, in Caversham, Reading.

1982 An exhibition of paintings and drawings by Betts is staged at the University Art Gallery, London Road.

1985 The Ruskin Collection returned to Sheffield City Art Galleries.

1994 The University purchases 14 drawings from Betts' personal collection from his son, Paul.

List of Exhibitions

1928 Mappin Exhibition, Hallamshire Sketch Club

1928 Exhibition at the Redfern Galleries, British Independent Society of Artists

1928 Mappin Exhibition, Sheffield Society of Artists

1929 Mappin Exhibition, Sheffield Society of Artists

1929 Mappin Exhibition, Hallamshire Sketch Club

1930 Mappin Exhibition, Sheffield Society of Artists

1933 Cooling Galleries, New Bond Street "Nineteen" Exhibition

1934 Kingston Public Library, New Kingston Group, Fifth Annual Exhibition

1936 Reading Guild of Artists Annual Exhibition

1940 Reading Guild of Artists Annual Exhibition

1941 Reading Guild of Artists Annual Exhibition

1963 University of Reading, Gallery Five Exhibition

1982 University Art Gallery, London Road

Catalogue

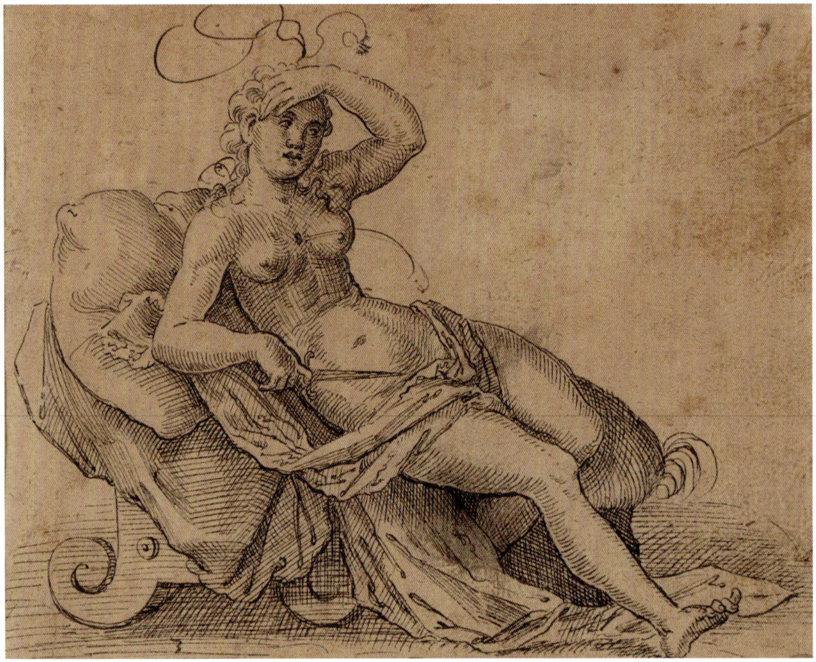

1. Jost Amman (1539–1591)

Lucretia

Ink, 114 × 146 mm

University of Reading Art Collection

UAC/10548

Inscription: 13 [?] *(top right, illegible, in ink)*; Jost Amman *(verso, in pencil)*

Provenance: Purchased from H. M. Calmann, 24 June 1953.

2. Jacopo Zanguidi, called Bertoia (1544–1573/1574)

Sheet of Studies with Seated Male Nude and Two Arms; (verso) An Ox, Seated Couple, Three Standing Male Nudes and an Anatomized Arm

Ink and chalk on blue paper, 350 × 271 mm

University of Reading Art Collection

UAC/10545

Inscriptions: Ernst Ilg. [?] Grahl, Dresden/ gek. 27. V. 22, Rome *(on mount, top right, in pencil)*; 5417599 *(on mount, top right, in pencil)*; 301 *(on mount, bottom left, in pencil)*; Dr LP *(on mount, bottom left, collector's mark, stamped in ink)* Doppelseitig *(on mount, bottom left, in pencil)*; No 4. Benvenuto Cellini *(verso, on mount, top centre, in antique hand in brown ink)*; Doppelseitig *(verso, on mount, top right, in pencil)*; 20½ x/ 25½ *(verso, on mount, right side, in pencil)*; VXX. *(verso, on mount, bottom centre, in pencil, circled)*; Doppelseitig *(verso, on mount, bottom centre, in pencil, underlined)*; Schule Michelangelo *(verso, on mount, bottom right, in pencil)*

Provenance: Dr Ludwig Pollak (1868–1943) (Lugt 788b); Purchased from H. M. Calmann, London, 24 June 1953.

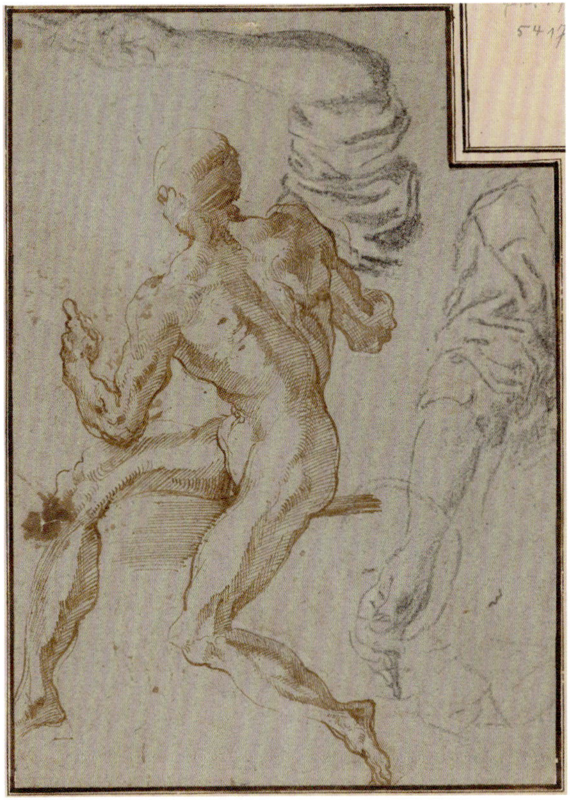
5417

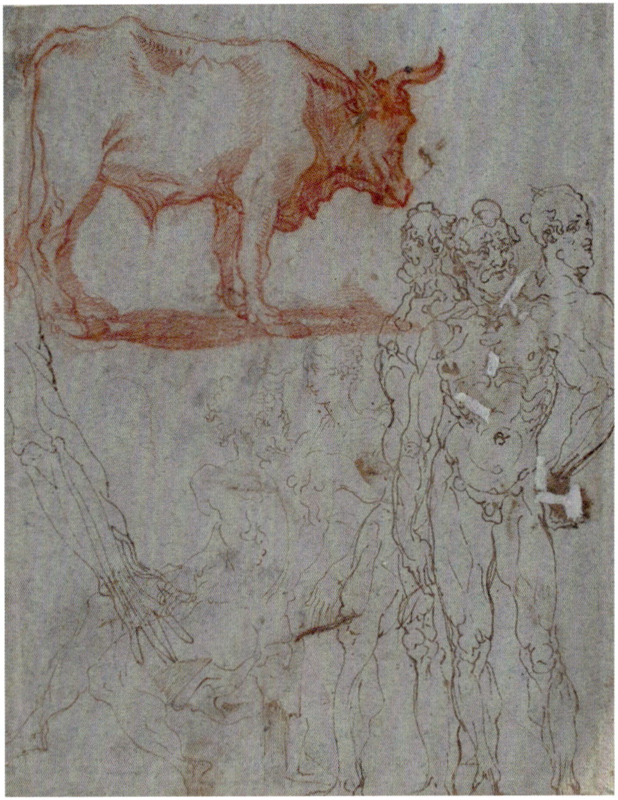

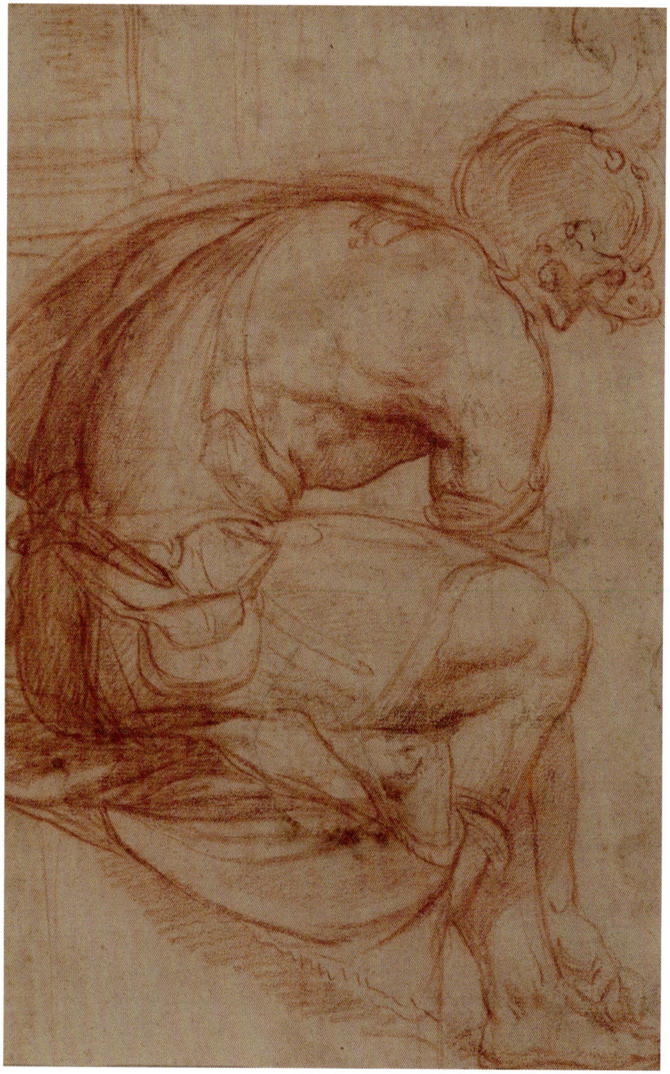

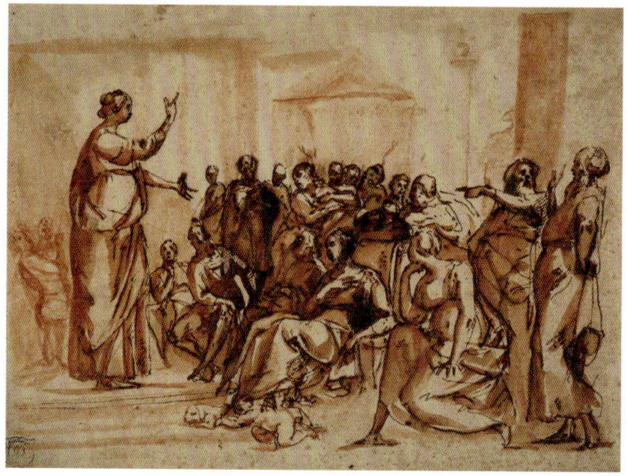

3. c16th Italian School

formerly attributed to Pelegrino Tibaldi (1527–1596)

Seated Roman Soldier

Chalk, 355 × 255 mm

University of Reading Art Collection

UAC/10576

Inscription: Da Rafaello *(verso, in pencil)*

Provenance: Purchased from H. M. Calmann, London, 24 June 1953.

4. attributed to Flaminio Allegrini (1587–1683) or Francesco Allegrini (1615/20–after 1679)

formerly attributed to Ventura Salimbeni (1568–1613)

St Catherine and the Philosophers (?)

Ink and wash, 254 × 344 mm

University of Reading Art Collection

UAC/10540

Inscription: CJD *(bottom left, collector's mark, stamped in ink)*

Provenance: Jean-Charles-Marie Jourdeuil (1811–1868) (Lugt 527); Sold, Sotheby's, London, 12-13 June 1868; Purchased from H. M. Calmann, London, 24 June 1953.

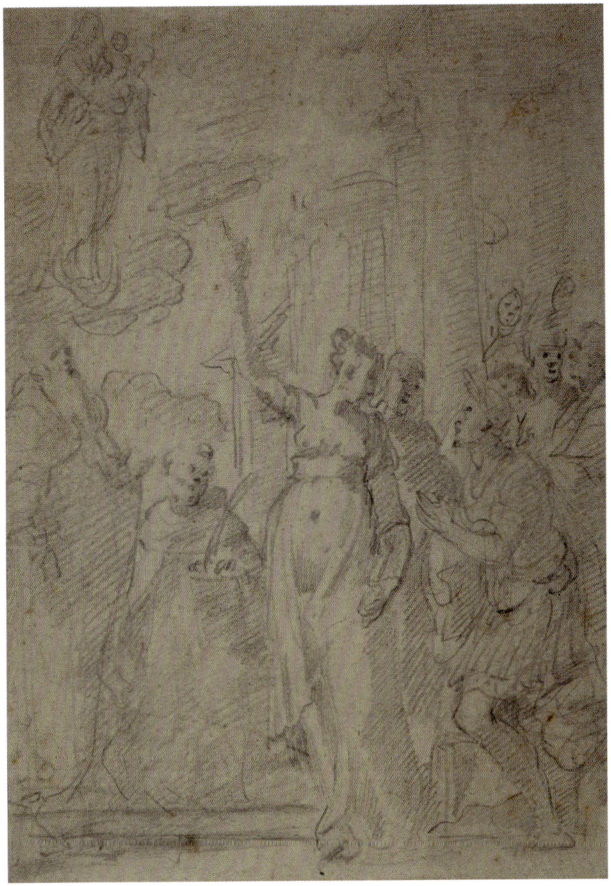

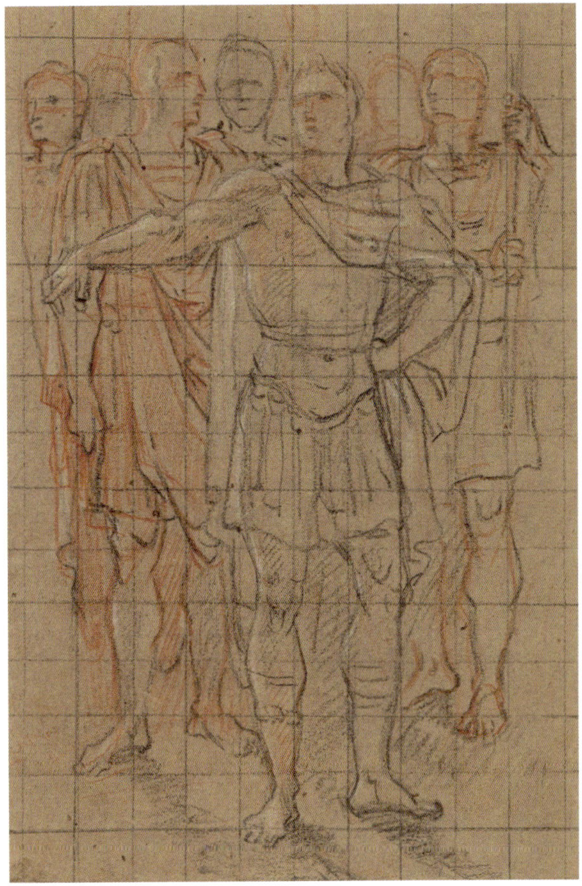

5. c16th Italian School

Tiburtine Sibyl Showing Emperor Augustus the Virgin and Christ Child, with St Anthony Abbot and an Unknown Martyr; (verso) Study for a Section of a Picture Frame (?)

Chalk; (verso) ink, 332 × 235 mm

University of Reading Art Collection

UAC/10541

Provenance: Purchased from H. M. Calmann, London, 24 June 1953.

6. Antoine Coypel (1661–1722)

Study of Silvius Aeneas for "Aeneas in the Underworld"

1716–1717

Chalk with white heightening on brown paper gridded for transfer, 274 × 187 mm

University of Reading Art Collection

UAC/10549

Provenance: Purchased from H. M. Calmann, London, 24 June 1953.

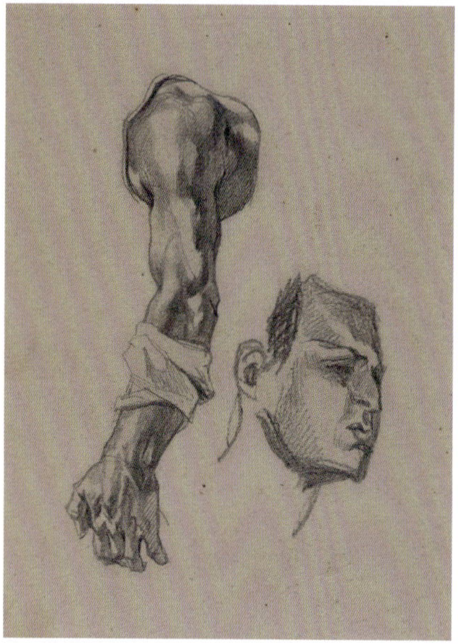

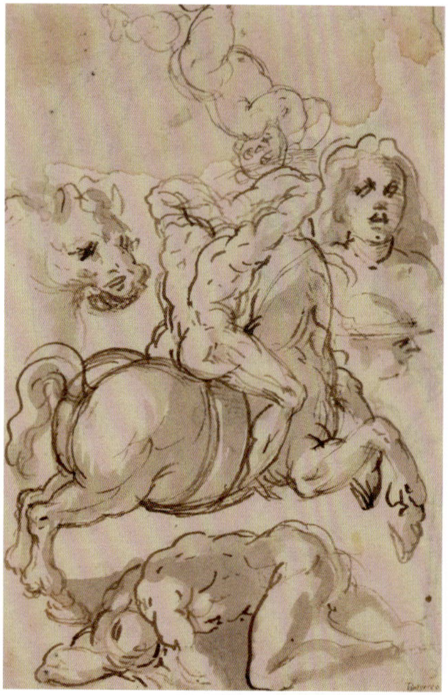

7. c19th French School
formerly attributed to Eugène Delacroix (1798–1863)

Study of a Head and Bandaged Arm; (verso) Two Soldiers

Chalk and pencil, 231 × 183 mm

University of Reading Art Collection

UAC/10543

Inscription: large [?] *(verso, in chalk, illegible notes annotate figures)*

Provenance: Purchased from H. M. Calmann, London, 24 June 1953.

8. c16th Italian School

Sheet of Studies with a Rider on Horseback; (verso) Head, Foot, Arm and Partial Study of a Standing Woman

Ink and wash, 316 × 216 mm

University of Reading Art Collection

UAC/10577

Inscription: Tintoreto *(bottom right, in ink)*

Provenance: Purchased from Alister Mathews, Bournemouth, 16 April 1956.

9. Giovanni Baglione (1566–1643)

Conversion of Mary Magdalene

Ink and wash, 177 × 135 mm

University of Reading Art Collection

UAC/10578

Inscription: Tintoretto Robusti *(bottom left, in ink)*; 48 = 578 *(verso, bottom centre, in pencil)*; PV *(verso bottom right, in pencil)*; Robusti Tintoretto 1518–1594 *(verso, bottom left, in pencil)*

Provenance: Purchased from Alister Mathews, Bournemouth, 16 April 1956.

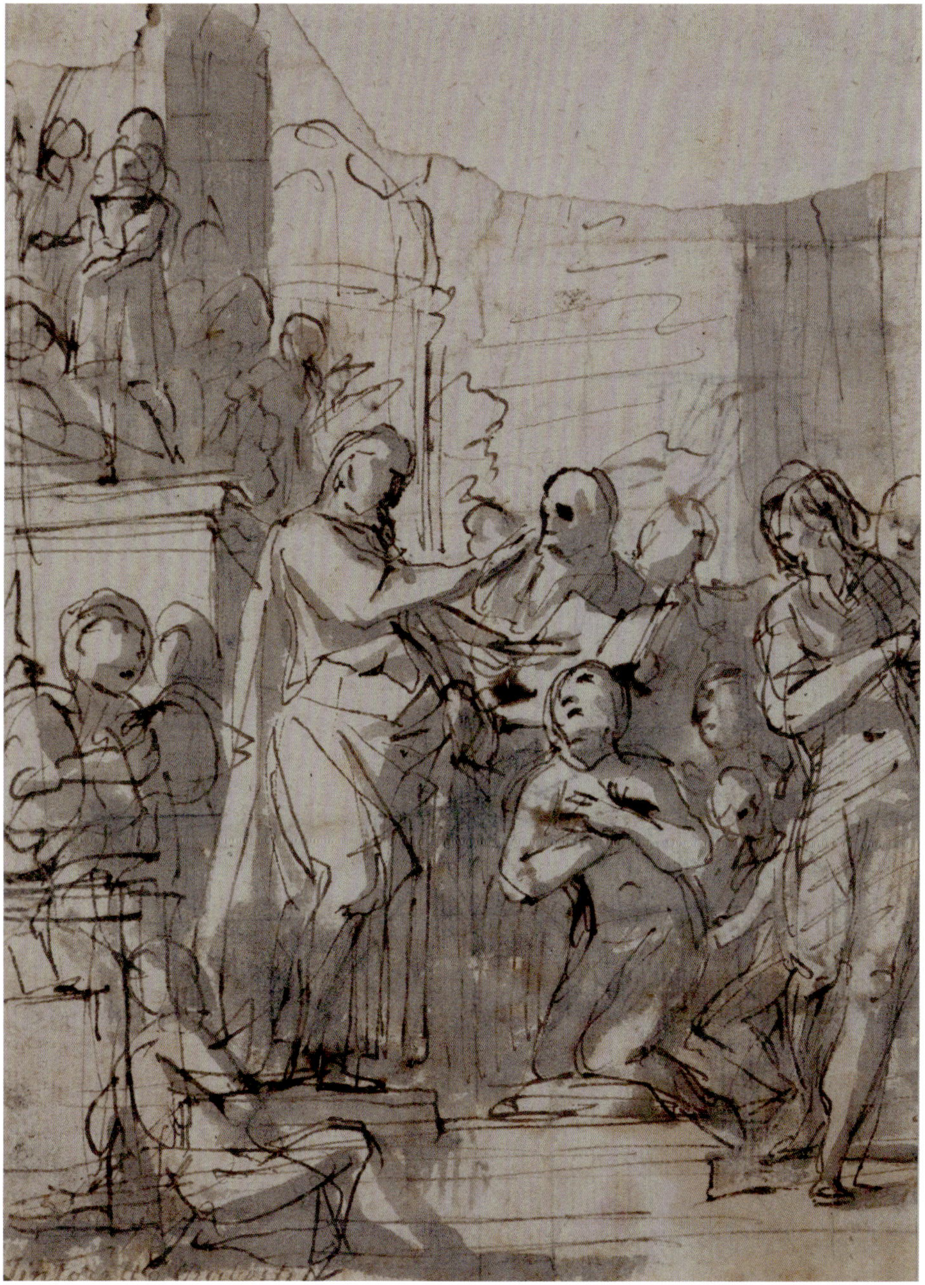

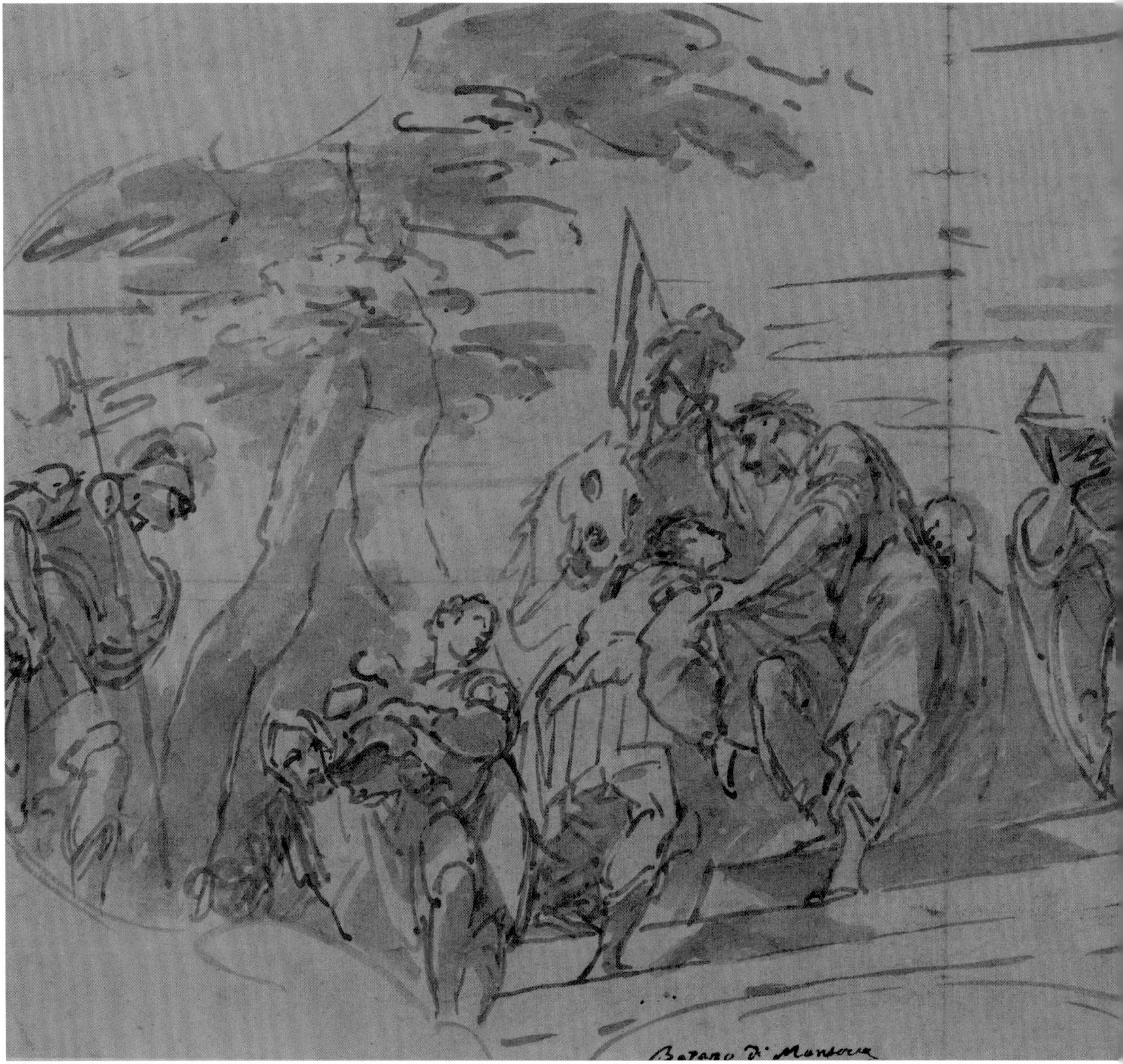

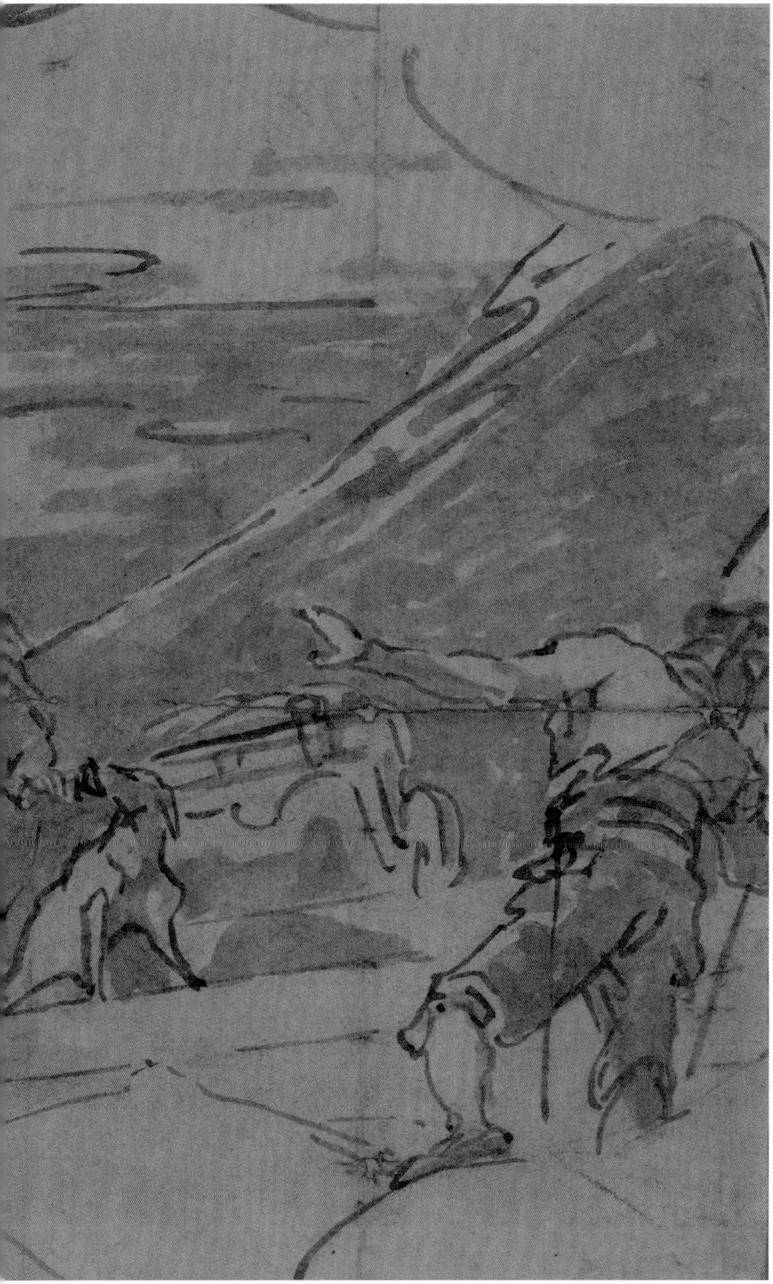

10. Giuseppe Bazzani (1690–1769)

Allegory of Liberality (Study for a Ceiling Panel with Alexander the Great and Diogenes); (verso) Head of a Woman Wearing a Bonnet

c.1740

Ink and wash; (verso) chalk, 223 × 379 mm

University of Reading Art Collection

UAC/10542

Inscription: Bazano di Mantua *(bottom centre, in ink)*

Provenance: Purchased from Matthiesen Gallery, London, 9 February 1954.

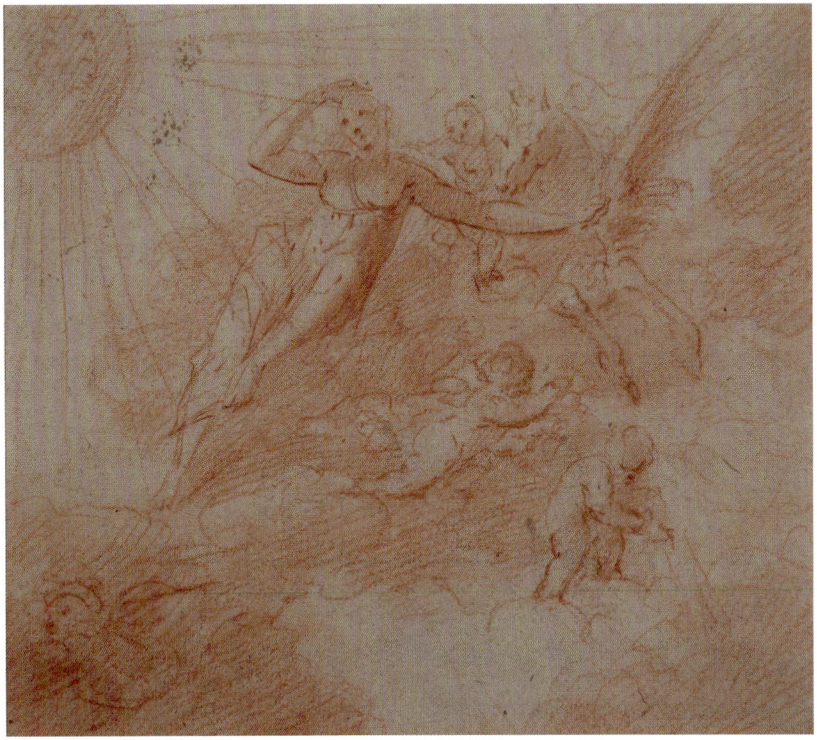

11. c18th French School, possibly circle of François Boucher (1703–1770)

formerly attributed to Jean-Honoré Fragonard (1732–1806)

Aurora and Pegasus attended by Putti

Chalk, 135 × 157 mm

University of Reading Art Collection

UAC/10579

Inscription: L'aurore. Fragonard. *(verso, bottom left, in pencil)*; 67–7 *(verso, bottom right, in pencil)*

Provenance: Purchased from Alister Mathews, Bournemouth, 16 April 1956.

12. Jean-Louis André Théodore Géricault (1791–1824)

Study of a Dead Soldier I

Pencil, 139 × 212 mm

University of Reading Art Collection

UAC/10556

Provenance: Purchased from Matthiesen Gallery, London, 9 February 1954.

13. Jean-Louis André Théodore Géricault (1791–1824)

Study of a Dead Soldier II

Pencil, 117 × 210 mm

University of Reading Art Collection

UAC/10559

Provenance: Purchased from Matthiesen Gallery, London, 9 February 1954.

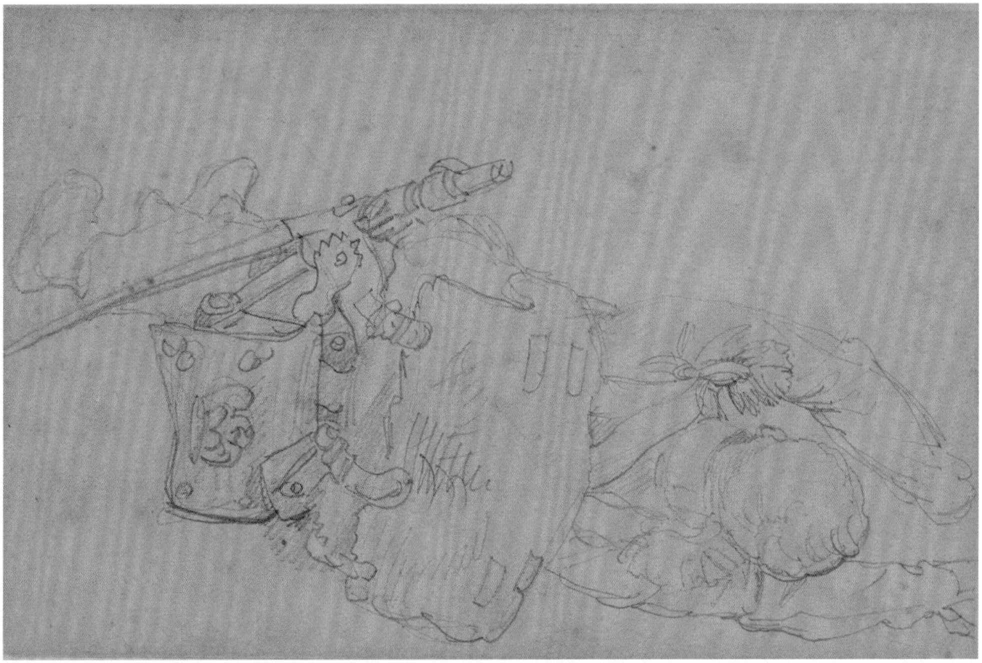

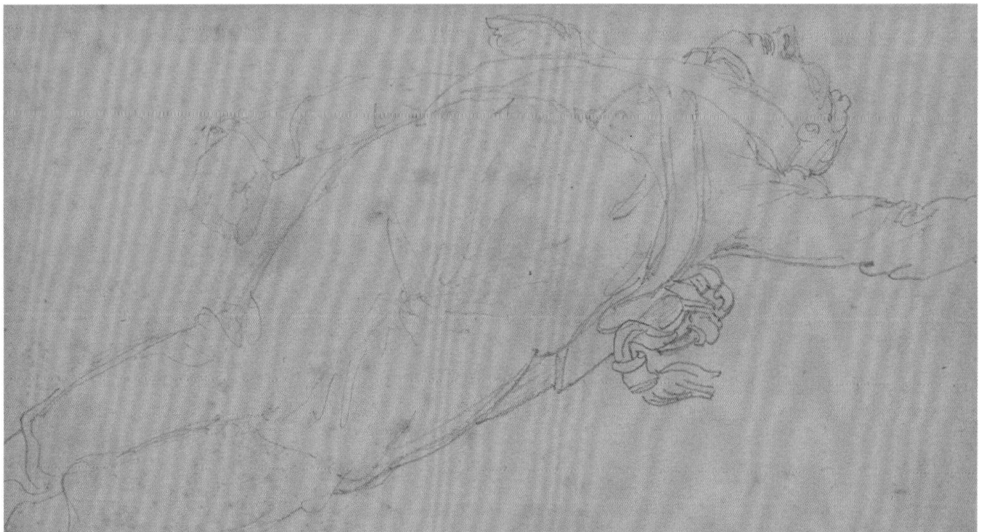

14. Peter Paul Rubens (1577–1640)

Portrait Sketch of Marie de' Medici (Study for The Meeting of Marie de' Medici and Henry IV at Lyon)

*c.*1622

Chalk, 108 × 89 mm

University of Reading Art Collection

UAC/10539

Inscription: [?] *(bottom right, illegible, in ink); R (bottom right, collector's mark, stamped in ink, in artists' pallet)*

Provenance: Jonathan Richardson (1667–1745) (Lugt 2183); Henry Wellesley (1794–1866); Gift of anonymous friend of James Anthony Betts, October 1954.

15. Augustin Théodule Ribot (1823–1891)

Landscape with a Farmhouse

Conté crayon, 91 × 142 mm

University of Reading Art Collection

UAC/10560

Inscription: Hirl...son [?] *(bottom left, illegible, in ink)*; t. R *(bottom left, in ink)*; Th. Ribot *(verso, in crayon)*

Provenance: Purchased from Leicester Galleries, London, 10 August 1954.

16. Augustin Théodule Ribot (1823–1891)

Landscape with Trees

Conté crayon, 91 × 142 mm

University of Reading Art Collection

UAC/10561

Provenance: Purchased from Leicester Galleries, London, 10 August 1954.

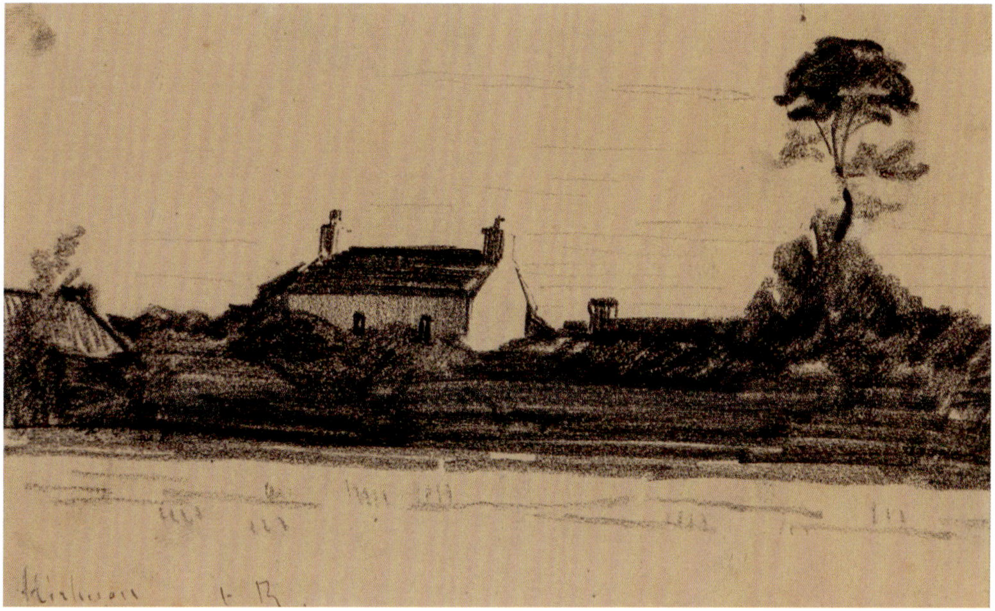

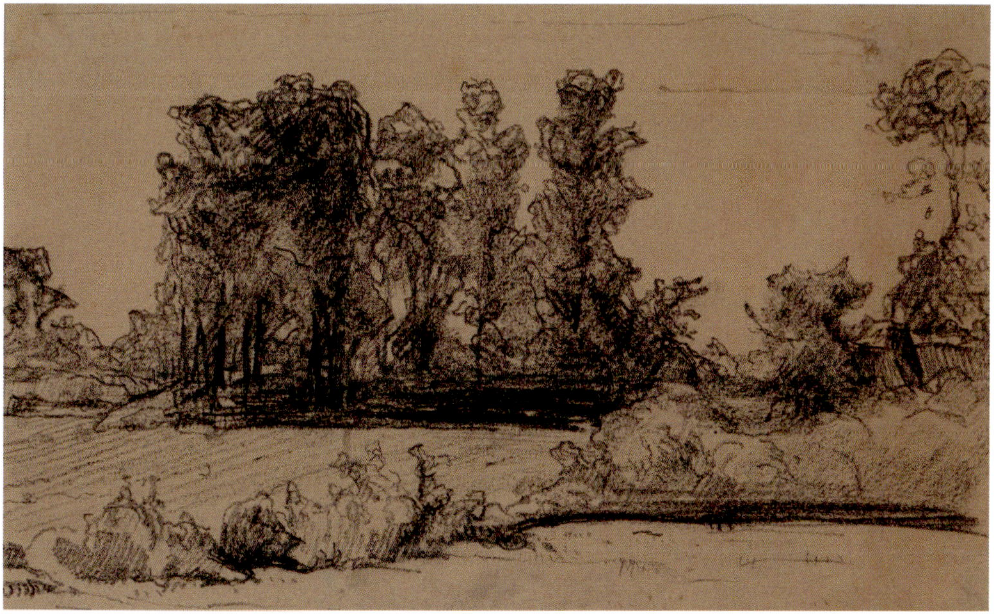

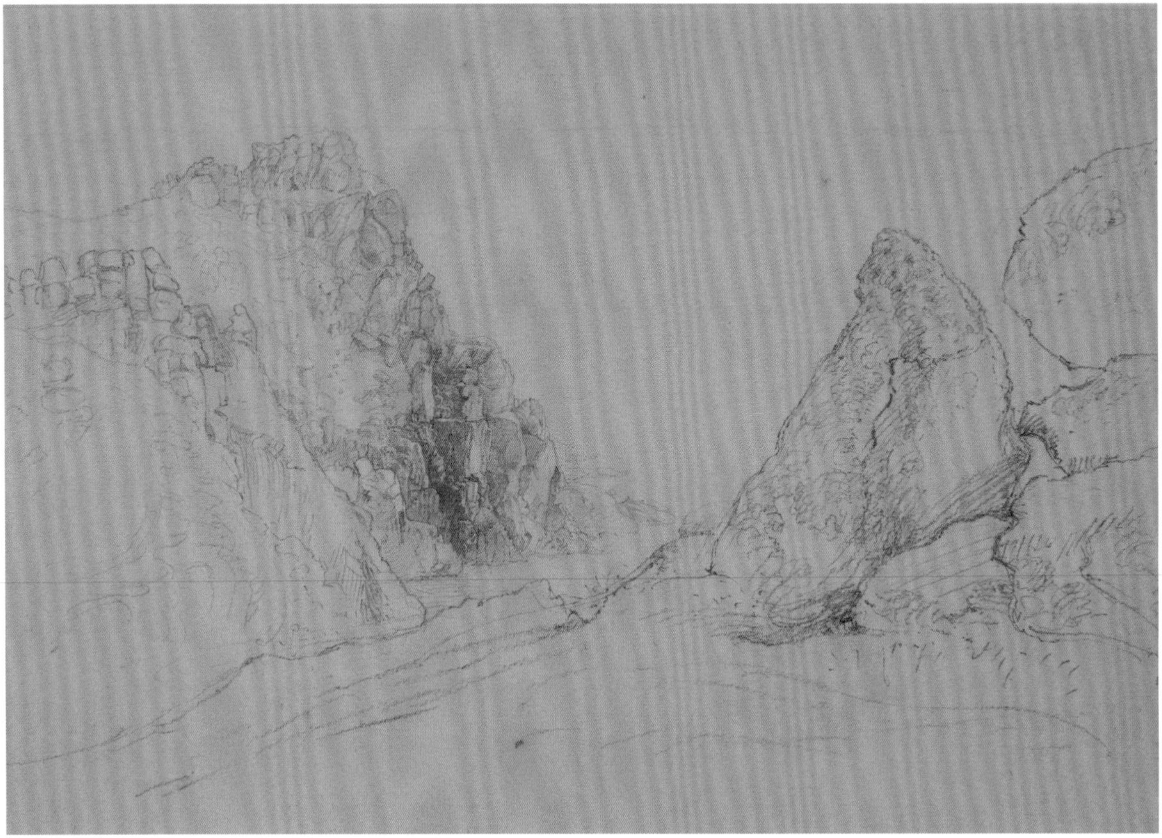

17. Samuel Palmer (1805–1881)

Near Land's End, Cornwall

1857

Chalk, 279 × 385 mm

University of Reading Art Collection

UAC/10563

Inscriptions: Near Lands End *(bottom left, in chalk)*; no gold green wash [?] *(bottom centre, illegible, in chalk)*; Lichen *(bottom right, in chalk, with arrow pointing upwards)*; 25 *(bottom right, in chalk)*; 01–01/ No 122/ 01–01 *(top left, sticker affixed with inscription printed and in pencil)*; Cornwall 1857 *(verso, centre, in pencil)*; £1 *(verso, centre left, in pencil)*; Nick W *(verso, right, in pencil)*; The writing above and on the Other Side is S. Palmer's/ Kensington Period./ A. H. P *(verso, bottom left, in pencil)*; A 21363 *(verso, bottom right, in pencil)*

Provenance: A. H. Palmer (1853–1932); Purchased from Colnaghi, London, 10 May 1956.

18. Edwin John Victor Pasmore (1908–1998)

River Landscape (Drawing for 'Suburban Gardens')

c.1947

Ink, 191 × 254 mm

University of Reading Art Collection

UAC/10571

Inscriptions: VP *(bottom right, in ink)*

Provenance: Purchased from Roland, Browse & Delbanco, London, 4 January 1955.

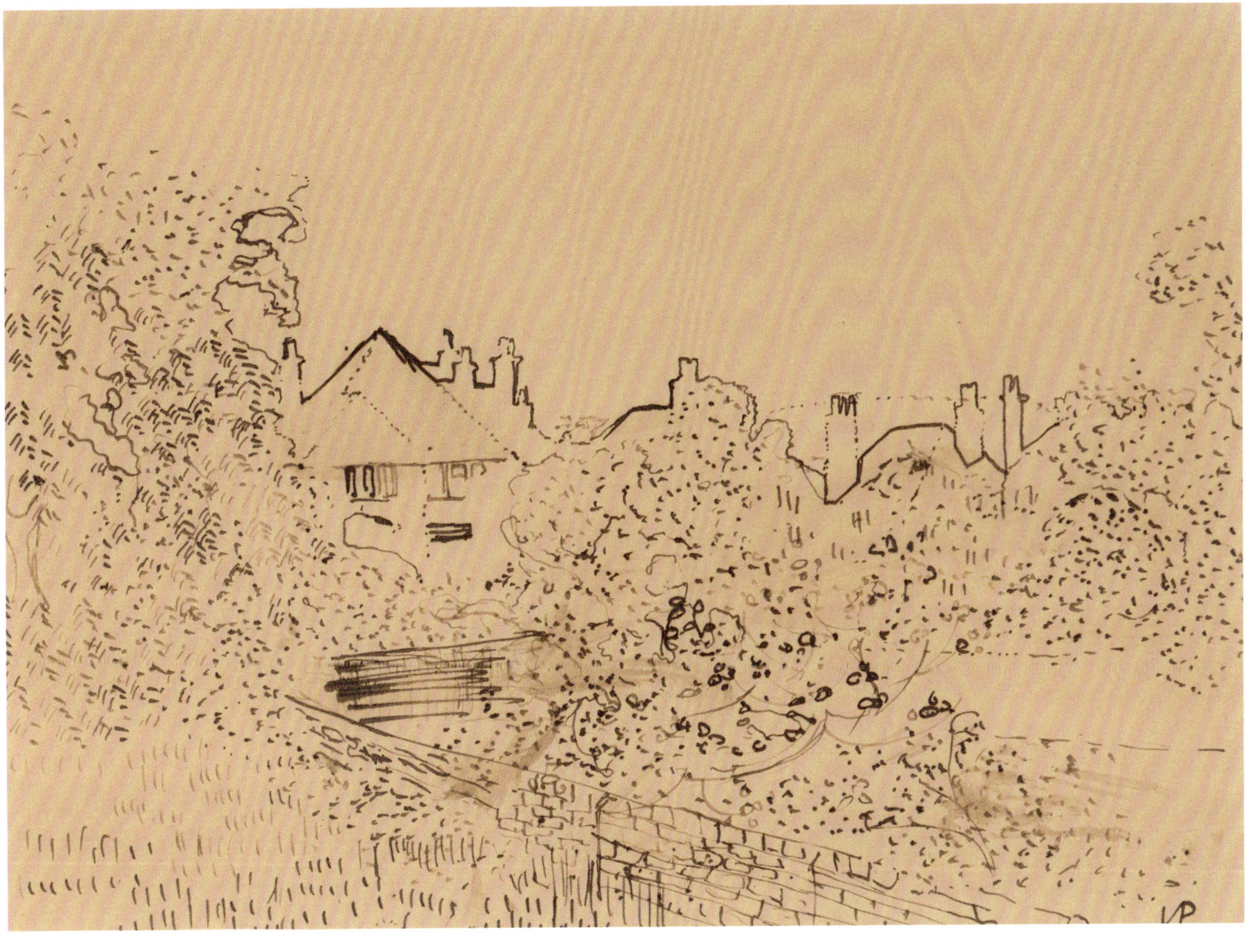

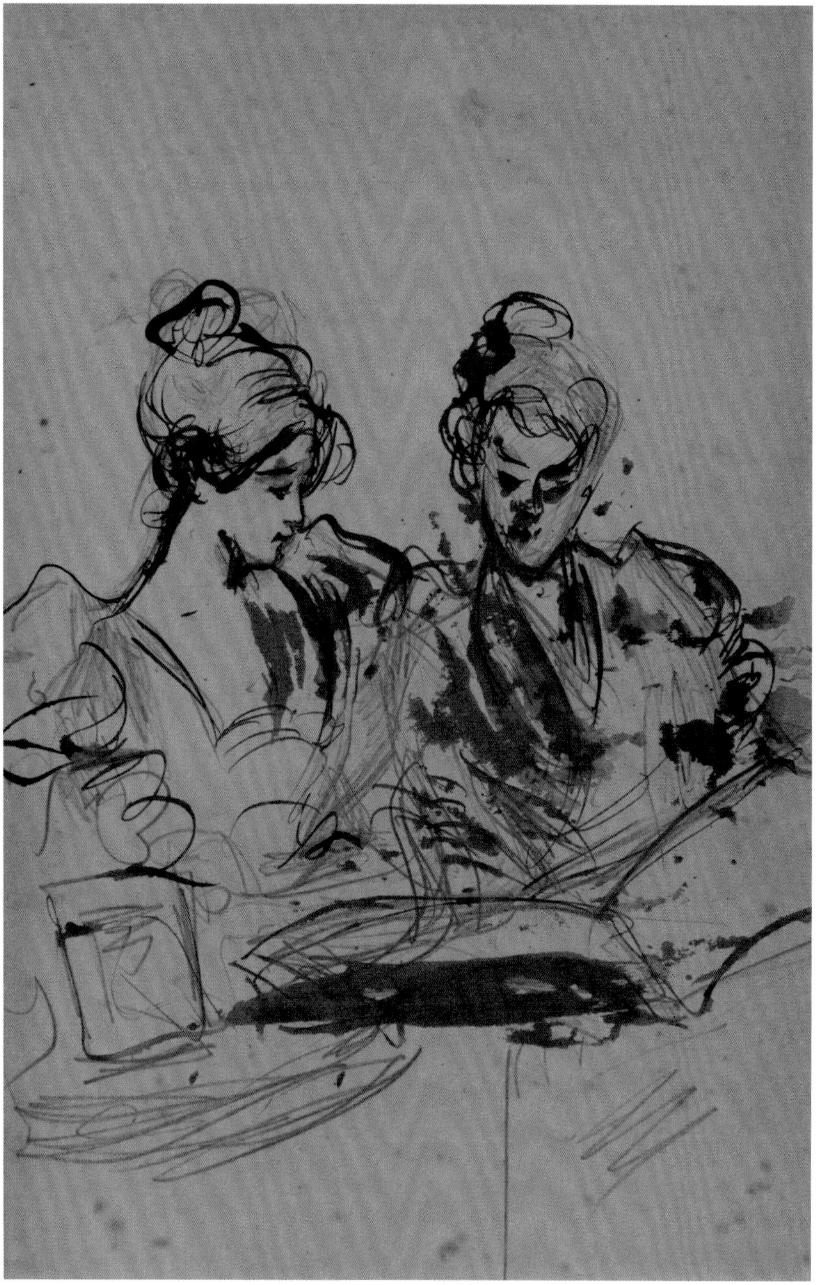

19. Albert de Belleroche (1864–1944)

Two Women Reading (Étude de Femme)

Ink over pencil, 203 × 124 mm

University of Reading Art Collection

UAC/10568

Provenance: Leicester Galleries, 1954; Professor James Anthony Betts (1897–1980); Purchased from Paul Betts, 1994.

20. Albert de Belleroche (1864–1944)

The Game of Checkers (La Partie de Dames) – Dr Demay & Friend

Chalk and pencil, 149 × 236 mm

University of Reading Art Collection

UAC/10569

Inscription: AB *(bottom right, in pencil)*

Provenance: Sold by Leicester Galleries, May-June 1954; Professor James Anthony Betts (1897–1980); Purchased from Paul Betts, 1994.

21. Albert de Belleroche (1864–1944)

Study from the Montparnasse Sketchbook: Portrait of Henri de Toulouse-Lautrec

Chalk, 102 × 76 mm

University of Reading Art Collection

UAC/10550

Inscriptions: 154 *(bottom left, in pencil)*; AR *(bottom right, in pencil)*

Provenance: Purchased from the artist's son, Count William de Belleroche (1913–1969), 22 March 1956.

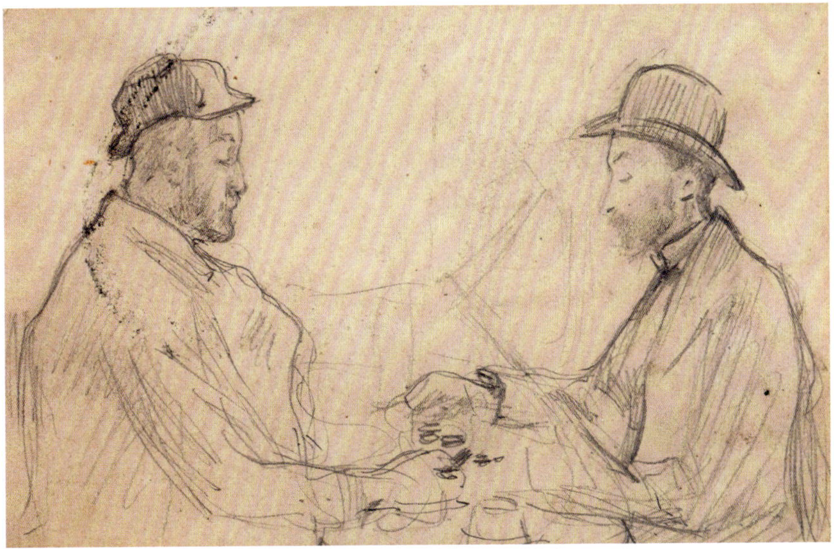

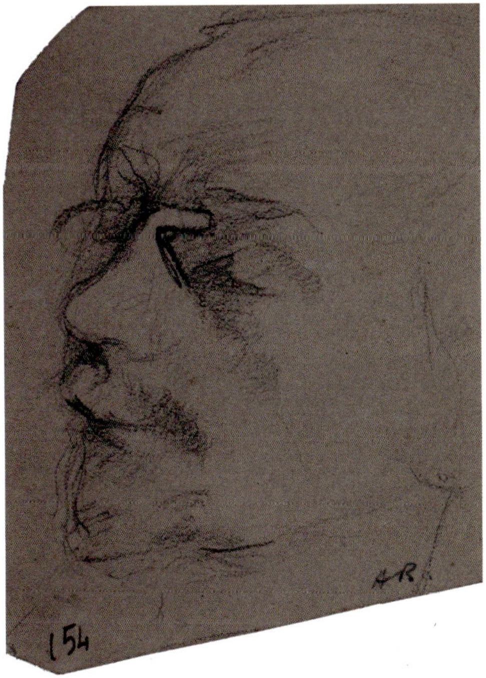
H.R.
154

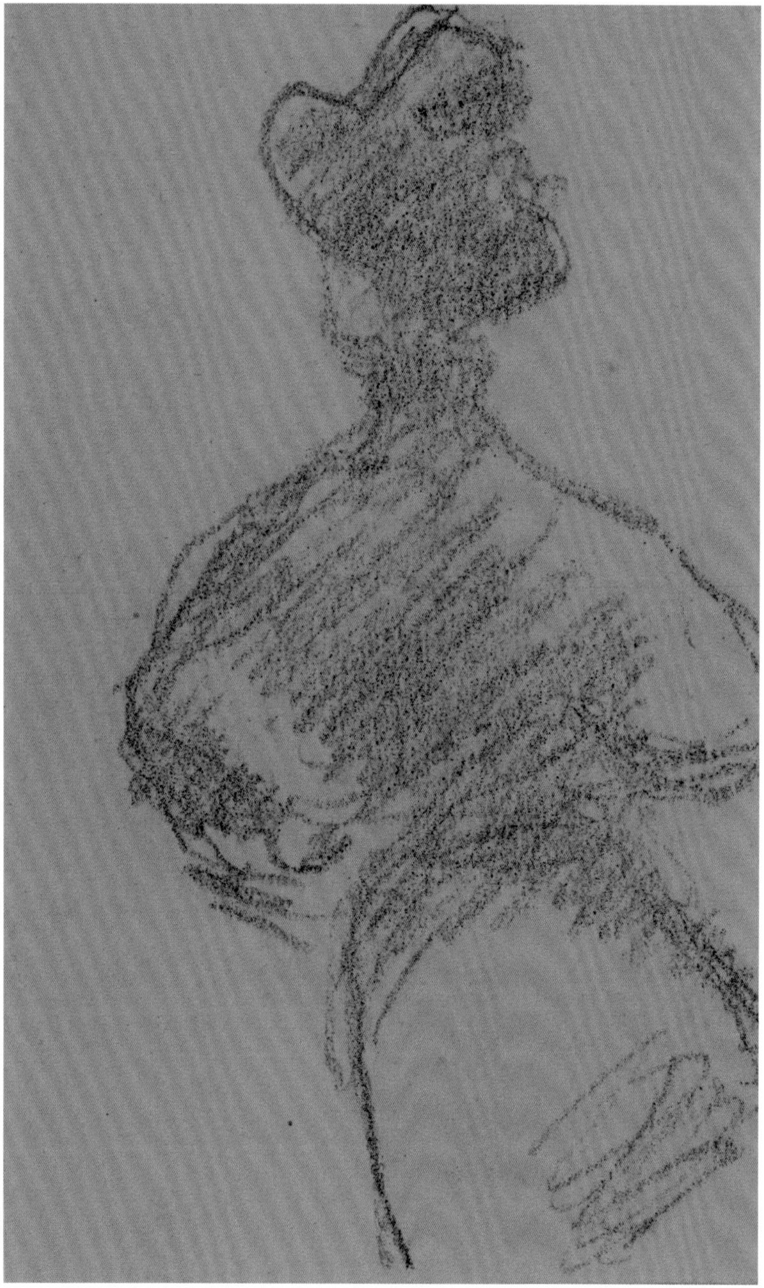

22. Albert de Belleroche (1864–1944)

Study from the Montparnasse Sketchbook: Woman in a Top Hat

Chalk, 117 × 74 mm

University of Reading Art Collection

UAC/10551

Provenance: Purchased from the artist's son, Count William de Belleroche (1913–1969), 22 March 1956.

23. Albert de Belleroche (1864–1944)

Study from the Montparnasse Sketchbook: Woman Sitting at a Table

Pencil, 156 × 197 mm (folded sheet)

University of Reading Art Collection

UAC/10552

Provenance: Purchased from the artist's son, Count William de Belleroche (1913–1969), 22 March 1956.

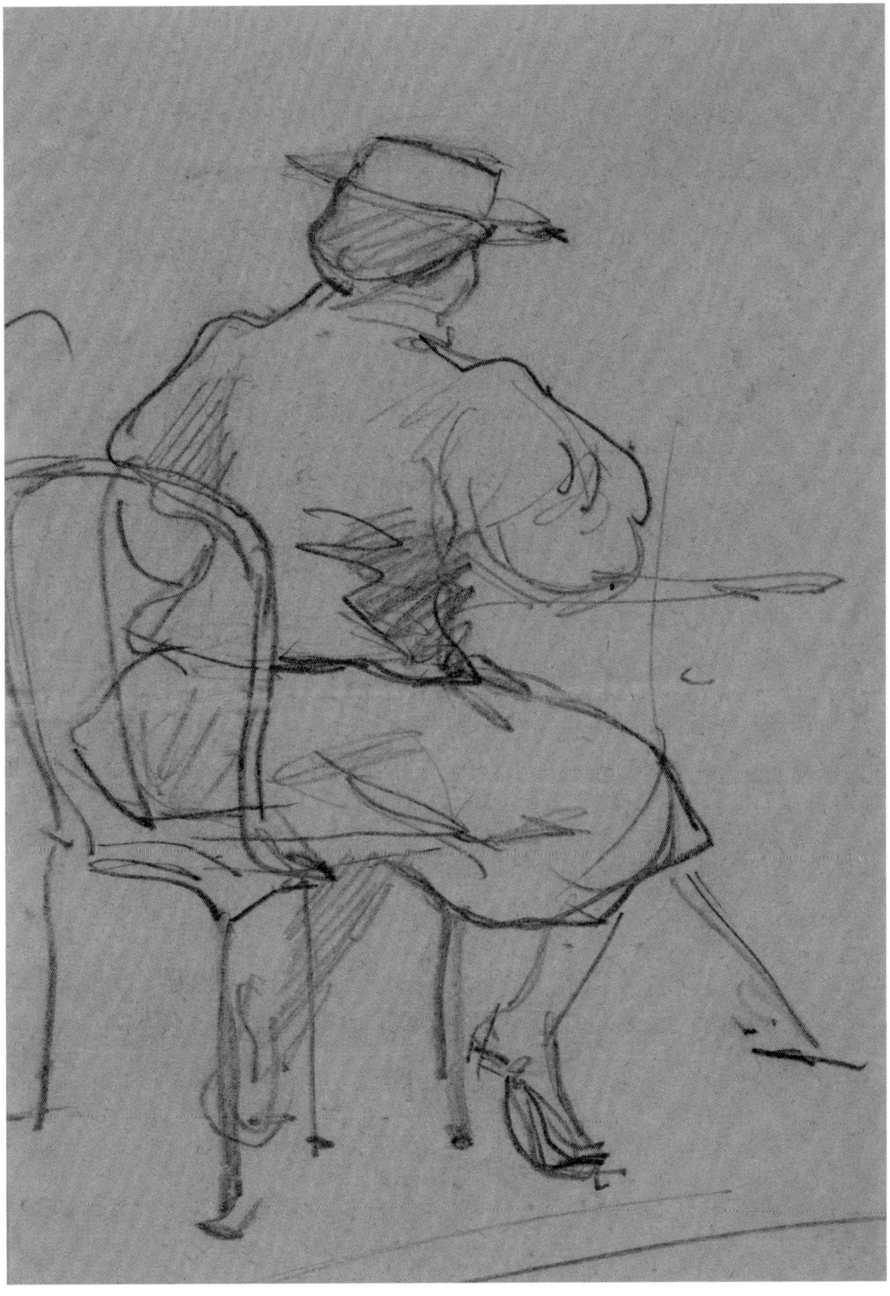

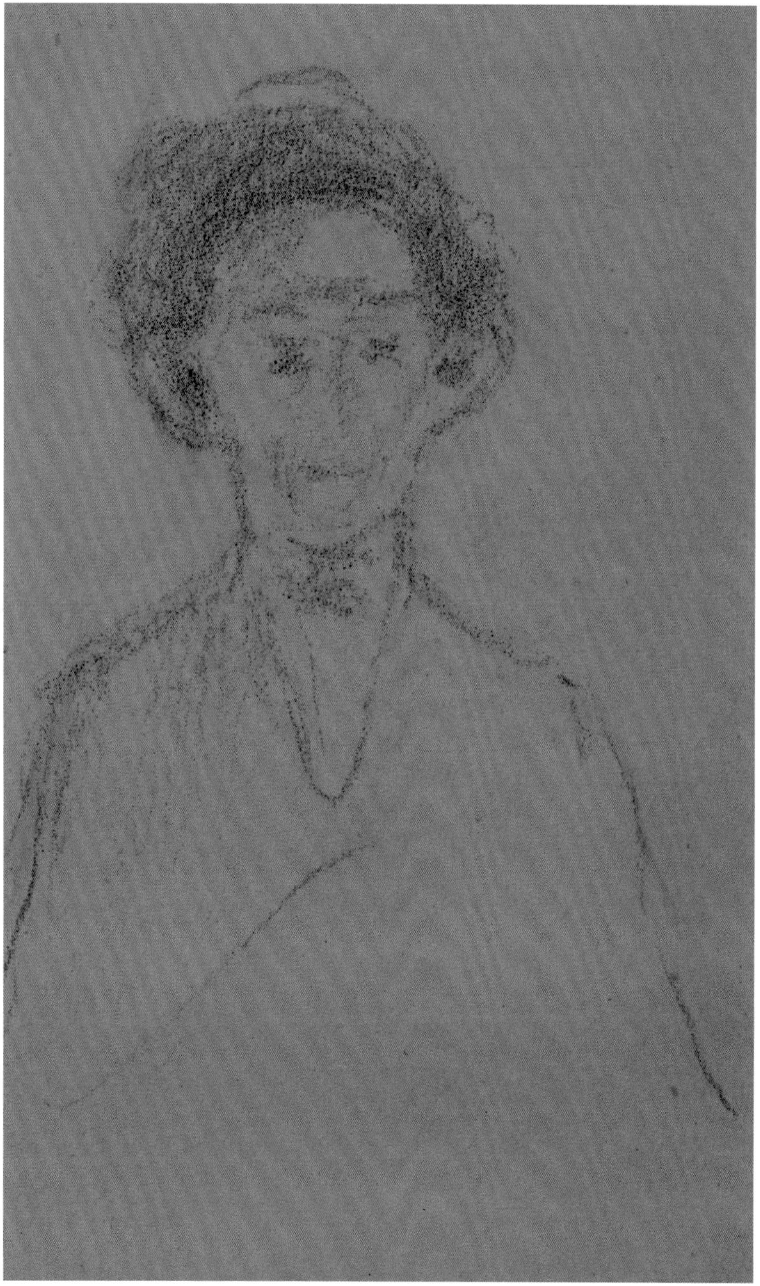

24. Albert de Belleroche (1864–1944)

Study from the Montparnasse Sketchbook: Man, in a Broad-Brimmed Hat

Chalk, 116 × 75 mm

University of Reading Art Collection

UAC/10553

Provenance: Purchased from the artist's son, Count William de Belleroche (1913–1969), 22 March 1956.

25. Albert de Belleroche (1864–1944)

Study from the Montparnasse Sketchbook: Man in a Top Hat

Chalk, 134 × 101 mm

University of Reading Art Collection

UAC/10554

Provenance: Purchased from the artist's son, Count William de Belleroche (1913–1969), 22 March 1956.

26. Jean-Louis Forain (1852–1931)

Man in Formal Attire

Chalk, 372 × 290 mm

University of Reading Art Collection

UAC/10580

Provenance: Ambroise Vollard (1866–1939); Purchased from K. E. Maison and Co, London, 9 February 1954.

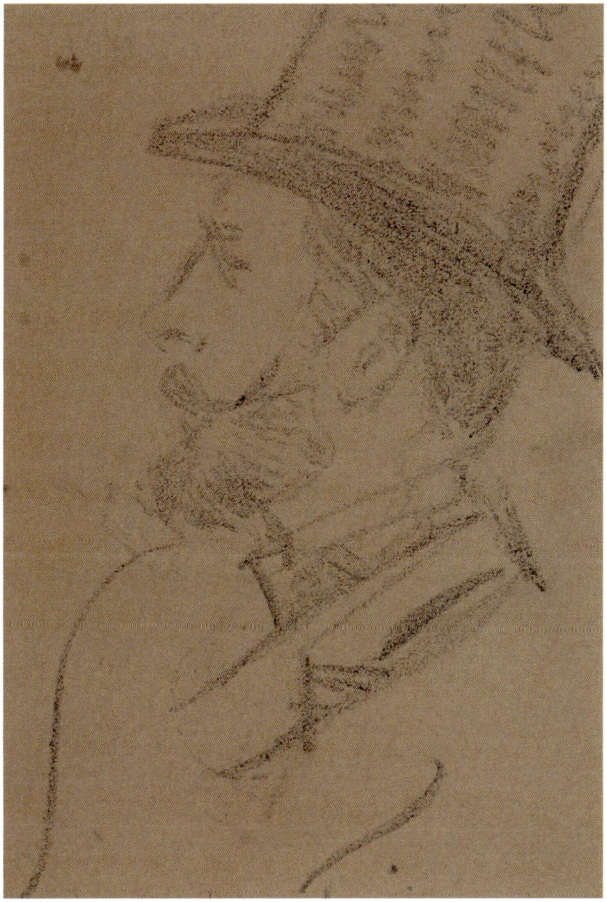

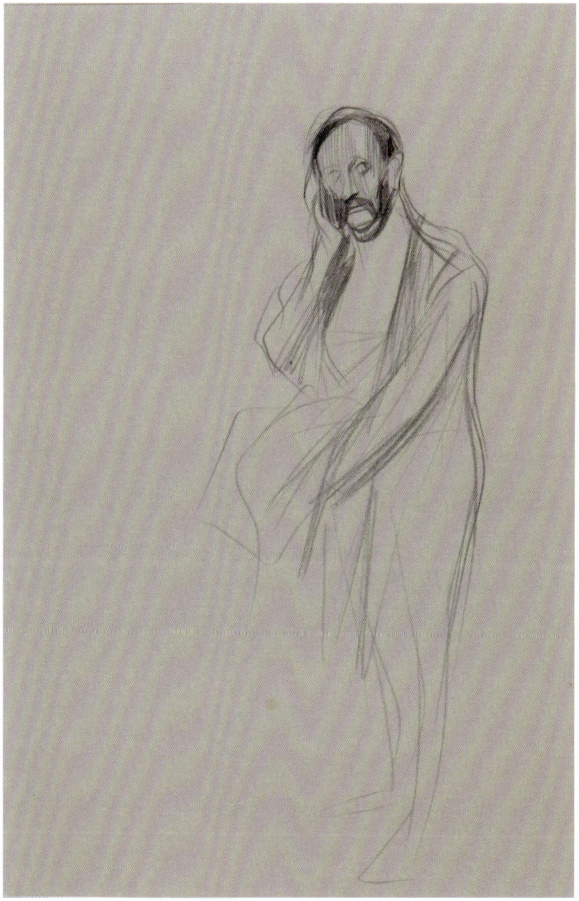

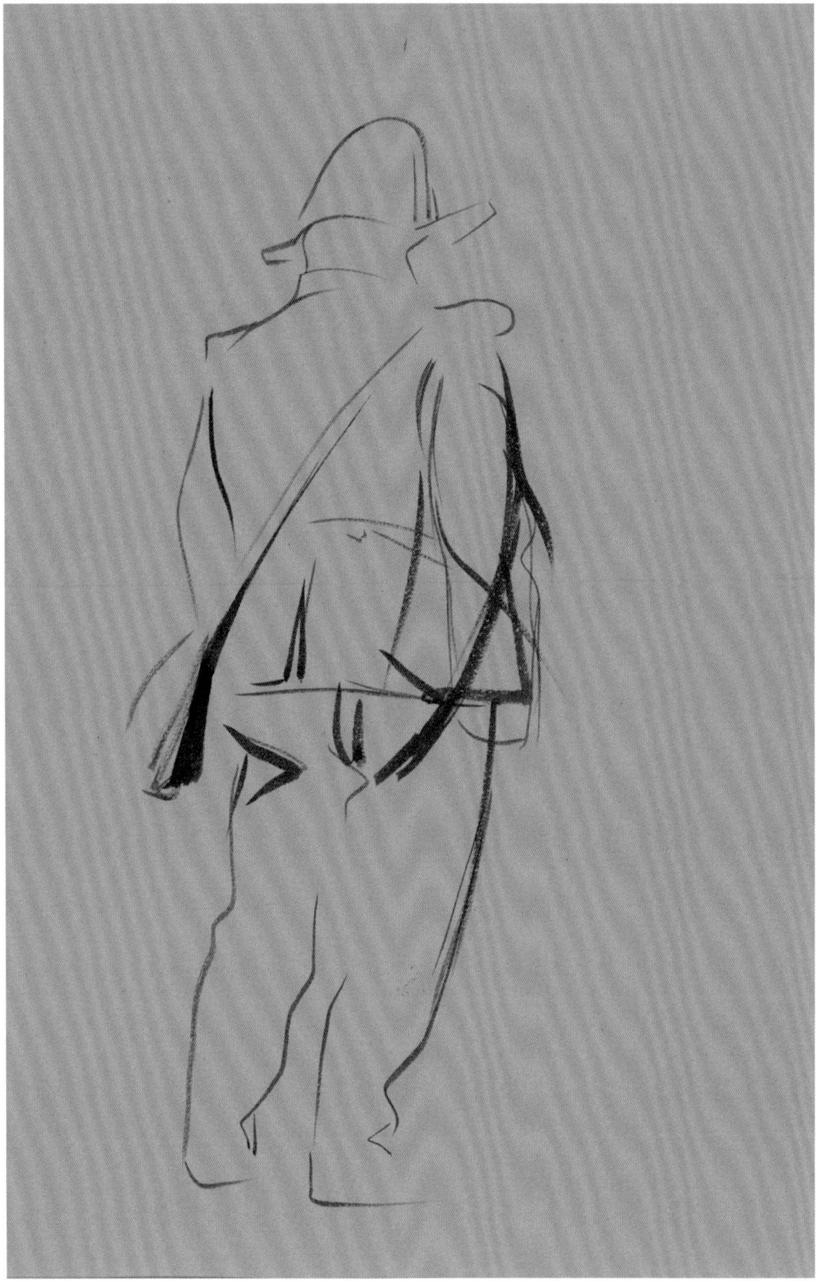

27. Jean-Louis Forain (1852-1931)

Military Officer

Ink, 375 × 274 mm

University of Reading Art Collection

UAC/10581

Provenance: Ambroise Vollard (1866-1939); Purchased from K. E. Maison and Co, London, 9 February 1954.

28. James Abbott McNeill Whistler (1834–1903)

The Fellow Traveller (Study of Ronald Murray Phillip)

1900–1901

Ink, 159 × 111 mm

University of Reading Art Collection

UAC/10519

Inscription: signed with butterfly *(centre left, in ink)*; Portrait of/ Ronald Philip *(verso, centre, in pencil)*; A. 20953 *(verso, bottom right, in pencil)*

Provenance: Whistler's studio at death; Miss Rosalind Bernie Philip, sister-in-law of the artist (1873–1958); sold to Colnaghi, London dealers, 25 June 1955; purchased from Colnaghi, London, 10 May 1956.

29. Gwendolen Mary John, called Gwen John (1976–1939)

Standing Female Nude; (verso) Seated Woman

Chalk, 229 × 181 mm

University of Reading Art Collection

UAC/10567

Provenance: Purchased from Colnaghi, London, 10 May 1956.

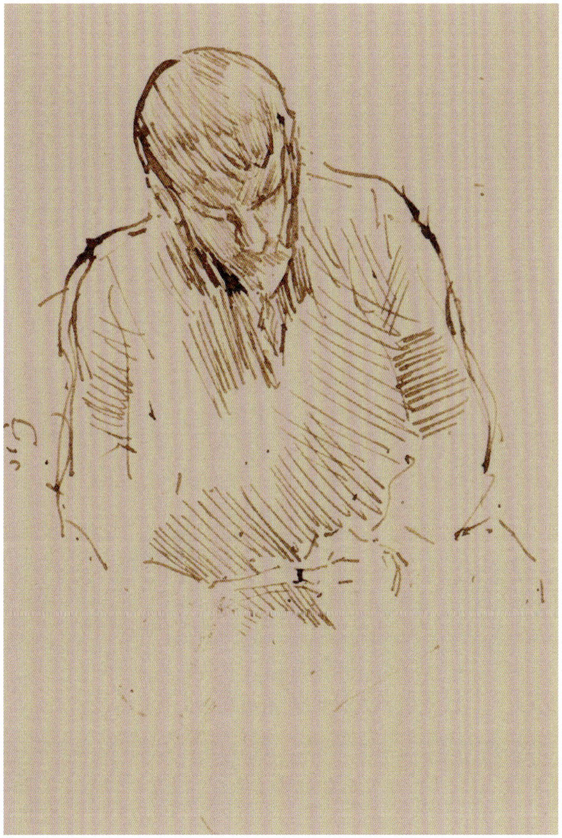

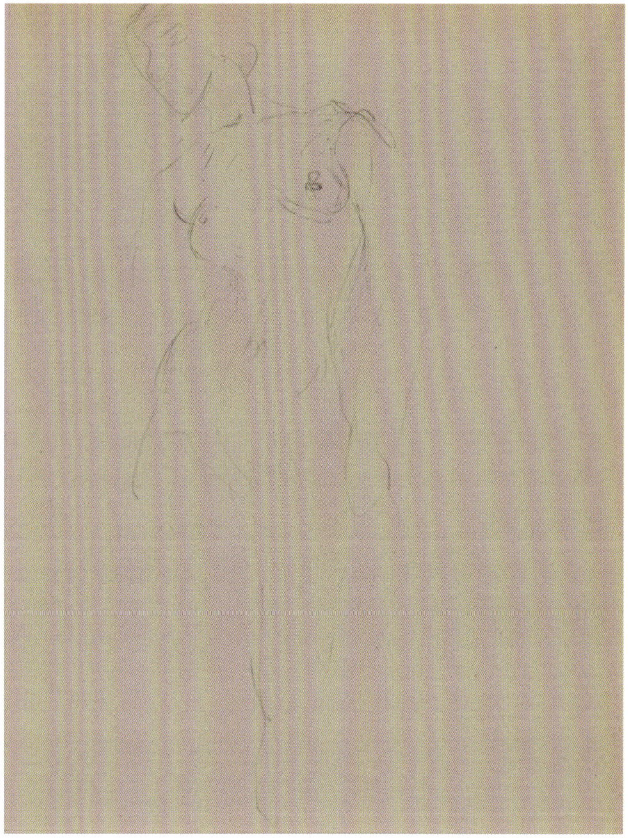

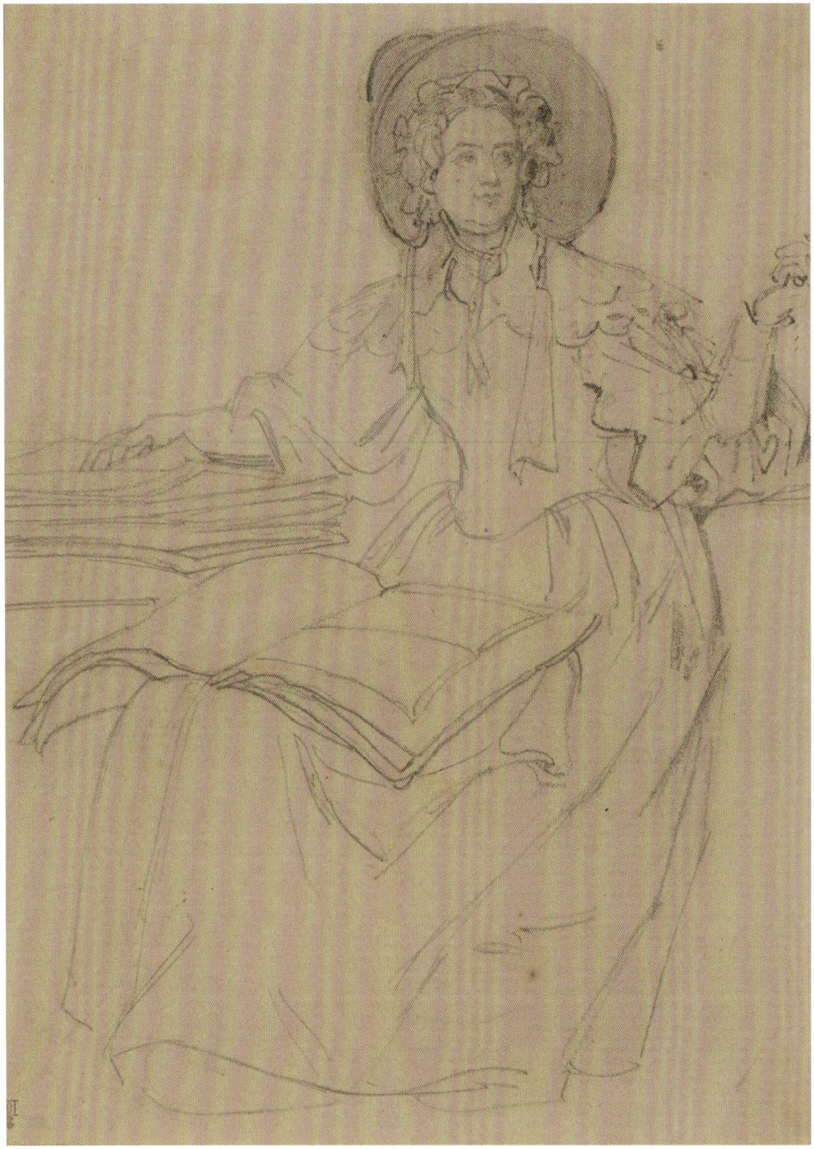

30. Daniel Maclise RA (1806–1870)

Study for a Portrait of Mary Russell Mitford (1787–1855)

*c.*1830

Pencil, chalk and wash, 199 × 152 mm

University of Reading Art Collection
UAC/10564

Inscription: DD *(bottom left, collector's mark, stamped in ink)*/ A17903 *(verso, bottom right, in pencil)*

Provenance: Sir William Richard Drake, F.S.A (1817–1890) (Lugt 736); Purchased from Colnaghi, London, 10 May 1956.

31. Edwin John Victor Pasmore (1908–1998)

Portrait of William Coldstream

Charcoal, 254 × 356 mm

University of Reading Art Collection
UAC/10570

Inscription: VP *(bottom right, signed, in crayon)*

Provenance: Purchased from Leicester Galleries, London, 5 February 1957.

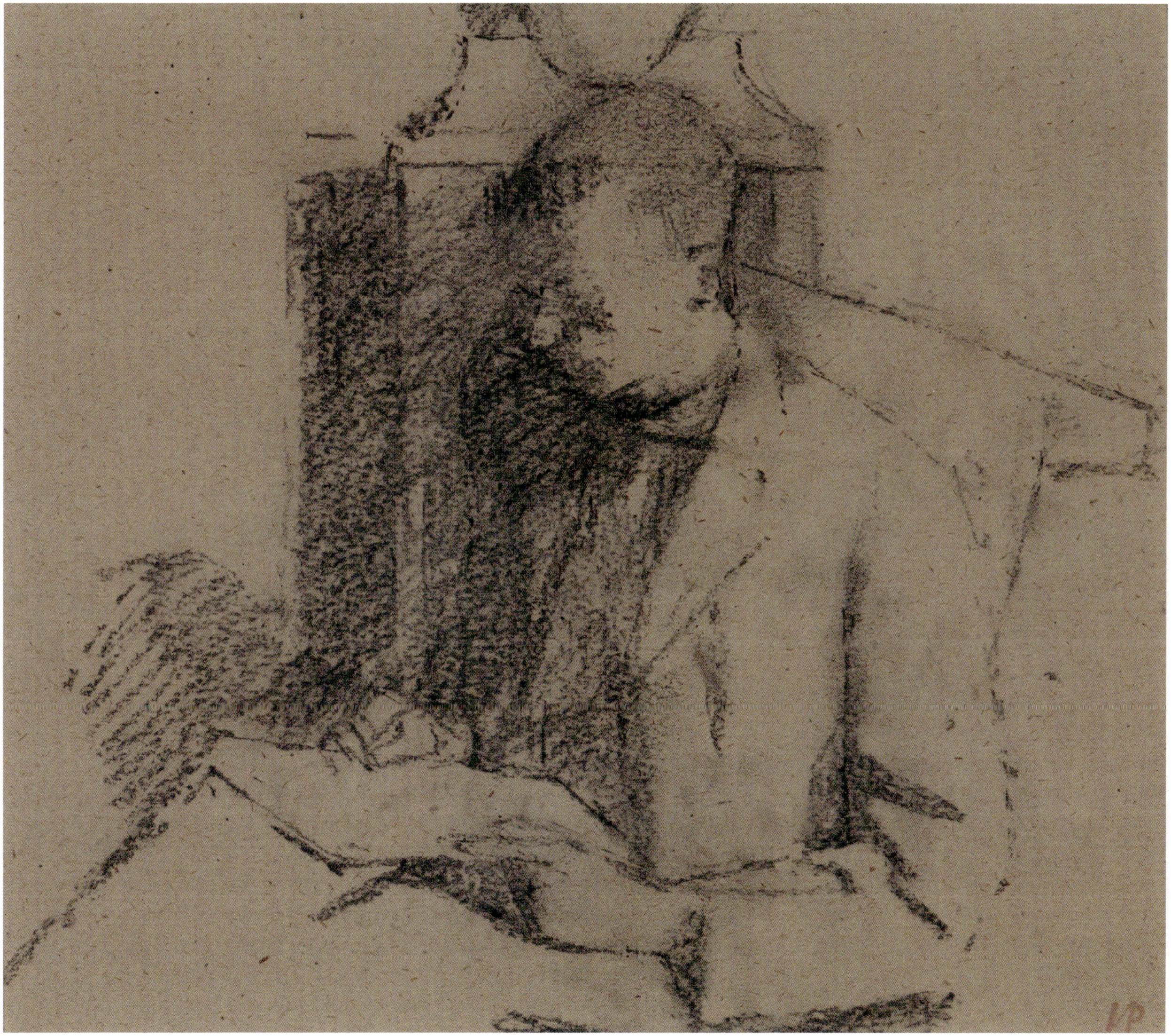

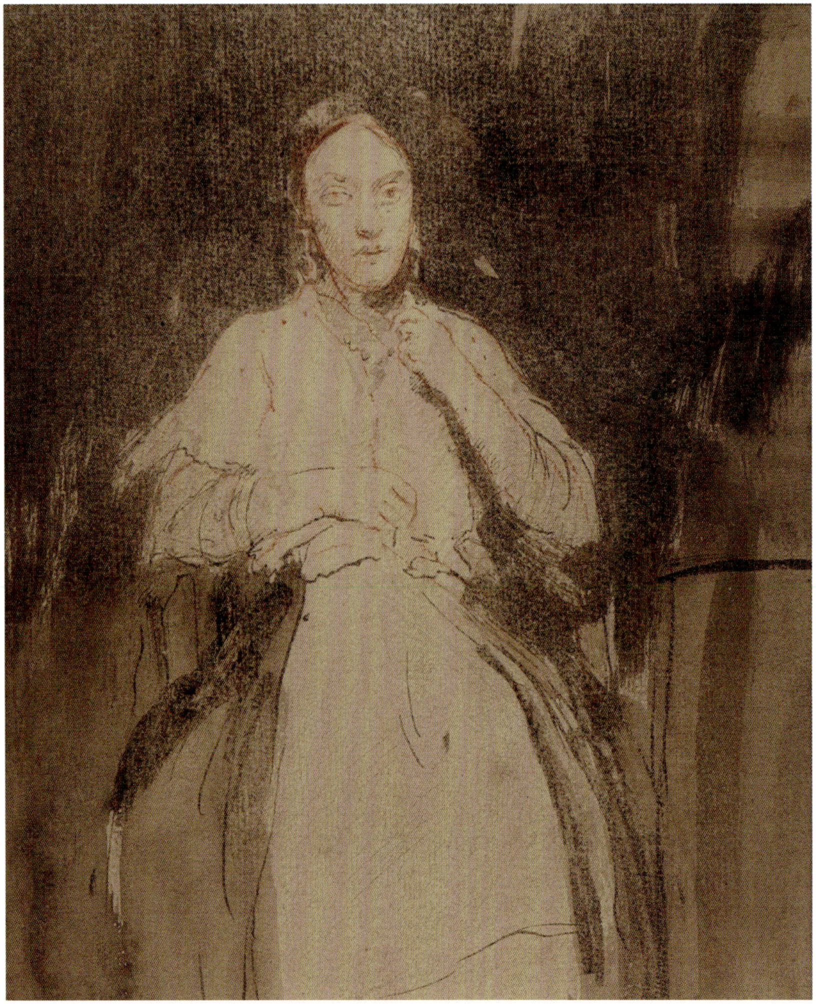

32. Ambrose McEvoy ARA (1878–1927)

Study for Phyllida

Ink, pencil, chalk and wash, 289 × 257 mm

University of Reading Art Collection

UAC/10565

Provenance: Mrs Claude Johnson; Purchased from Leicester Galleries, London, 11 December 1953.

33. Barnett Freedman (1901–1958)

Standing Female Nude

1929

Ink and wash over pencil, 411 × 216 mm

University of Reading Art Collection

UAC/10546

Inscription: Barnett Freedman, 1929 *(bottom right, signed and dated, in ink)*; Nude Study *(verso, centre, in ink)*; for Anthony Betts *(verso, centre left, in pencil)*

Provenance: Professor James Anthony Betts (1897–1980); Purchased from Paul Betts, 1994.

34. John Egerton Christmas Piper (1903–1992)

Standing Female Nude

Ink, wash and white heightening, 465 × 239 mm

University of Reading Art Collection

UAC/10582

Inscription: John Piper *(bottom right, signature, in ink)*

Provenance: Purchased from the artist, 1 January 1956.

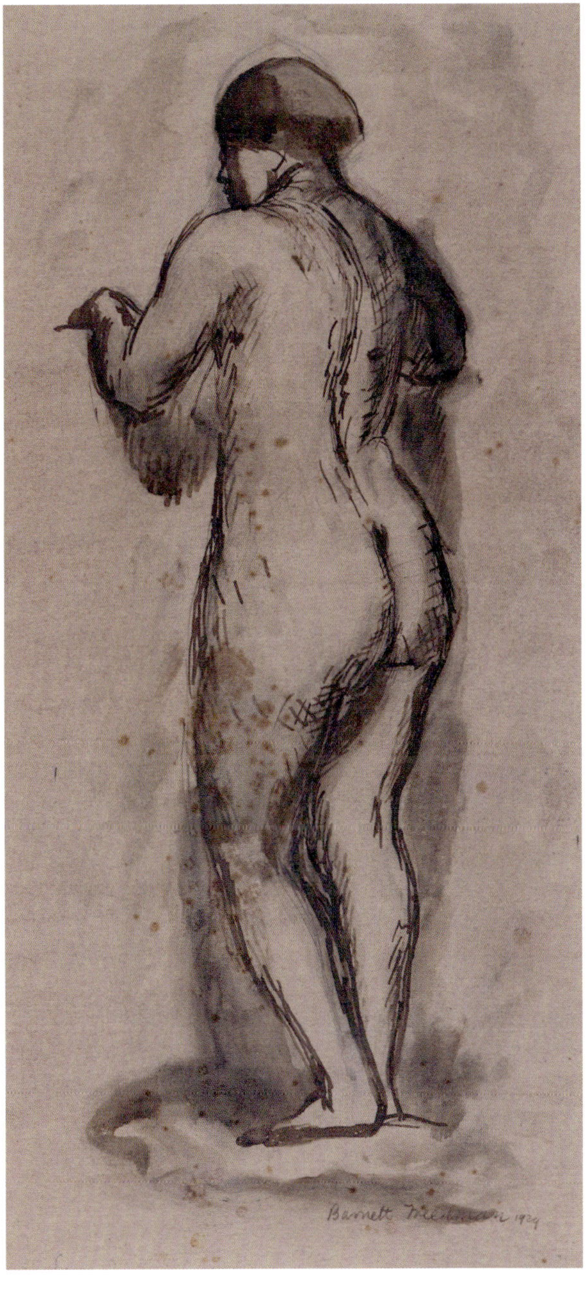

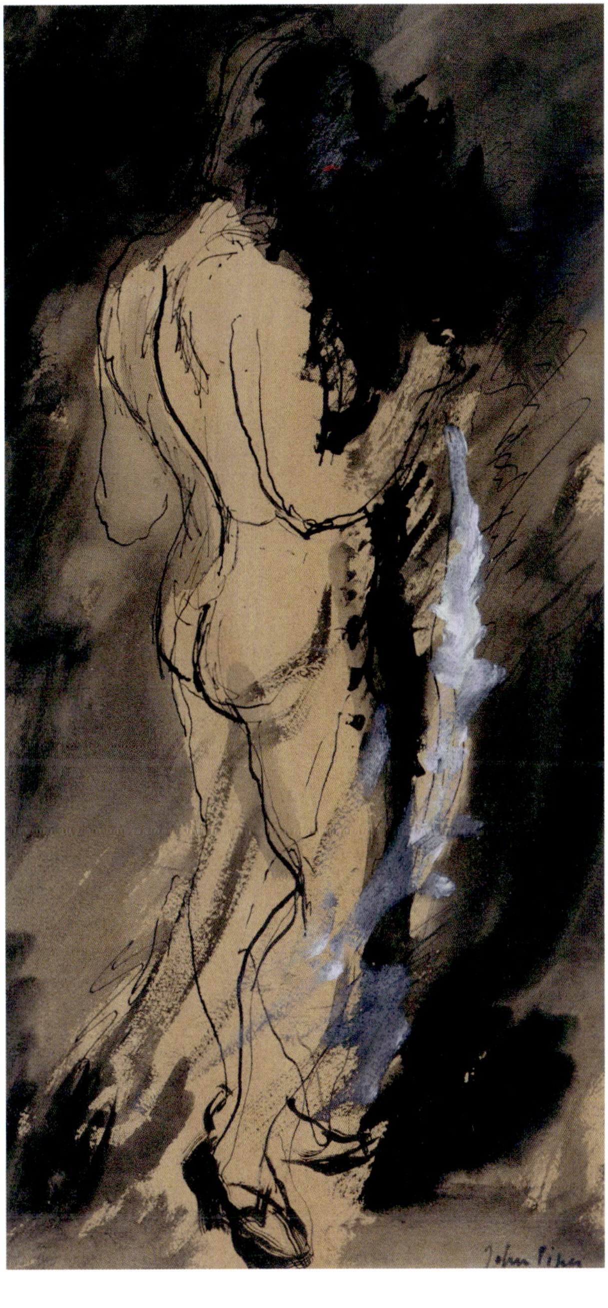
John Piper

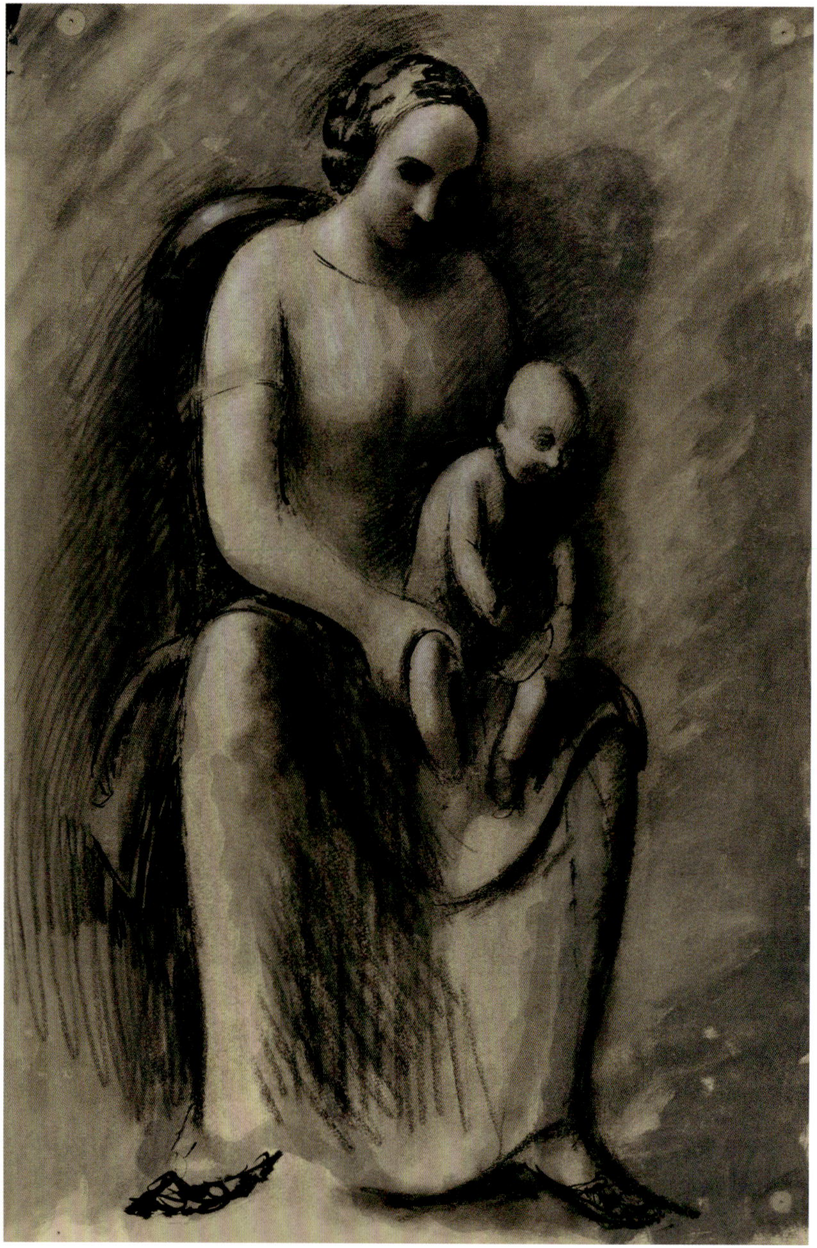

35. James Anthony Betts (1897–1980)

Mother and child

*c.*1928

Watercolour, charcoal, ink and white heightening, 559 × 379 mm

University of Reading Art Collection UAC/10851

Provenance: Gift of the family of the artist, 2006.

© Estate of J. Anthony Betts.

36. James Anthony Betts (1897–1980)

Baby Betts

*c.*1929–1930

Pastel, 560 × 430 mm

Reading Museum 1981.17.1

Inscription: Anthony Betts *(bottom left, signed, in image, in pencil)*; Baby Betts *(verso, in pencil)*

Provenance: Purchased from Abbot & Holder, 1981.

© Estate of J. Anthony Betts.

37. James Anthony Betts (1897–1980)

Man Sitting on a Bar Stool

1927

Ink, 382 × 294 mm

Reading Museum 1981.15.1

Inscription: Betts/ 1927 *(bottom right, signed and dated, in ink)*; Anthony Betts/ Professor of Art/ Reading *(verso, in centre, on mount board, in ink)*; Mike O'Halloran [?] Esq (Tramp) *(verso, bottom, in pencil)*; G0651 *(verso [sheet], in pencil)*

Provenance: Purchased from Abbot & Holder, 1981.

© Estate of J. Anthony Betts.

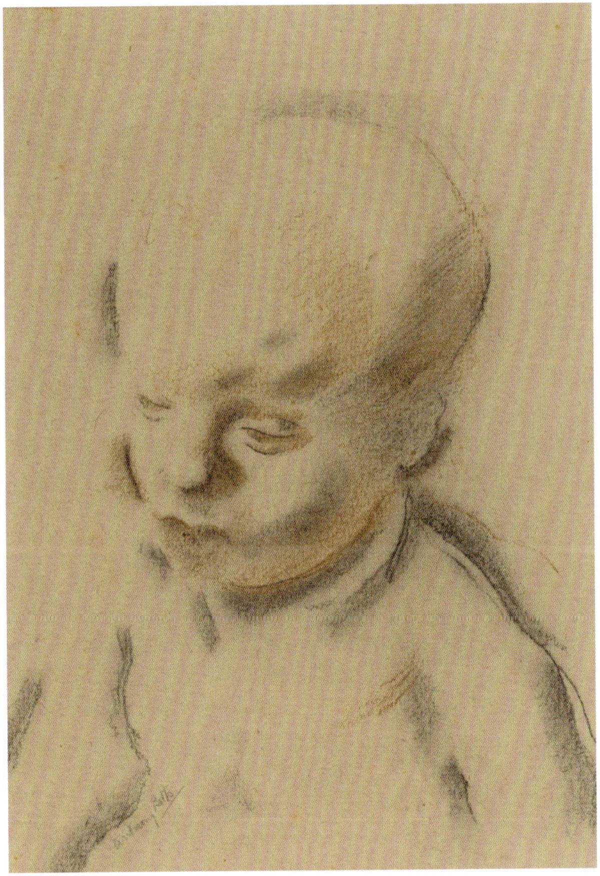

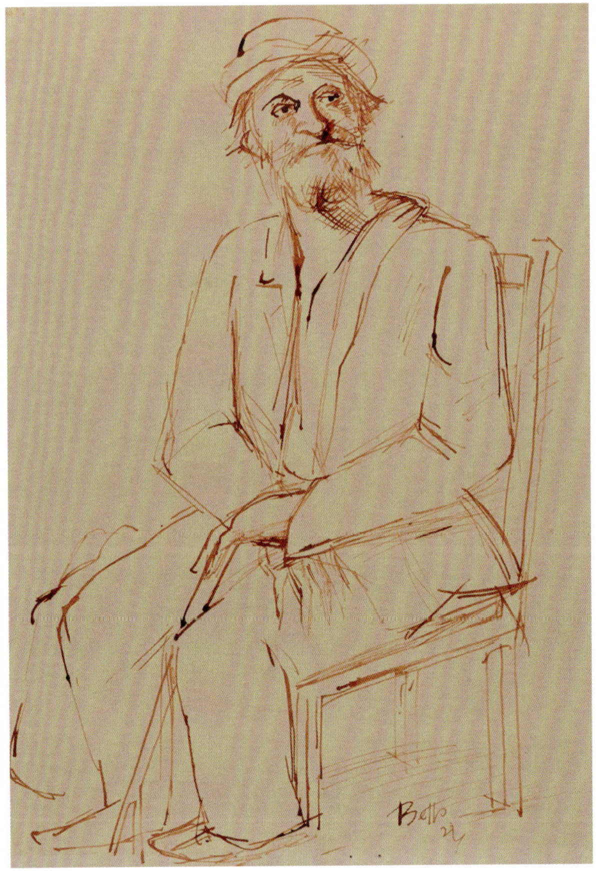

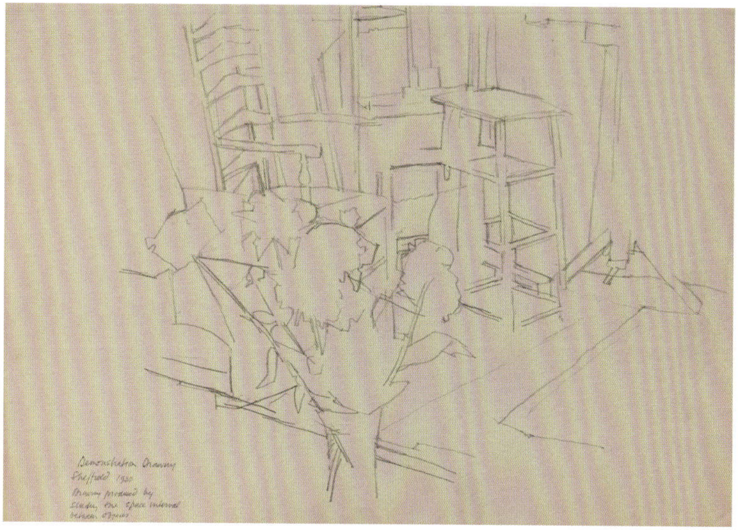

38. James Anthony Betts (1897–1980)

Demonstration Drawing

1930

Pencil, 350 × 500 mm

University of Reading Art Collection

UAC/10794

Inscription: Demonstration drawing/ Sheffield 1930/ Drawing produced by/ studying the space interval/ between objects *(bottom left, in ink)*

Provenance: Gift of the family of the artist, 2006.

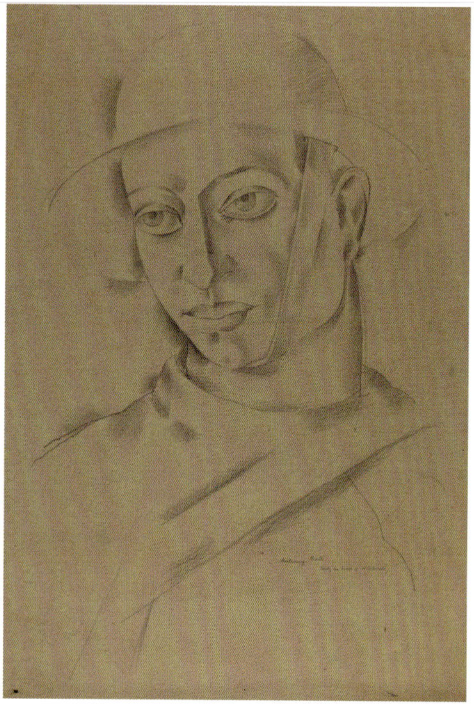

39. James Anthony Betts (1897–1980)

Study for the Head of a Soldier

*c.*1929

Pencil, 545 × 381 mm

University of Reading Art Collection

UAC/10852

Inscription: Anthony Betts/ Study for head of a soldier *(bottom right, signed, in pencil)*

Provenance: Gift of the family of the artist, 2006.

40. James Anthony Betts (1897–1980)

Standing Female Nude

*c.*1928

Watercolor, bodycolour, ink, charcoal, 565 × 405 mm

University of Reading Art Collection

UAC/10853

Provenance: Gift of the family of the artist, 2006.

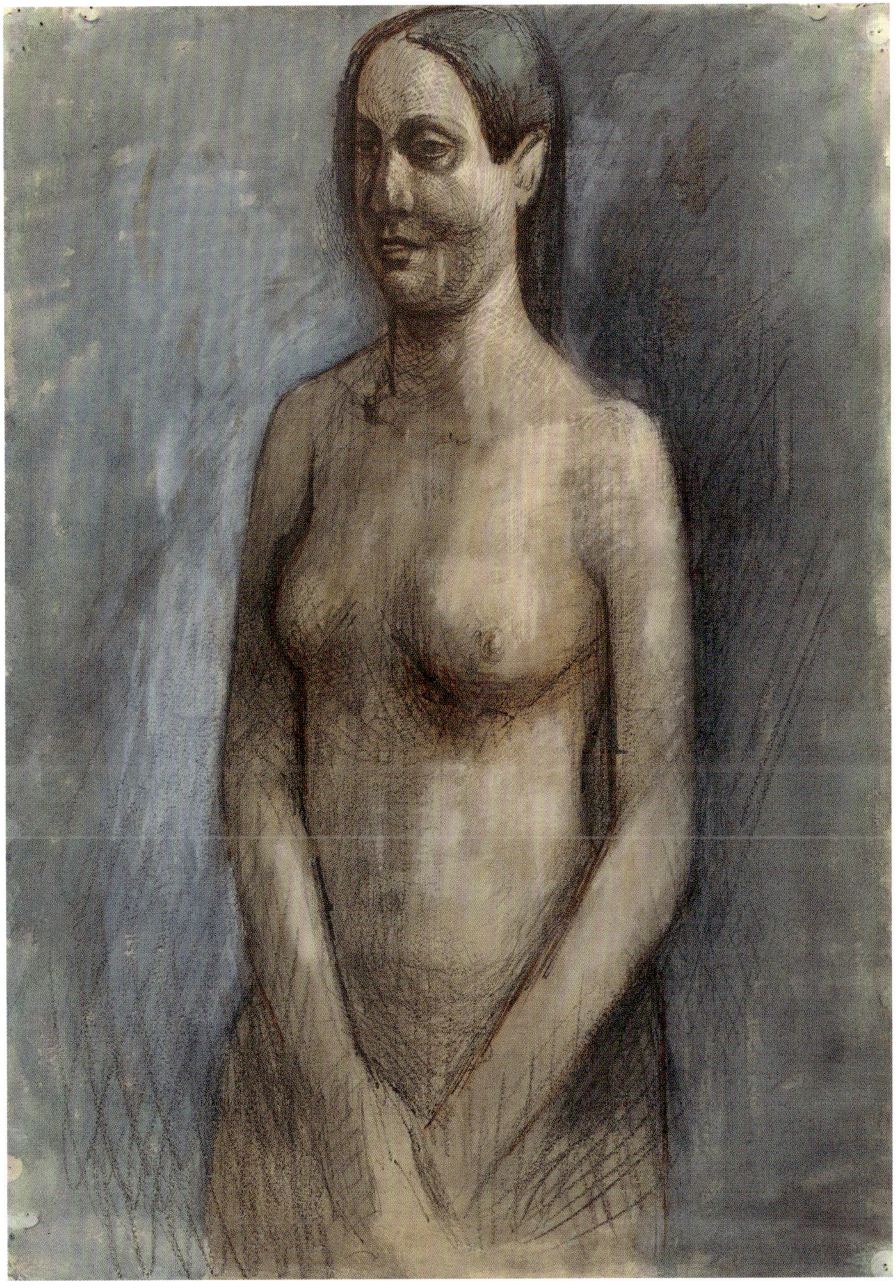

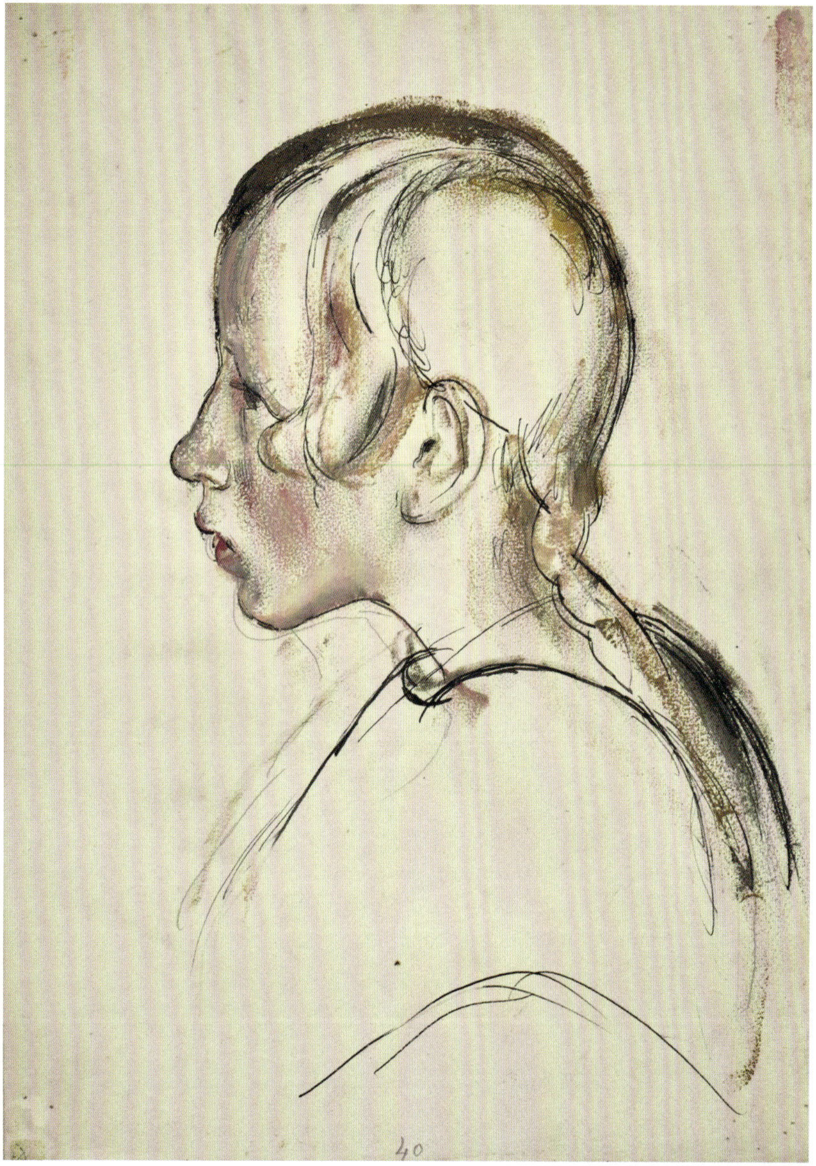

41. Leon Underwood (1890–1975)

Icelandic Girl

1923

Ink, pencil, bodycolour, 392 × 284 mm

British Museum 1996,0928.6

Provenance: In Underwood's studio at death; purchased from Emily Underwood, 1996.

42. Leon Underwood (1890–1975)

Standing Nude

1924

Conté crayon with white heightening, 615 × 460 mm

Private Collection

Inscription: Leon U. '24. *(right of figure, signed and dated, in crayon)*; L'academie Julian *(bottom centre-right, in ink)*

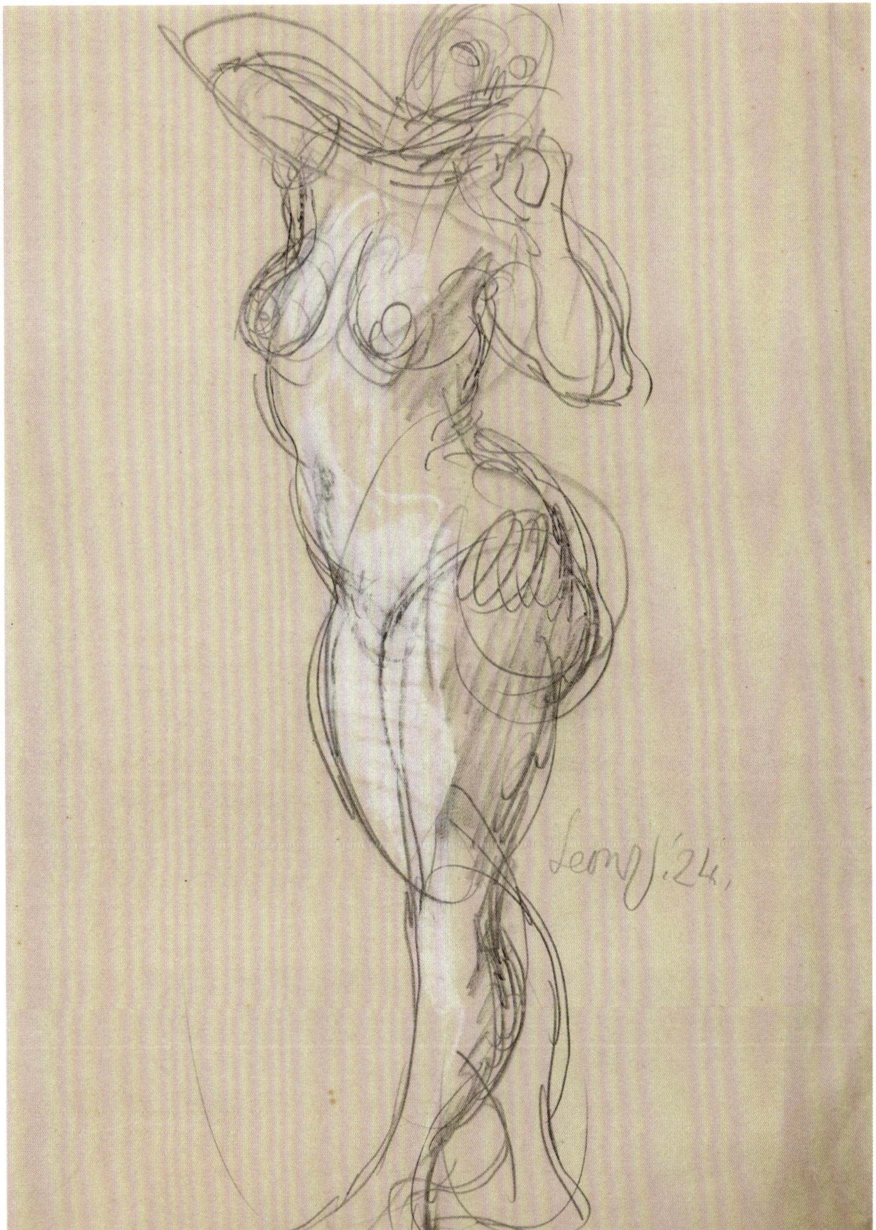

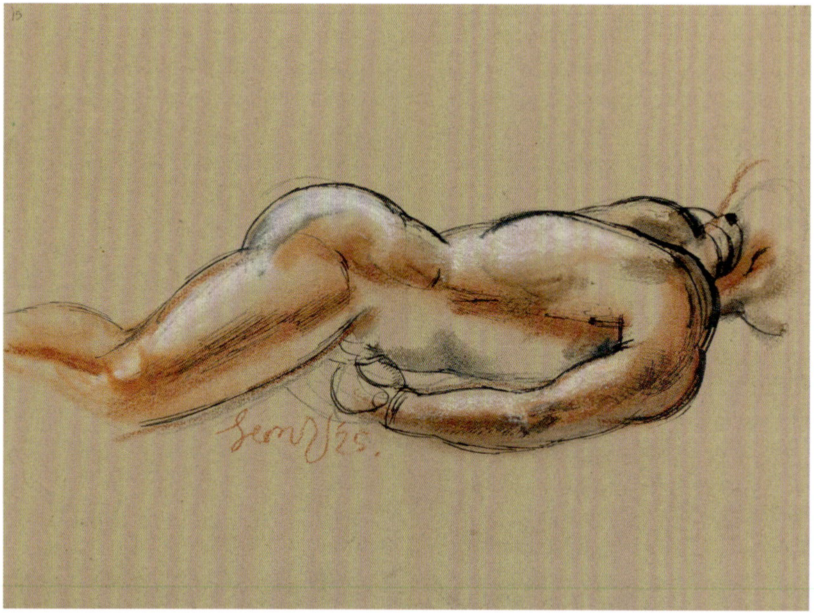

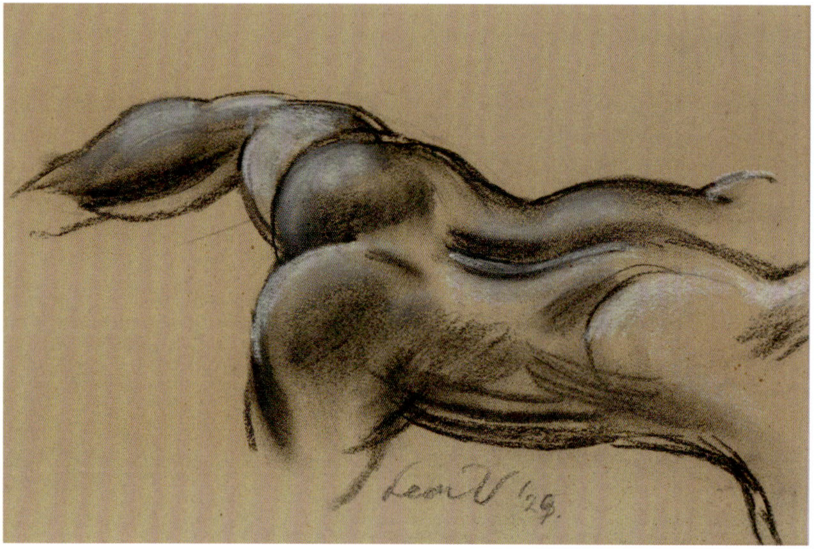

43. Leon Underwood (1890–1975)

Study for "Swimmers"

1925

Conté crayon with white heightening, 288 × 391 mm

Private Collection

Inscription: Leon U 25 *(bottom centre, signed and dated, in crayon)*

© Estate of Leon Underwood.

44. Leon Underwood (1890–1975)

Study for "Swimmers"

1925

Conté crayon with white heightening, 248 × 385 mm

Private Collection

Inscription: Leon U 25 *(bottom centre, signed and dated, in crayon)*

© Estate of Leon Underwood.

45. Leon Underwood (1890–1975)

Leaping Figure

*c.*1930s

Conté crayon, 379 × 256 mm

Private Collection

Inscription: Leon U. *(bottom right, signed, in crayon)*

© Estate of Leon Underwood.

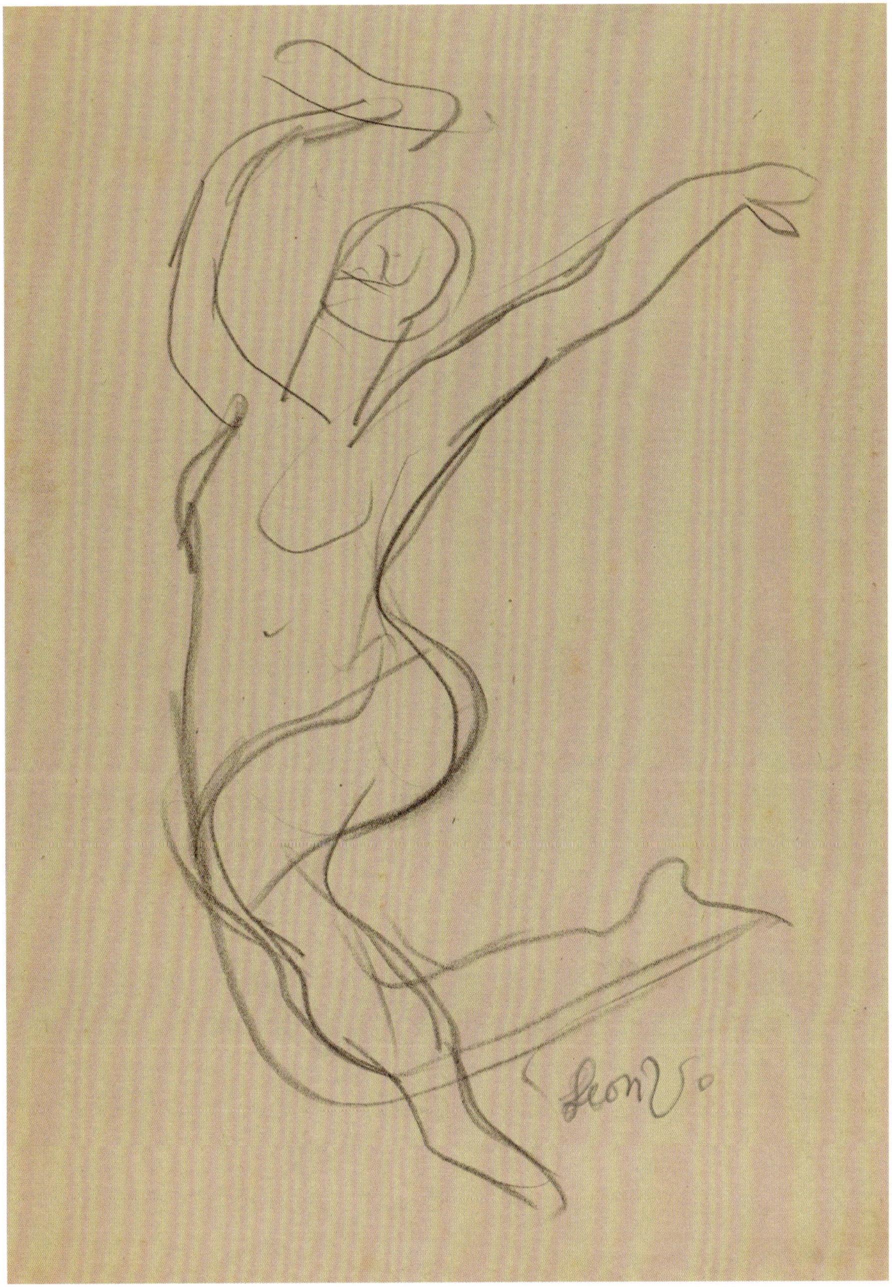

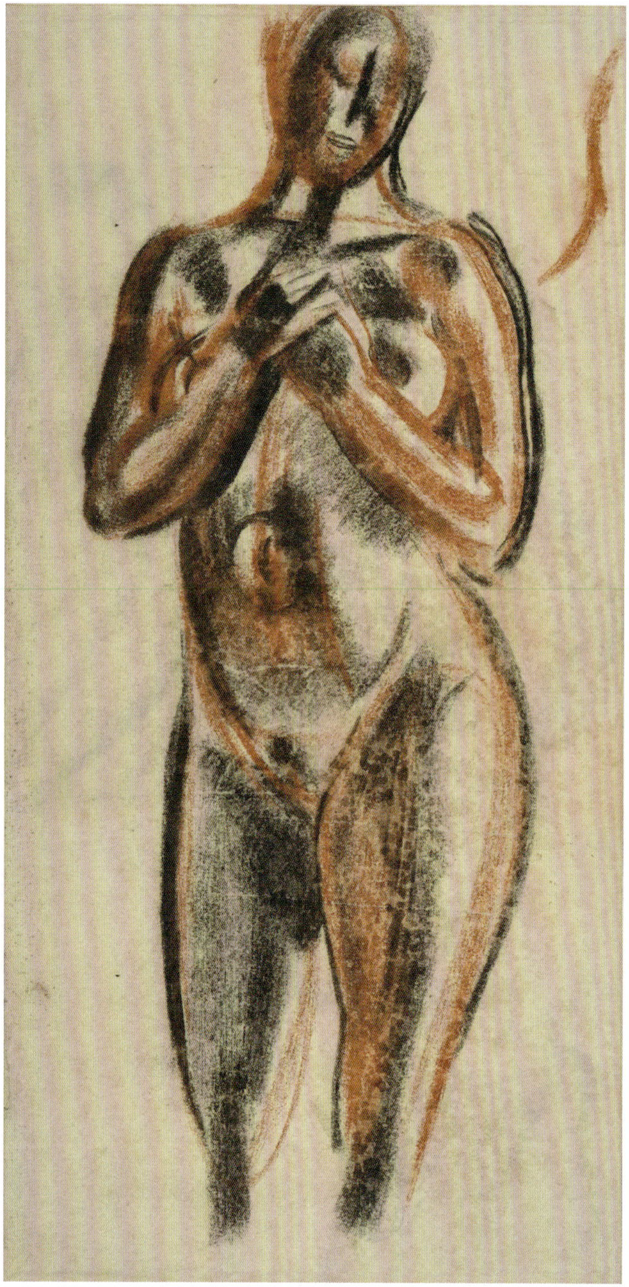

46. Blair Hughes-Stanton (1902–1981)

Standing Female Nude

*c.*1924

Chalk, 389 × 195 mm

British Museum 1940,0817.1

Provenance: Presented by Campbell Dodgson, 1940.

47. James Anthony Betts (1897–1980)

Reclining Nude

Bodycolour, 270 × 340 mm

British Museum 1927,0212.80

Inscription: Betts *(bottom centre-right, signed, in pencil)*

Provenance: Presented by Leon Underwood via the Contemporary Art Society, 1927.

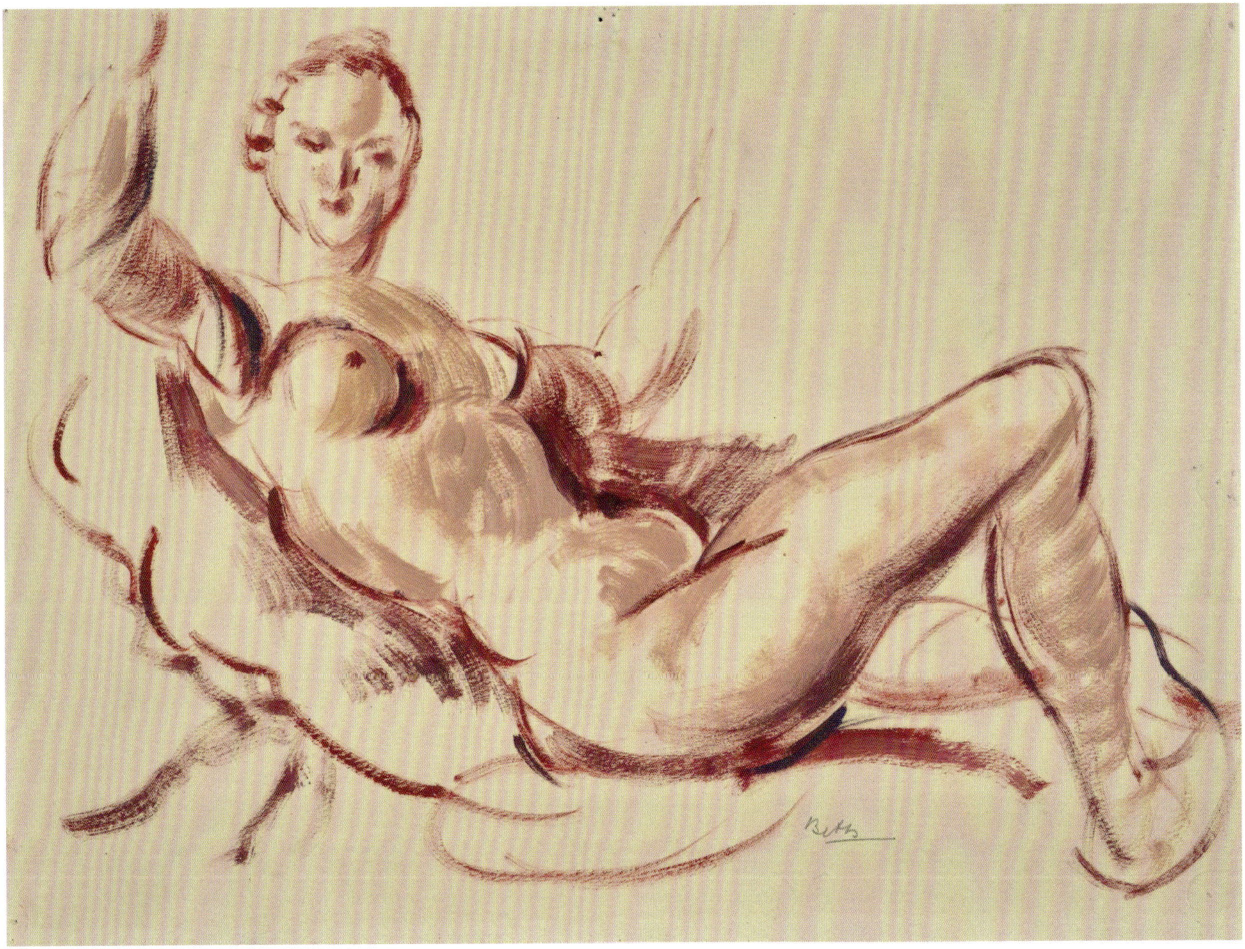

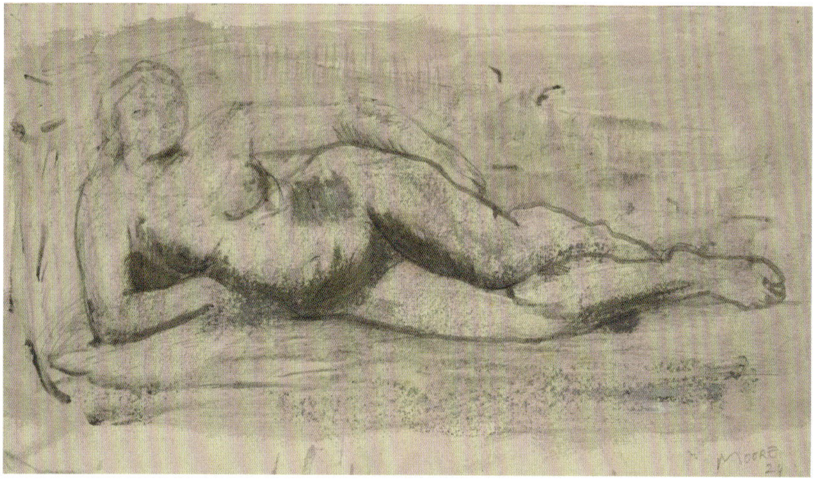

48. Henry Moore (1898–1986)

Reclining Nude

1924

Pencil, gouache and wash, 298 × 423 mm

British Museum 1969,0315.23

Inscription: Moore/ 24 (bottom right, in pencil)

Provenance: Purchased from Henry Moore, 1969.

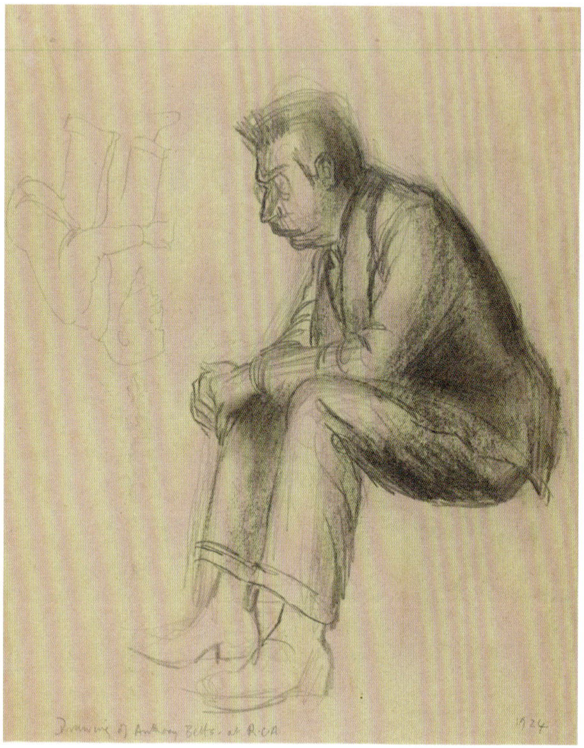

49. Henry Moore (1898–1986)

Anthony Betts at the R.C.A

1924

Pencil and chalk, 334 × 271 mm

The Henry Moore Foundation HMF 213

Inscription: Drawing of Anthony Betts at the R.C.A. *(bottom left, in pencil)*

Provenance: Gift of the artist, 1977.

50. James Anthony Betts (1897–1980)

Devastation After War; (verso) Figure Studies

1922

Watercolour, bodycolour, pencil; (verso) chalk, 380 × 354 mm

University of Reading Art Collection

UAC/10854

Inscription: Sketch for mural/ decoration for/ Prix de Rome 1922/ did not enter!!!! AB *(bottom left, in ink)*; Subject / Devastation after War *(bottom left centre, in ink)*

Provenance: Presented by the family of the artist, 2006.

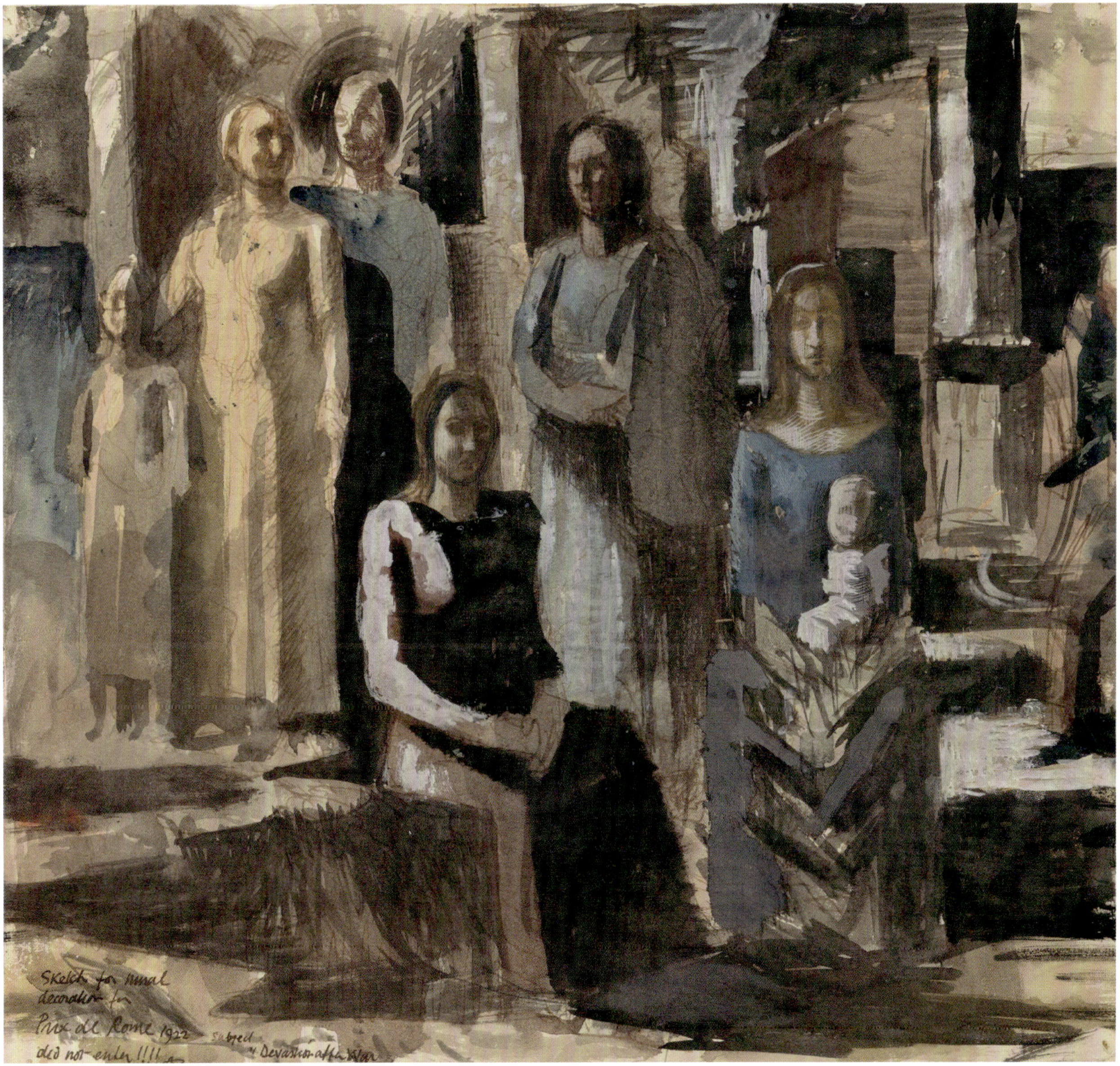
Sketch for mural
decoration for
Prix de Rome 1922
did not enter!!!!
Subject
"Devastation after War

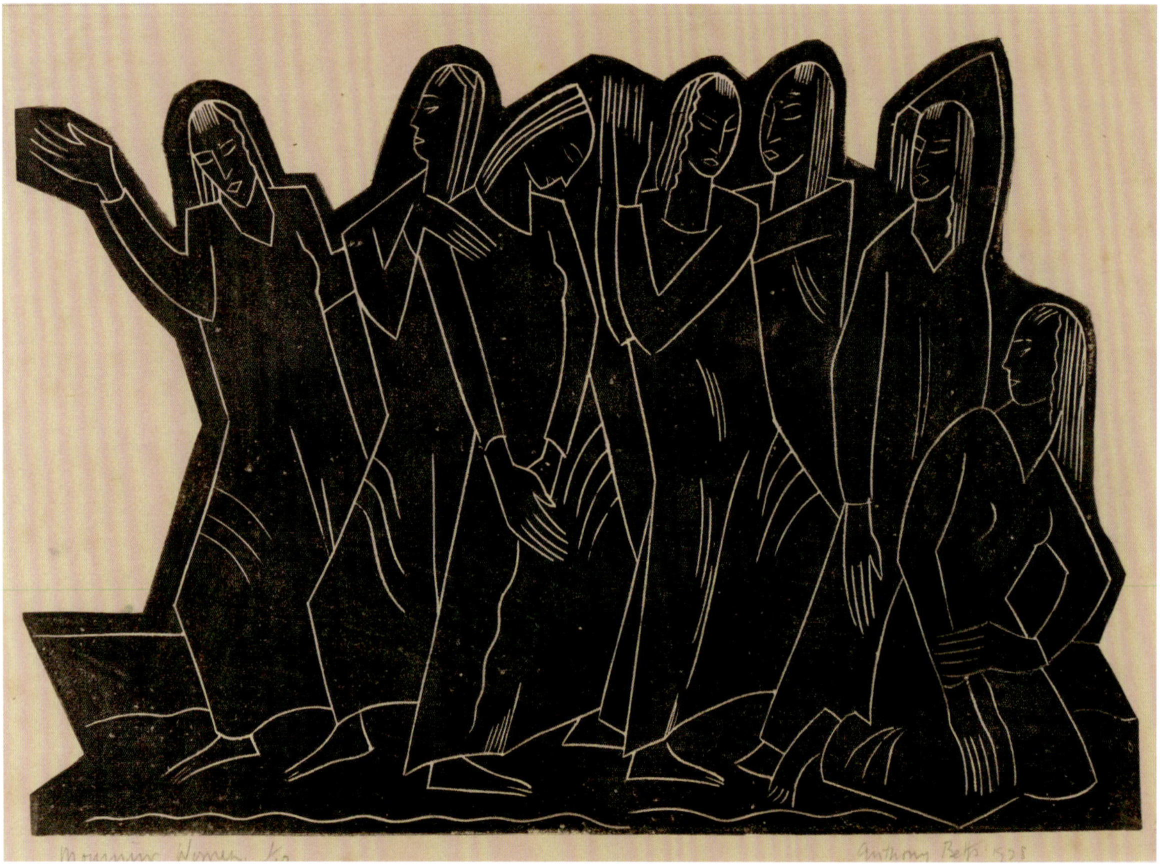

51. James Anthony Betts (1897–1980)

Mourning Women

1928

Wood-engraving, 265 × 407 mm

University of Reading Art Collection

UAC/10772

Inscription: Mourning Women. 1/10 *(bottom left, in pencil)*; Anthony Betts. 1928 *(bottom right, in pencil)*

Provenance: Presented by the family of the artist, 2006.

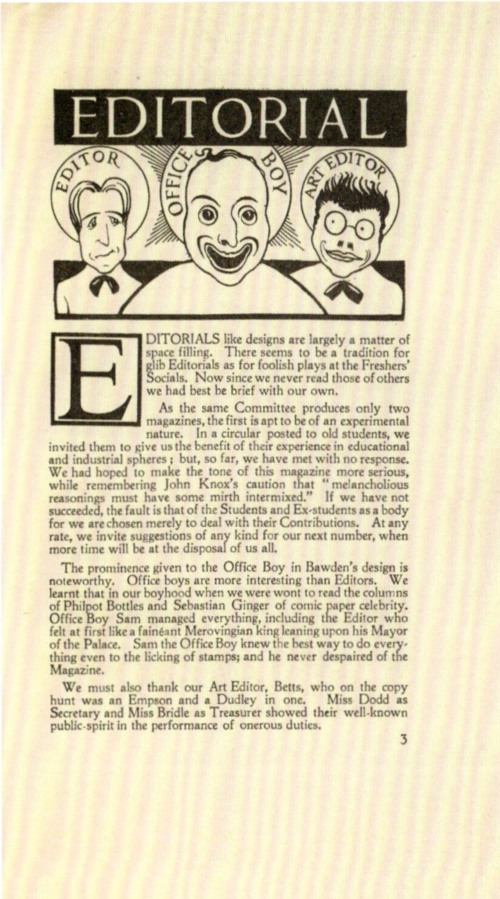
EDITORIAL

EDITORIALS like designs are largely a matter of space filling. There seems to be a tradition for glib Editorials as for foolish plays at the Freshers' Socials. Now since we never read those of others we had best be brief with our own.

As the same Committee produces only two magazines, the first is apt to be of an experimental nature. In a circular posted to old students, we invited them to give us the benefit of their experience in educational and industrial spheres; but, so far, we have met with no response. We had hoped to make the tone of this magazine more serious, while remembering John Knox's caution that "melancholious reasonings must have some mirth intermixed." If we have not succeeded, the fault is that of the Students and Ex-students as a body for we are chosen merely to deal with their Contributions. At any rate, we invite suggestions of any kind for our next number, when more time will be at the disposal of us all.

The prominence given to the Office Boy in Bawden's design is noteworthy. Office boys are more interesting than Editors. We learnt that in our boyhood when we were wont to read the columns of Philpot Bottles and Sebastian Ginger of comic paper celebrity. Office Boy Sam managed everything, including the Editor who felt at first like a fainéant Merovingian king leaning upon his Mayor of the Palace. Sam the Office Boy knew the best way to do everything even to the licking of stamps; and he never despaired of the Magazine.

We must also thank our Art Editor, Betts, who on the copy hunt was an Empson and a Dudley in one. Miss Dodd as Secretary and Miss Bridle as Treasurer showed their well-known public-spirit in the performance of onerous duties.

3

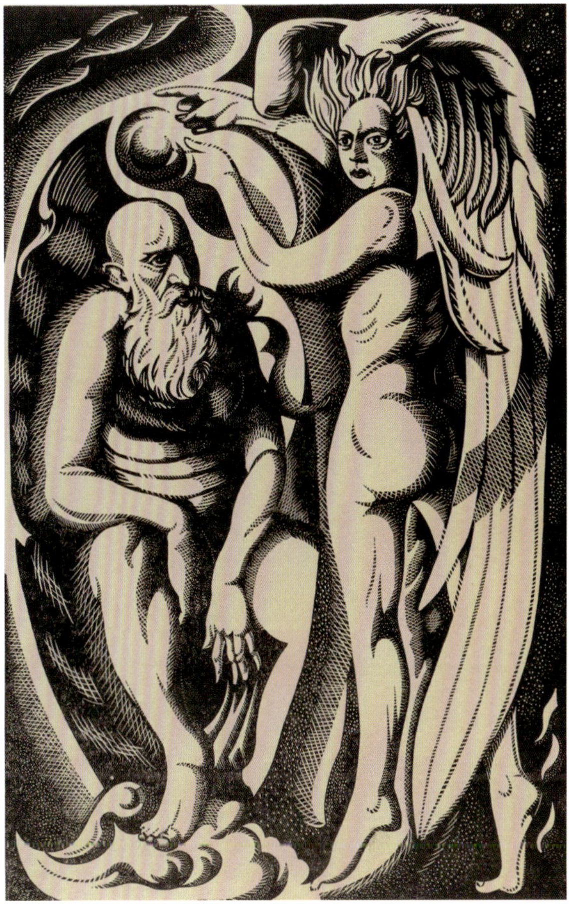

52. The Royal College of Art Student Magazine,

(Vol.2 December 1923. No.7)

The Royal College of Art Archive

53. James Anthony Betts (1897–1980)

Illustration to Milton's Paradise Lost

1938

Wood-engraving, 378 × 255 mm

Private Collection

© Estate of J. Anthony Betts.

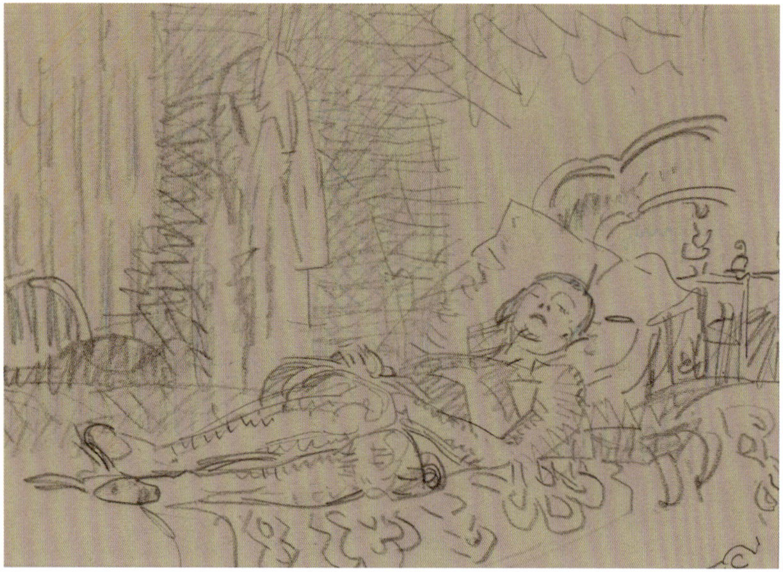

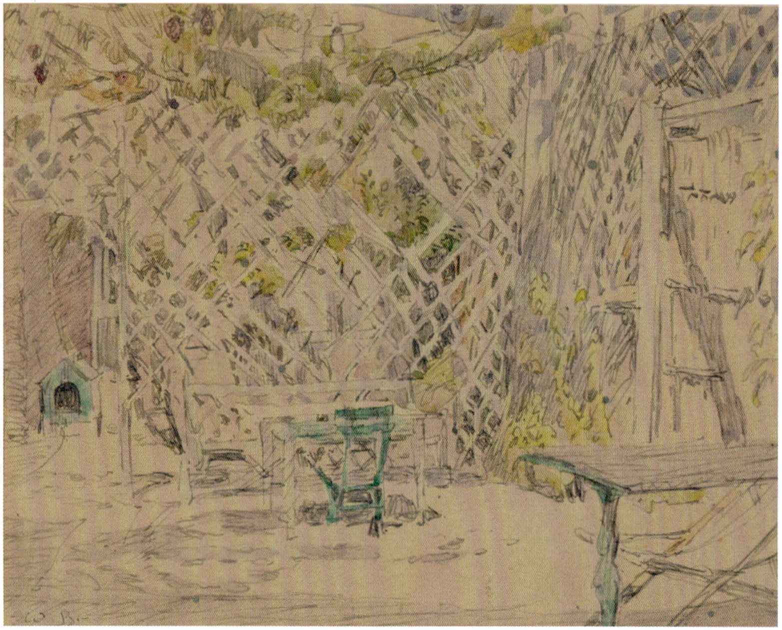

54. Walter Bayes (1869–1956)

Kitty on a Bed

Conté Crayon, 279 × 330 mm

University of Reading Art Collection

UAC/10574

Provenance: Professor James Anthony Betts (1897–1980); Purchased from Paul Betts, 1994.

55. Walter Bayes (1869–1956)

French Garden

Ink and watercolour, 194 × 244 mm

University of Reading Art Collection

UAC/10574

Provenance: Professor James Anthony Betts (1897–1980); Purchased from Paul Betts, 1994.

56. Walter Richard Sickert (1860–1942)

The Little Bed

1902

Pencil and chalk, 238 × 315 mm

University of Reading Art Collection

UAC/10520

Inscription: Sickert-Neuville 1902 *(bottom left, in ink)*; 13 *(right side of image, in crayon)*

Provenance: Professor James Anthony Betts (1897–1980); Purchased from Paul Betts, 1994.

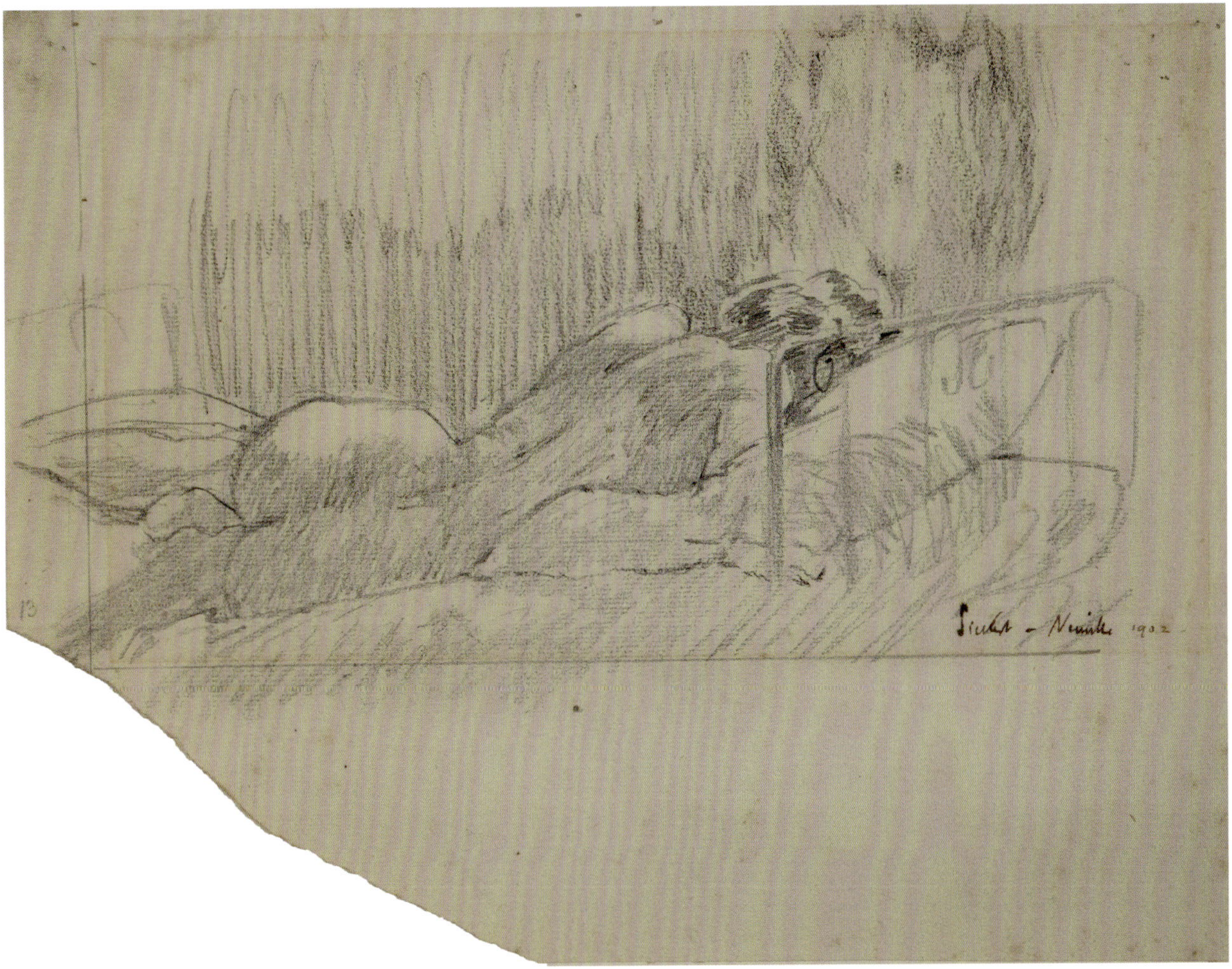
Sickert – Neuville 1902

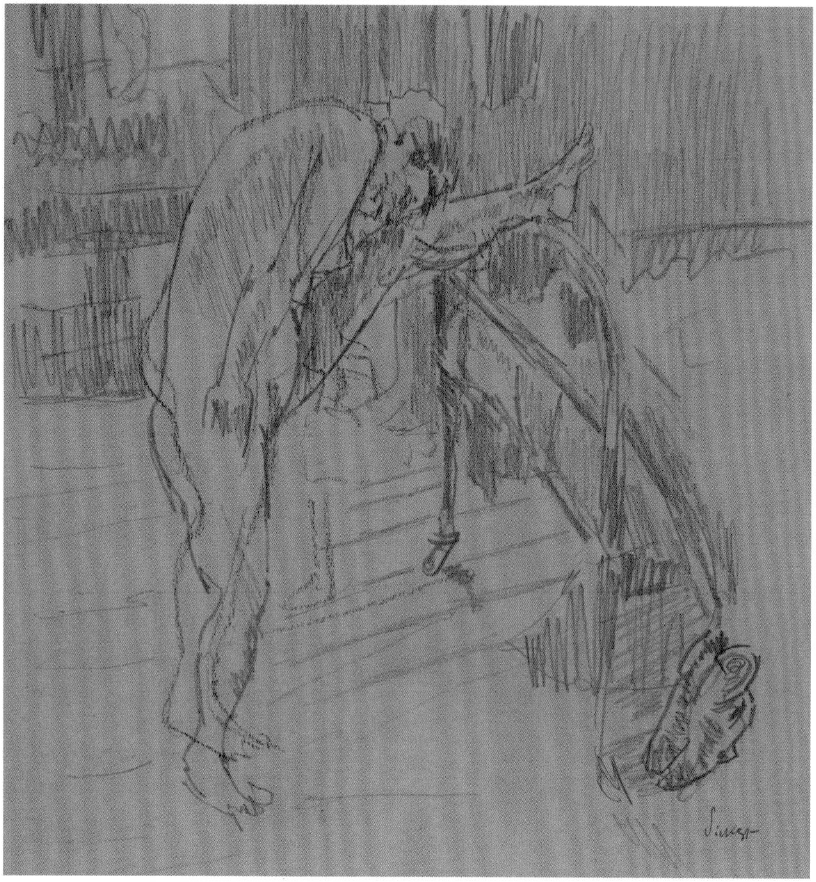

57. Walter Richard Sickert (1860–1942)

Practice

*c.*1909

Pencil and chalk, 379 × 284 mm

University of Reading Art Collection

UAC/10538

Inscription: Sickert *(bottom right, signed, in ink)*; 23 *(bottom centre, in crayon, in circle)*; RU5 *(verso, bottom right, in pencil)*; 6 *(verso, bottom right, in pencil)*

Provenance: Purchased from Leicester Galleries, London, 20 September 1955.

58. Walter Richard Sickert (1860–1942)

Marie Seated on a Bed

*c.*1911–1912

Pencil, chalk and white heightening on grey paper, 380 × 282 mm

University of Reading Art Collection

UAC/10536

Inscription: The discussion *(bottom centre, in chalk)*; Sickert *(bottom right, signed, in ink)*; Sickert *(bottom right, signed, under image, in ink)*; 6 *(bottom right, in chalk)*

Provenance: Purchased from Leicester Galleries, London, 6 June 1953.

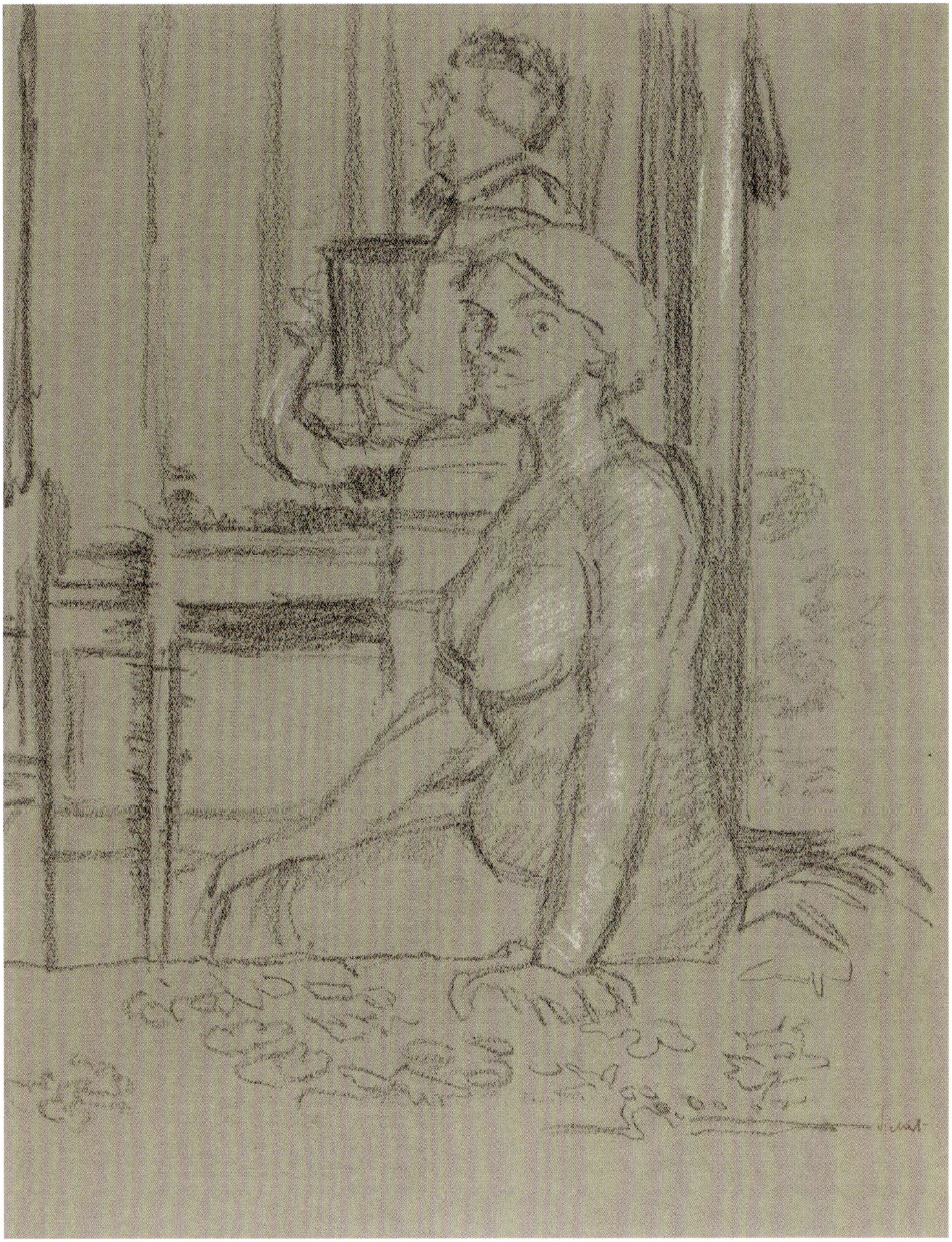

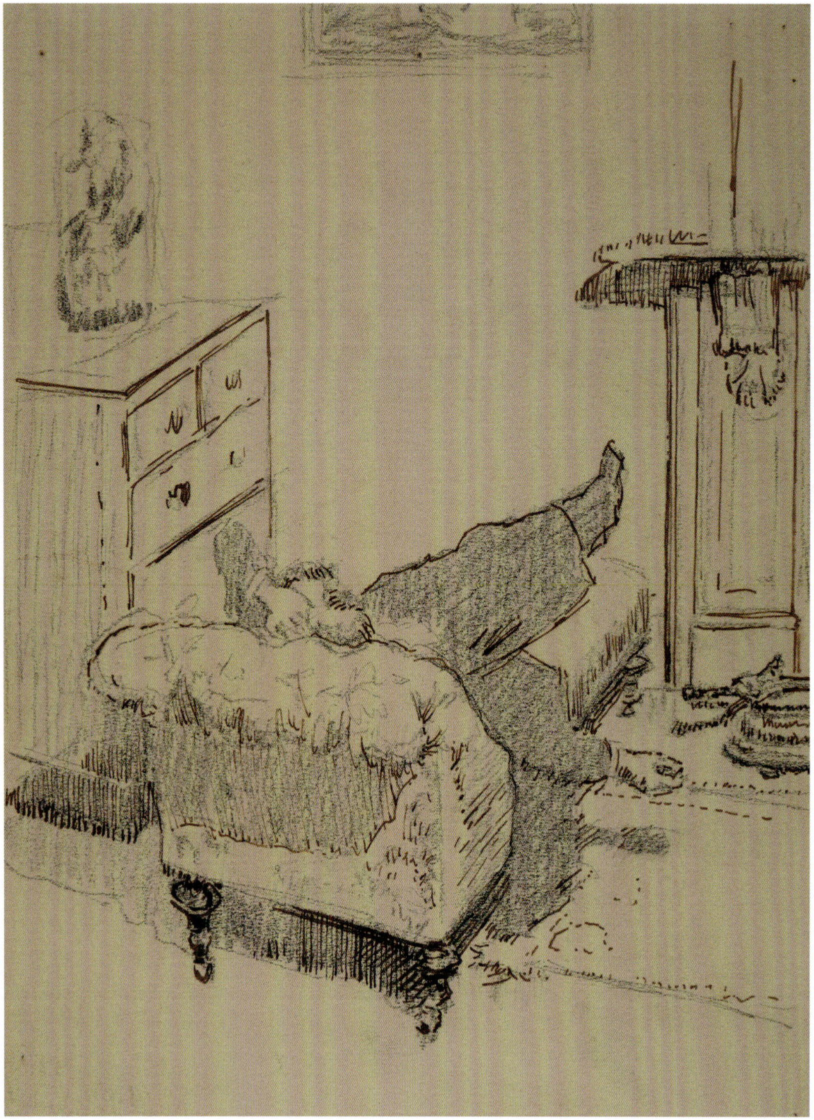

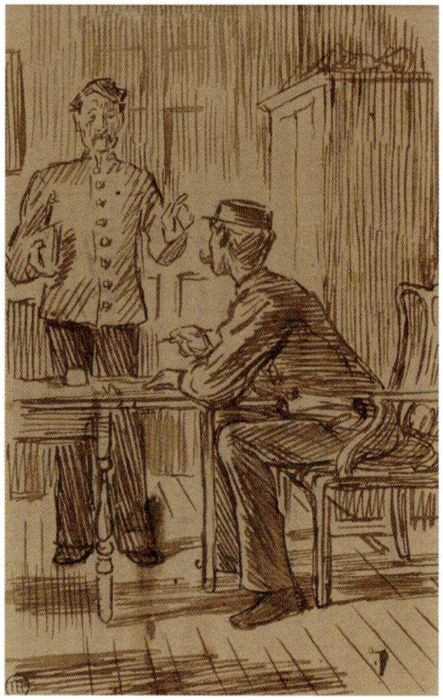

59. Walter Richard Sickert (1860–1942)

Woman Lying on a Couch (Study for Ennui)

*c.*1912

Chalk and ink, 382 × 280 mm

University of Reading Art Collection
UAC/10524

Inscription: upstairs etching *(verso, top centre, in pencil)*

Provenance: Stubbing; Purchased from Roland, Browse & Delbanco, London, 1 July 1957.

60. Charles Keene (1823–1891)

Soldier Talking to an Officer in the Orderly Room

Ink, 180 × 114 mm

University of Reading Art Collection
UAC/10555

Inscription: TAL *(bottom left, collector's mark, stamped in ink)*

Provenance: Thomas Esmond Lowinsky (1892–1947) (Lugt 2420a); Sold Leicester Galleries, November 1952; Professor James Anthony Betts (1897-1980); Purchased from Paul Betts, 1994.

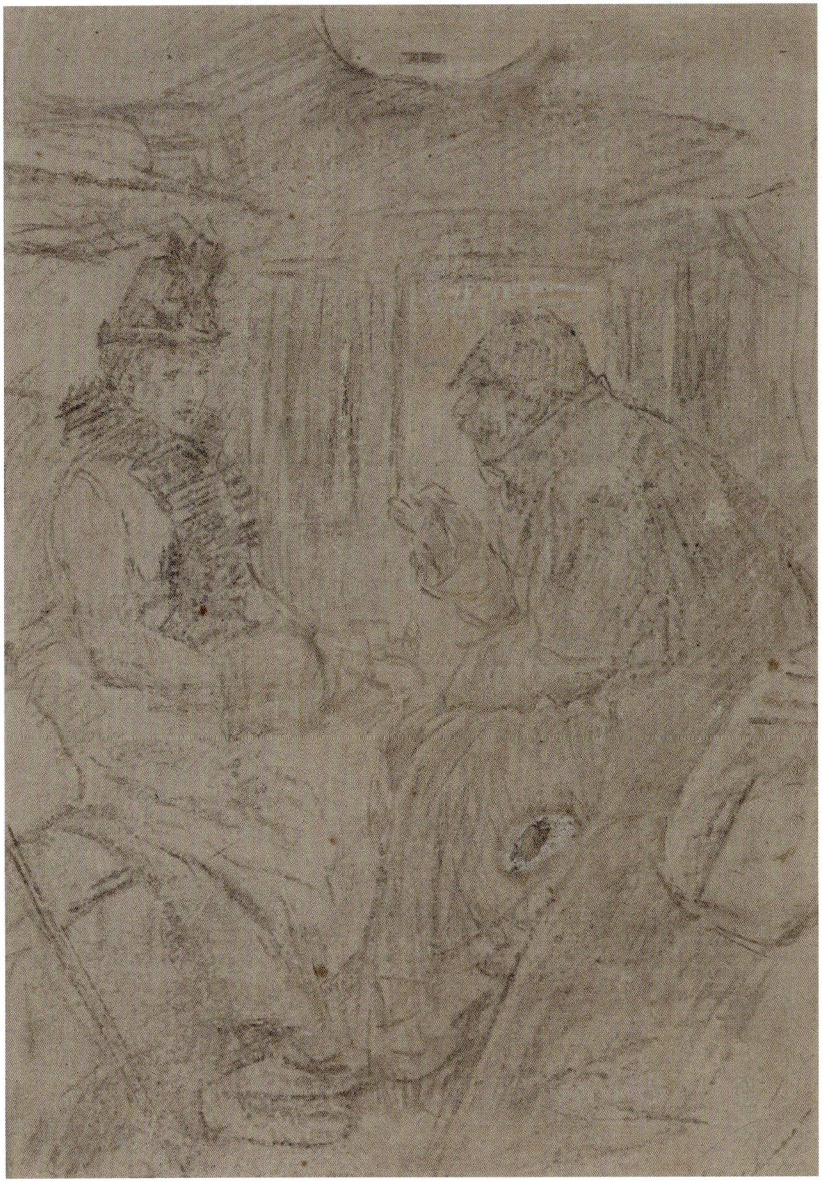

61. Charles Keene (1823–1891)

Number One

1888

Chalk and heightening on paper prepared with a white ground, 191 × 151 mm

University of Reading Art Collection

UAC/10557

Inscription: mount – show inscription *(right edge, in ink)*; TAL *(bottom right, collector's mark, stamped in ink)*; J. Crawhall *(bottom left, on paper affixed to sheet, in ink)*; Mar. 20/ 1888 *(bottom left, on paper affixed to sheet, in ink)*; from C. Keene *(bottom left, in ink)*; Number One/ Bridegroom *(on their way to Paris)* – "You are sure you're quite warm and comfortable/ love!"....Bride "Oh yes, Dear – Quite."/ Bridegroom " I don't like to see you sitting with your back to the engine, dar/ ling. You don't feel any draught!"...Bride "Oh, not the slightest!"/ Bridegroom *(who does!)* "Then, sweetest, would you mind changing places -!!!"*(bottom, on paper affixed to sheet and backboard, printed in ink)*

Provenance: Thomas Esmond Lowinsky (1892–1947) (Lugt 2420a); Sold Leicester Galleries, November 1952; Professor James Anthony Betts (1897–1980); Purchased from Paul Betts, 1994.

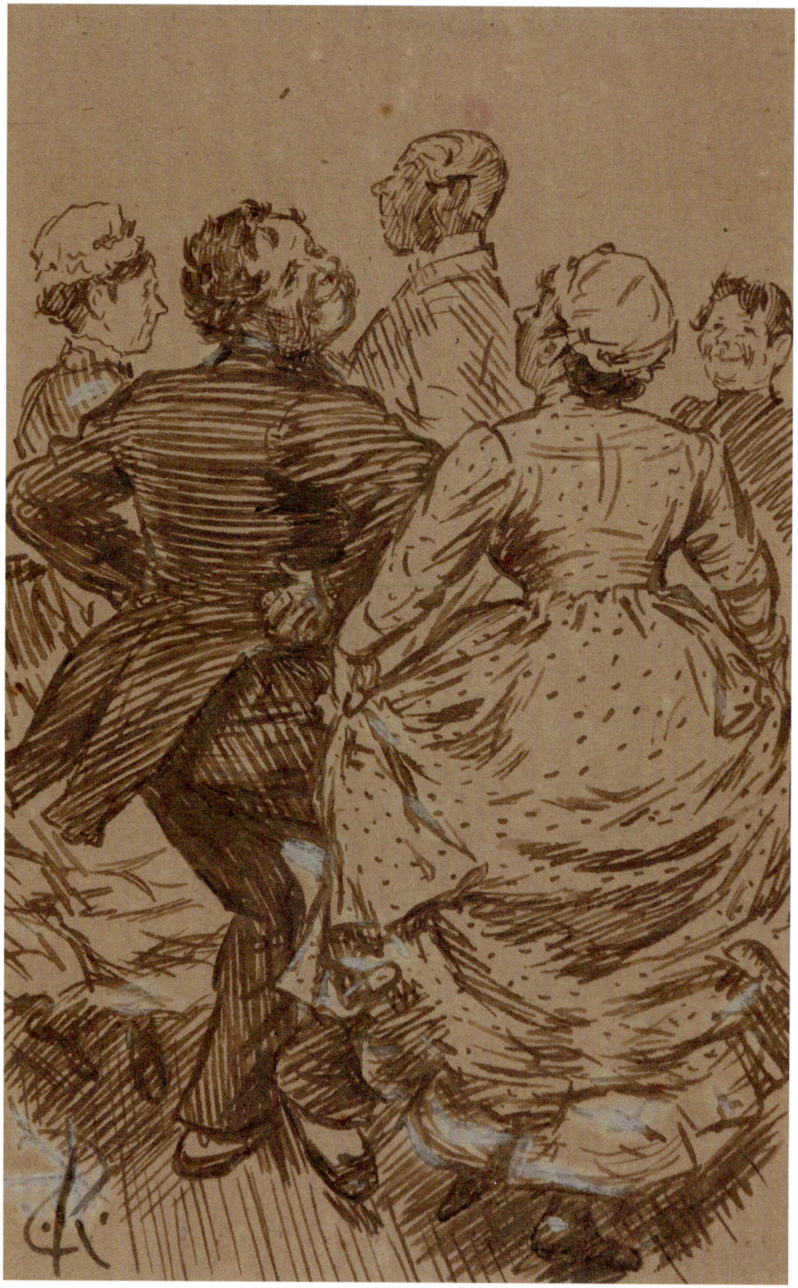

62. Charles Keene (1823–1891)

Robert, at Cook's Little Swarry

1886

Ink and white heightening, 177 × 107 mm

University of Reading Art Collection

UAC/10575

Inscription: CK *(bottom left, signed, in ink)*; Robert at the Servants 'all *(top centre, in pencil)*; As large as you can *(bottom left, in pencil)*; A 13387 *(bottom right, in pencil)*; A 13387 *(verso, top left corner, in pencil)*; 337 *(verso, top left, in pencil)*; The Servant's Ball *(verso, in centre, in pencil, crossed out)*; Robert, at Cook's "Little Swarry"/ (Punch, Oct. 1886) *(verso, in centre, in pencil)*

Provenance: Professor James Anthony Betts (1897–1980); Purchased from Paul Betts, 1994.

63. Spencer Frederick Gore (1878–1914)

Ballet at the Alhambra; (verso) Dancing Figures

Pastel, 223 × 278 mm

University of Reading Art Collection

UAC/10566

Provenance: Professor Donald J. Gordon (died 1977); Gift of Professor James Anthony Betts (1897–1980).

64. Spencer Frederick Gore (1878–1914)

Dancing Figures: (verso) Landscape in Black and Yellow

Pastel, 206 × 279 mm

University of Reading Art Collection

UAC/10547

Provenance: Professor James Anthony Betts (1897–1980); Purchased from Paul Betts, 1994.

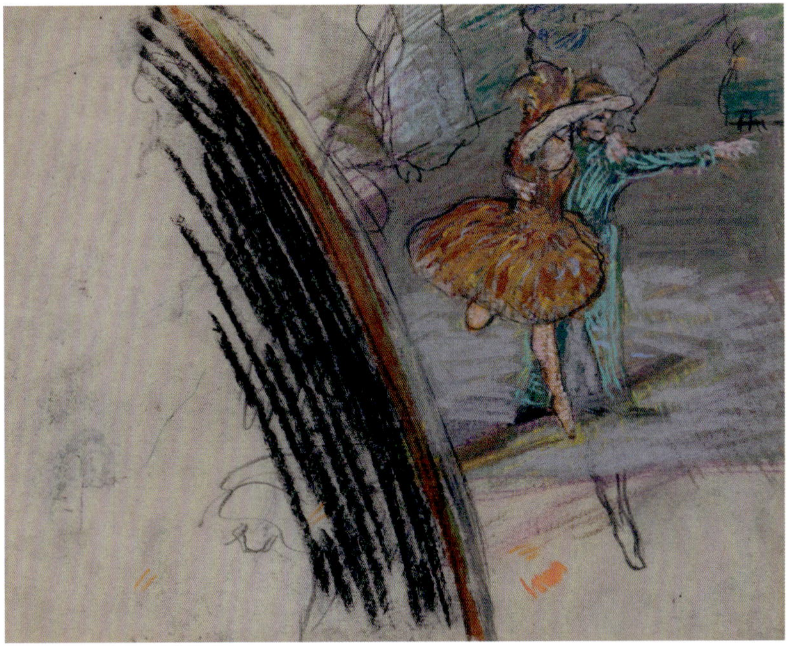

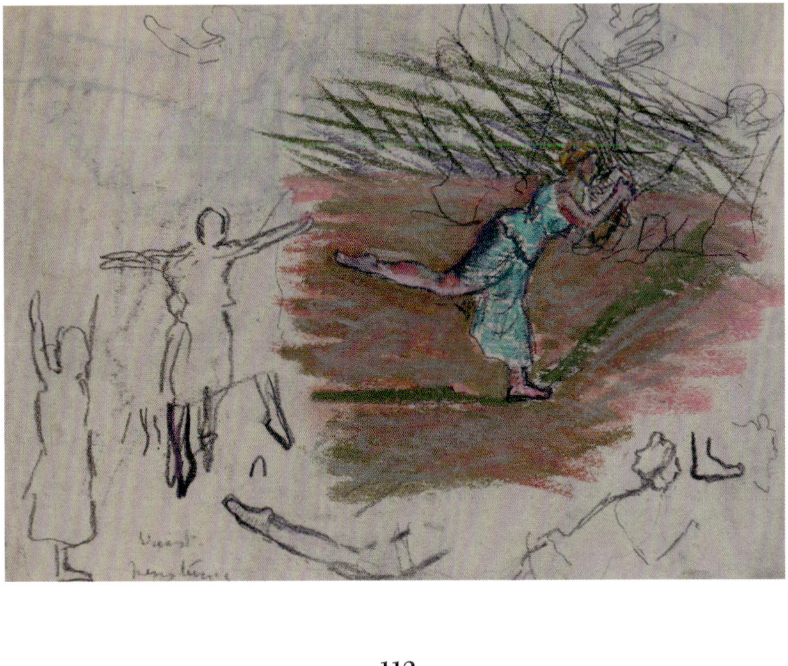

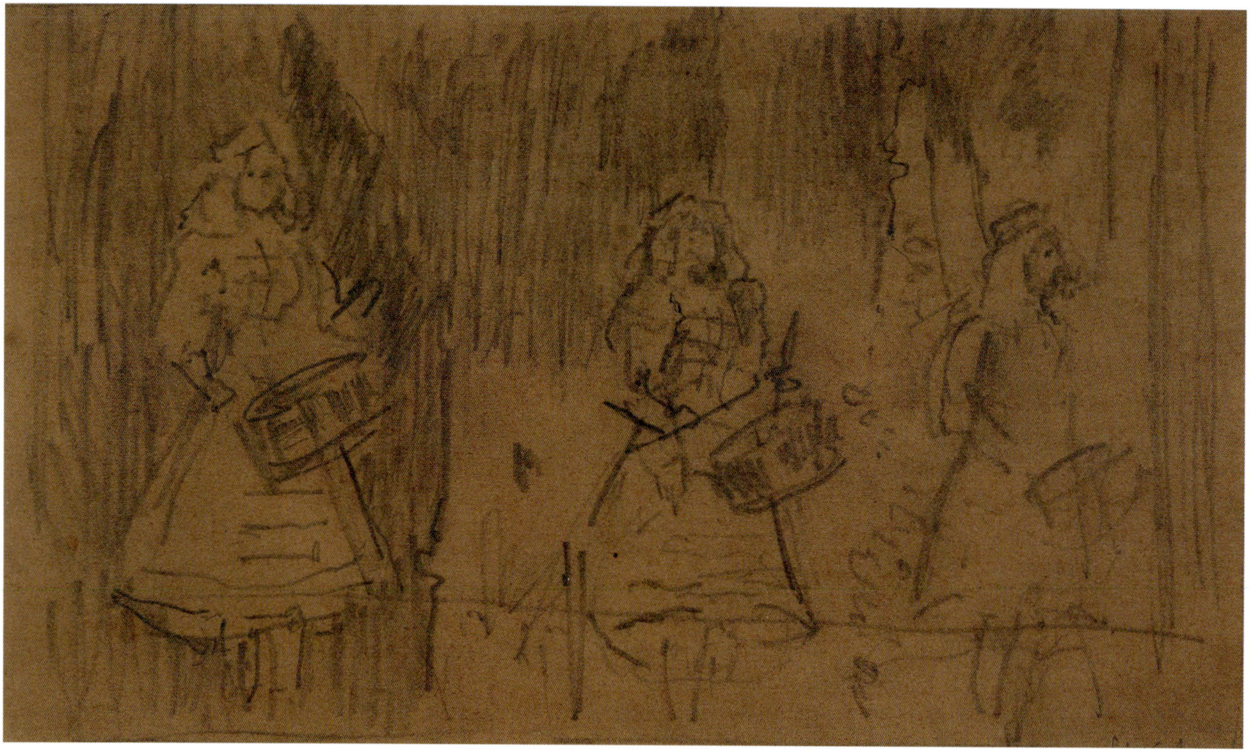

65. Walter Richard Sickert (1860–1942)

The Three Drummers (The Sisters X)

*c.*1890

Pencil, 255 × 328 mm

University of Reading Art Collection

UAC/10532

Inscription: Sickert *(bottom right, signed, in ink)*; Sickert W. Richard *(bottom right, in ink)*; Sickert Old Bedford *(bottom right, in ink)*; The Drummer Trio *(bottom centre, in chalk)*; 7 by 11/ 47 *(bottom left, in pencil)*

Provenance: Purchased from Leicester Galleries, London, 10 July 1953.

66. Walter Richard Sickert (1860–1942)

The New Oxford Music Hall (The New Bedford)

*c.*1907–1908

Pencil, 114 × 179 mm

University of Reading Art Collection

UAC/10522

Inscription: Sickert New Oxford *(bottom left and centre, signed, in ink)*

Provenance: Robinson Firster; Purchased from Roland, Browse & Delbanco, London, 4 January 1955.

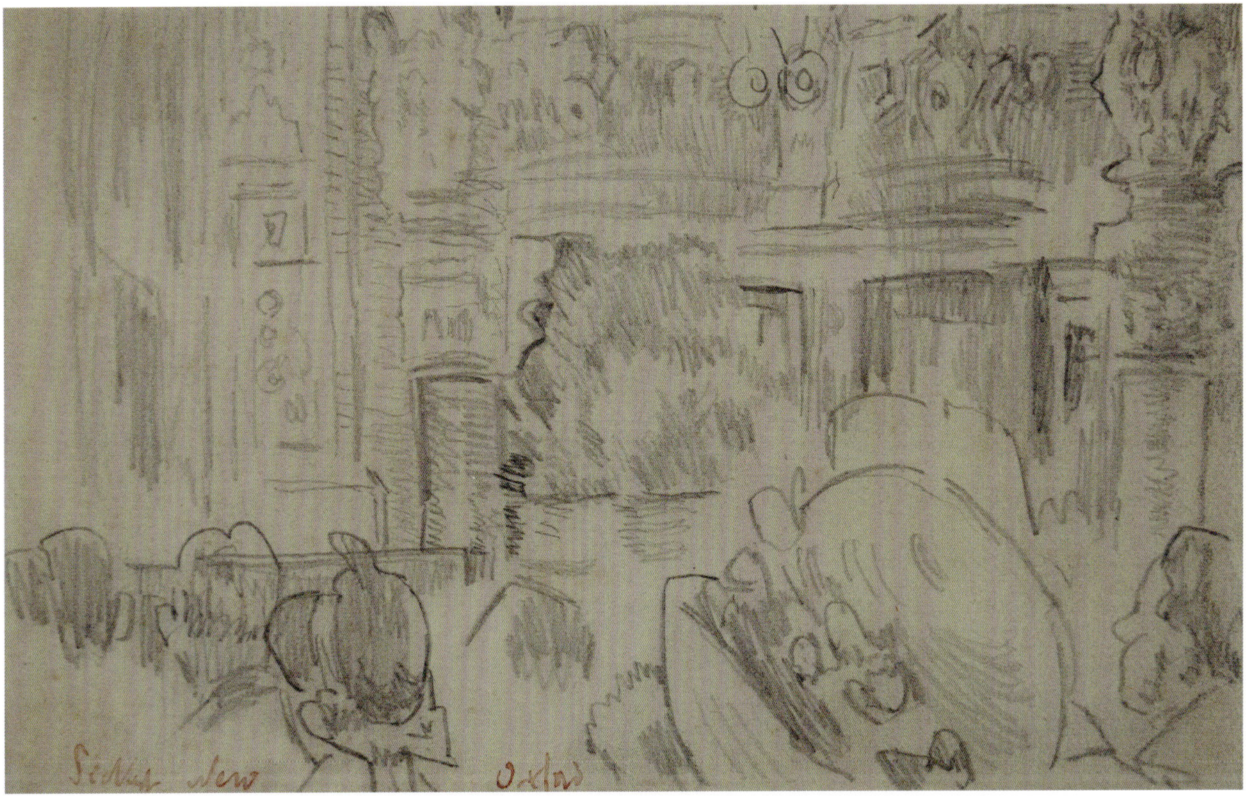

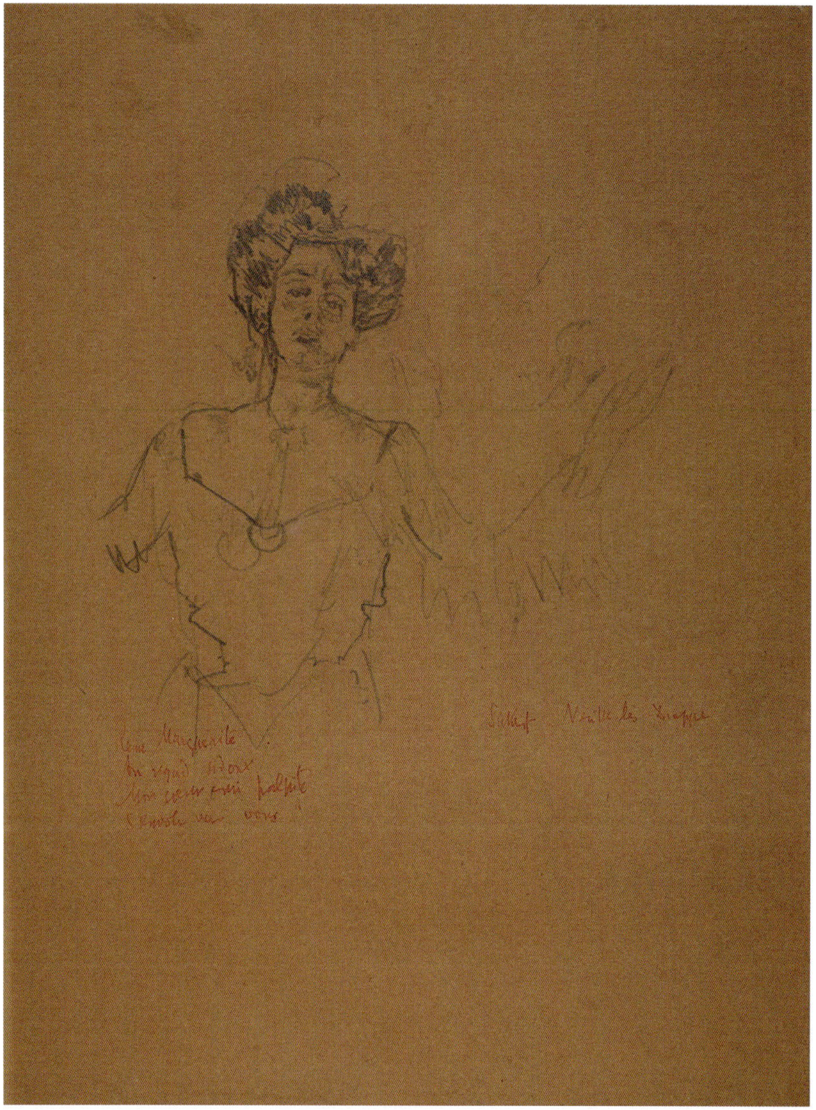

67. Walter Richard Sickert (1860–1942)

Café Chanteuse (Woman singing)

*c.*1904

Pencil, 324 × 235 mm

University of Reading Art Collection

UAC/10531

Inscription: Sickert - Neuville les Dieppe *(bottom right, signed, in ink)*; Reine Marguerite/ Au Regard si doux/ Mon coeur qui palpite/ S'envoie vers vous. [Queen Marguerite/ with gentle glance/ my heart beats/ flies towards you] *(bottom left, in ink)*

Provenance: Professor James Anthony Betts (1897–1980); Purchased from Paul Betts, 1994.

68. Walter Richard Sickert (1860–1942)

The Middlesex

*c.*1888–1889

Pencil, 310 × 238 mm

University of Reading Art Collection

UAC/10521

Inscription: Sickert Middlesex *(bottom right, in ink)*

Provenance: Graham; Purchased from Roland, Browse & Delbanco, London, 18 May 1957.

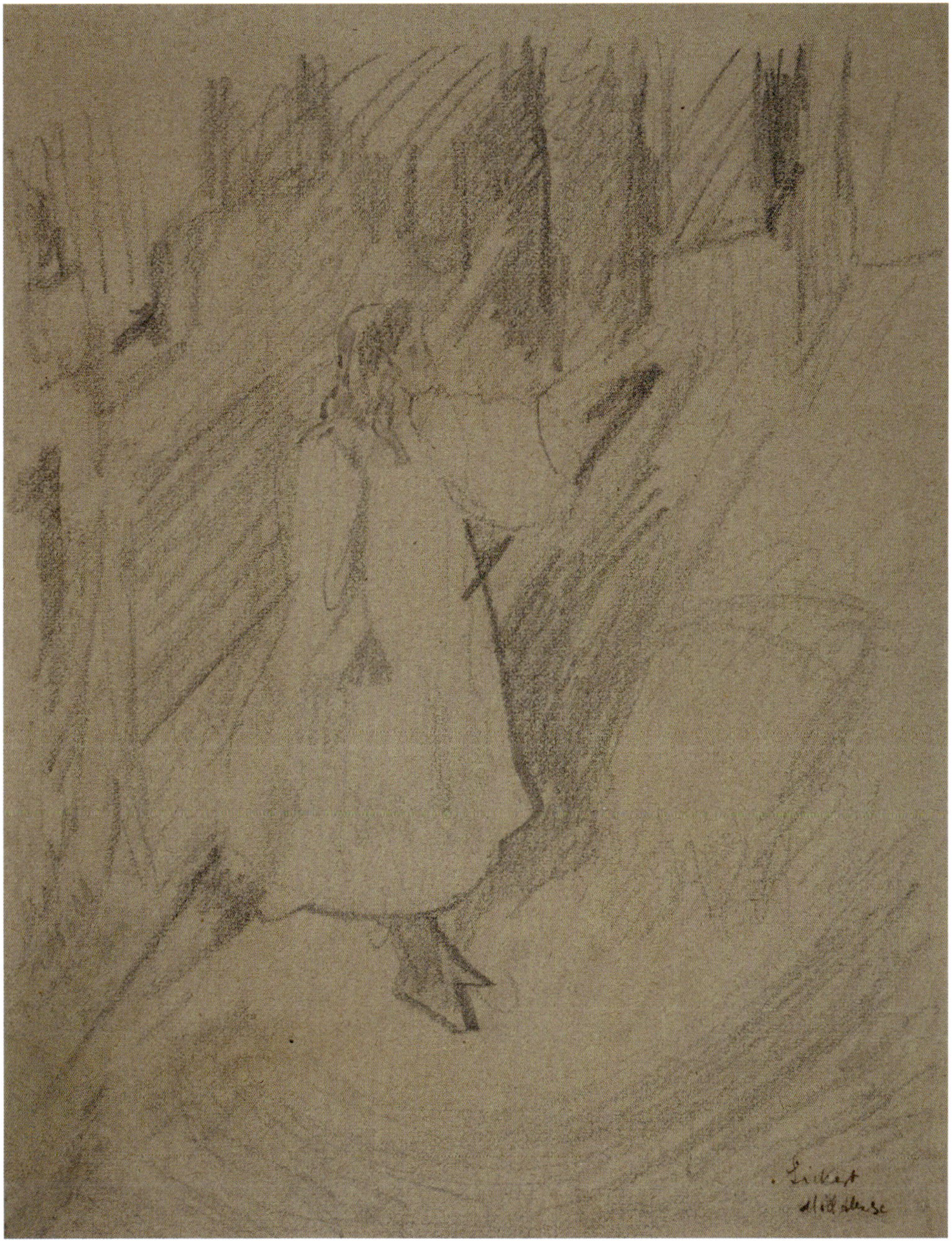

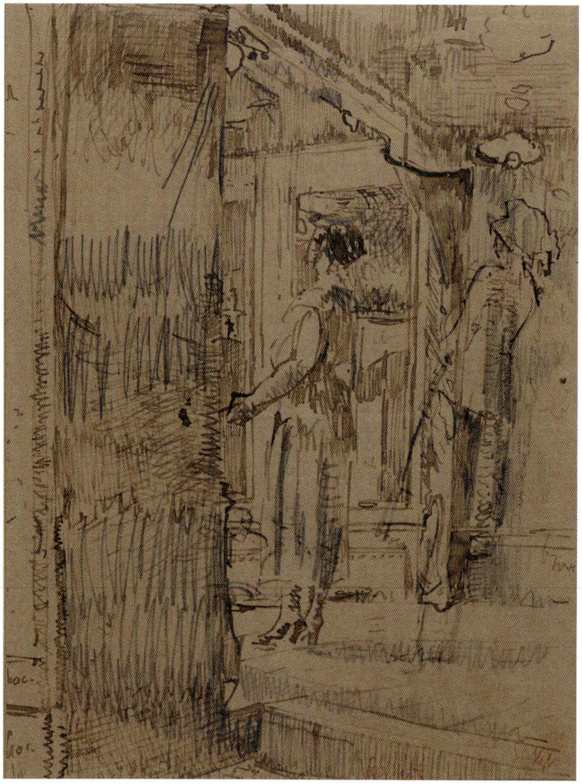

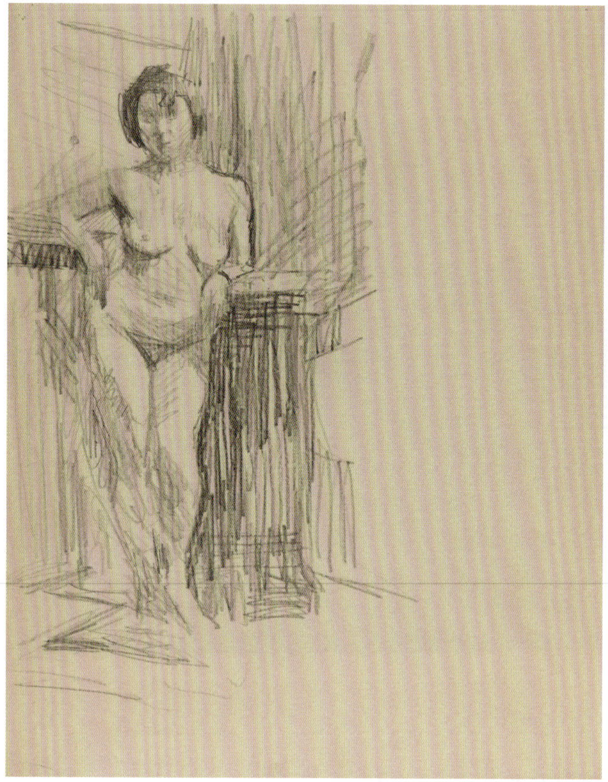

69. Walter Richard Sickert (1860–1942)

Vernets (Study for "Au Caboulet au Bout du Quai")

*c.*1920

Pencil, ink and wash, 280 × 229 mm

Reading Museum 1942.9.1

Inscription: Sickert *(bottom right, signed, in red ink)*; Vernets *(bottom centre-right, in ink)*; colour notes bottom left.

Provenance: Purchased from Leicester Galleries, 1942.

70. James Anthony Betts (1897–1980)

Standing Female Nude

Conté crayon, 478 × 383 mm

University of Reading Art Collection

UAC/10779

Provenance: Gift of the family of the artist, 2006.

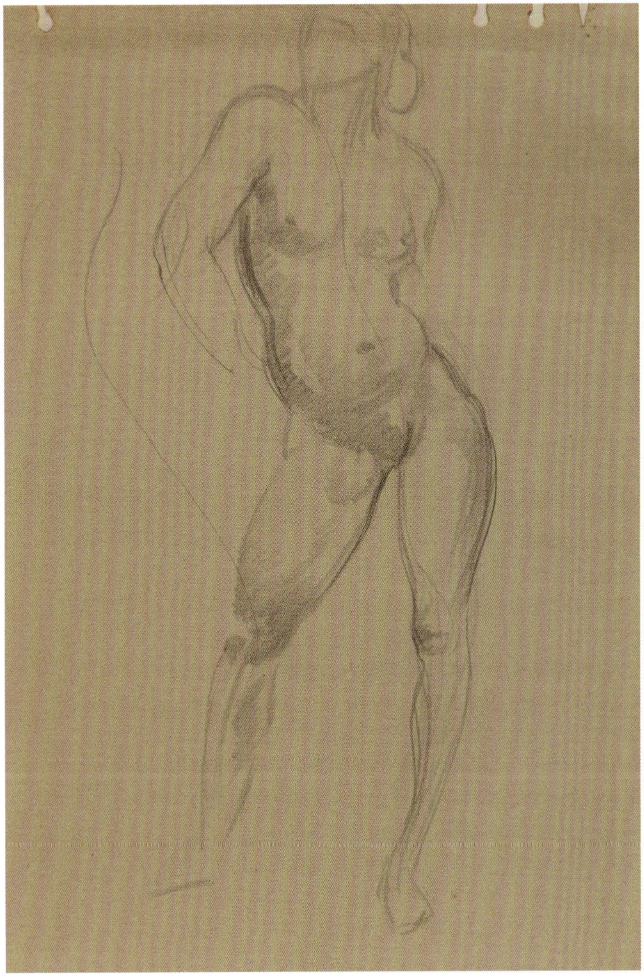

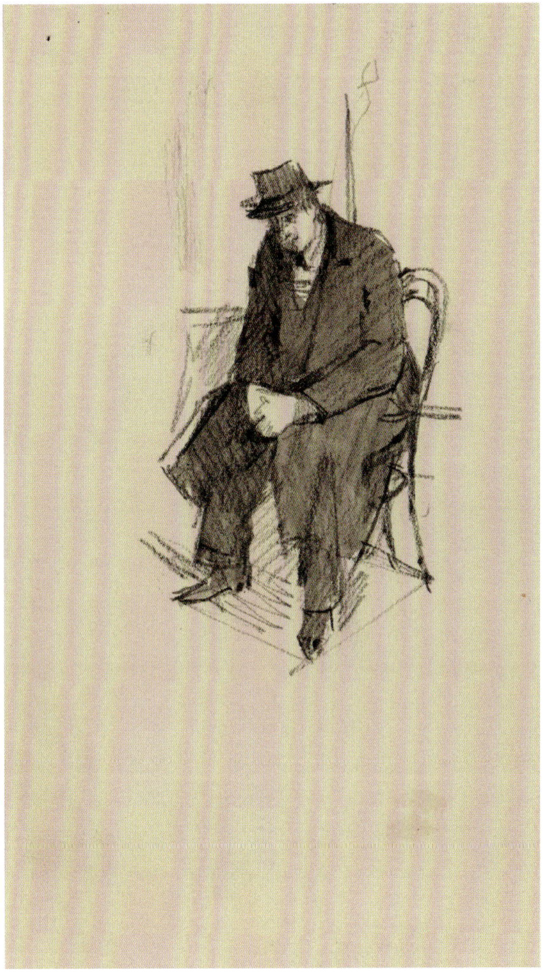

71. Robert Gibbings (1889–1958)
Nude Study
*c.*1950s
Pencil, 400 × 280 mm
Private Collection

72. Harry Redman (1920–1994)
Man Sitting on a Stool
Charcoal and ink, 220 × 134 mm
Private Collection

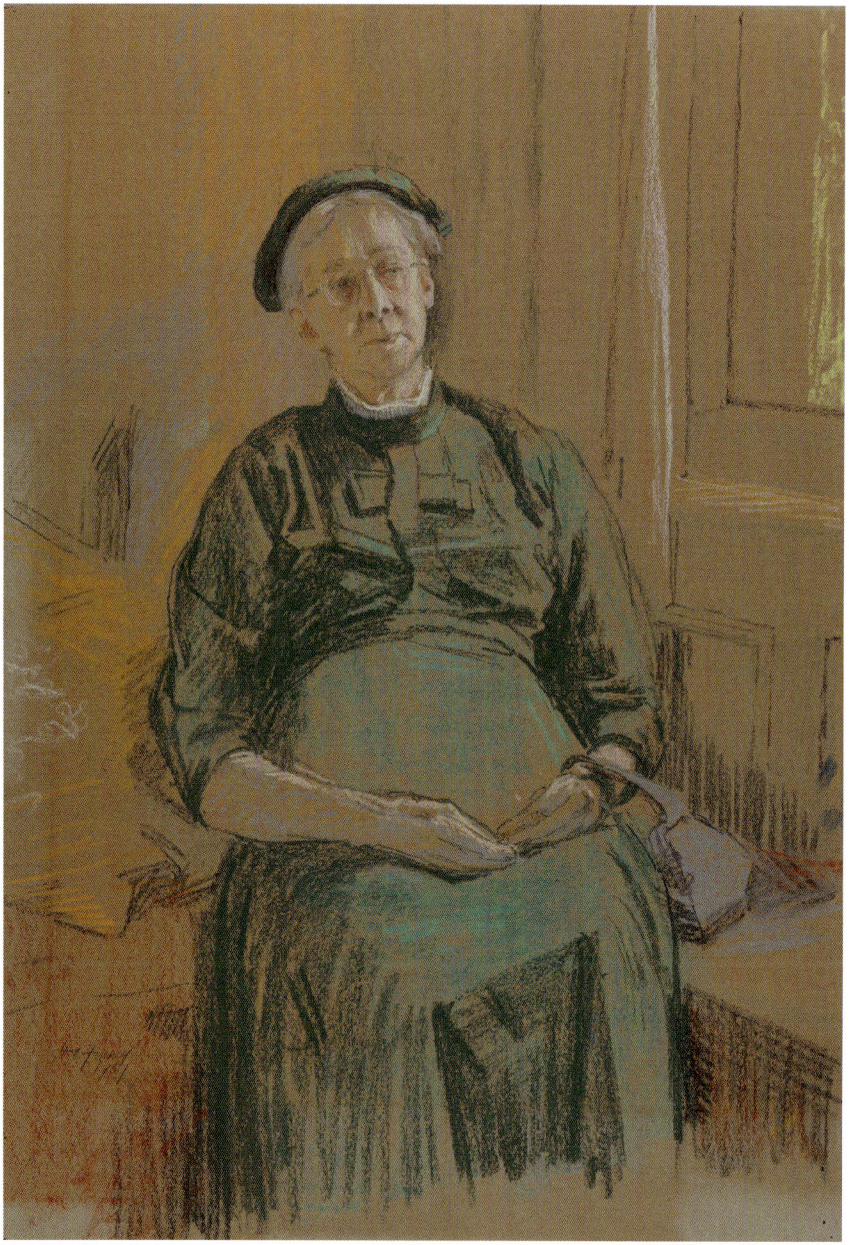

73. Hugh Finney (1905–1991)

Miss E M Skrimshire

1957

Pastel, 550 × 394 mm

Reading Museum 1958.241.1

Provenance: Purchased from the artist, 1958.

74. Hugh Finney (1905–1991)

Reclining Female Nude

Conté crayon on Japanese paper, 280 × 409 mm

Private Collection

Inscription: Study of nude in Conte crayon/ no 443 *(verso, top left, in pencil)*

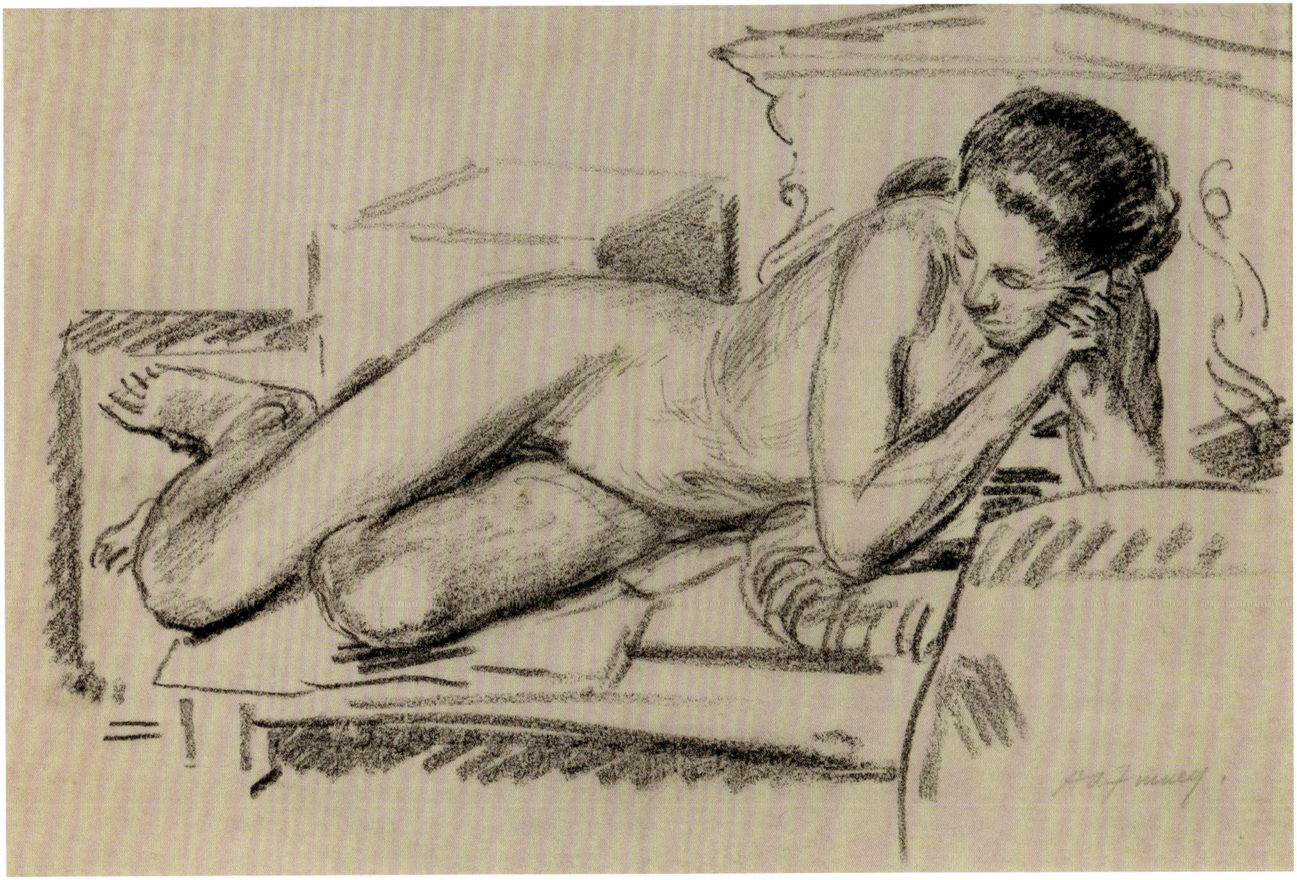

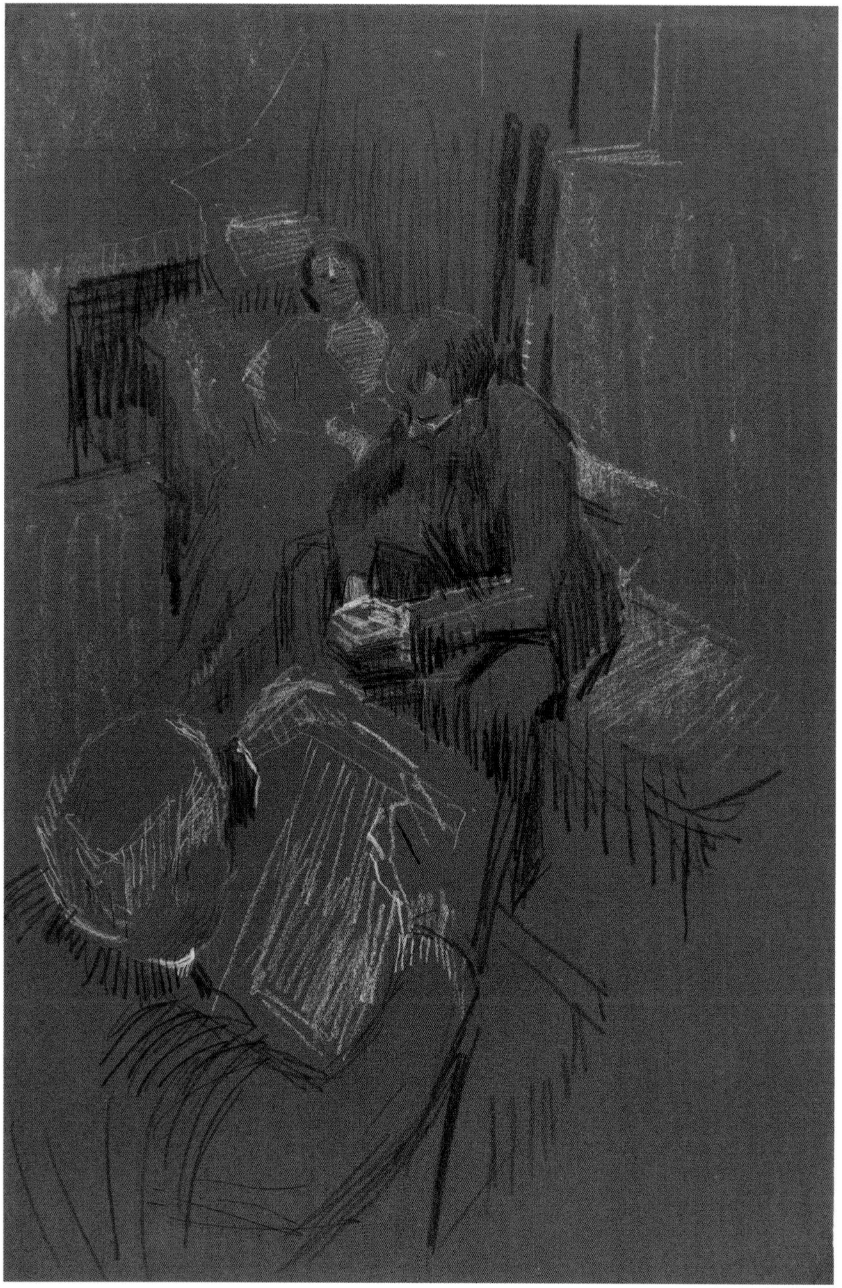

75. Anthony Harris (b.1931)

Professor Betts in a Life Drawing Class

1952

Conté crayon on grey paper, 560 × 386 mm

Collection of the Artist

76. Anthony Harris (b.1931)

Man Sitting on a Bed (University of Reading School of Art)

1952

Conté crayon on grey paper, 215 × 315 mm

Collection of the Artist

Inscription: Last Term 1952 *(bottom right, in pencil)*

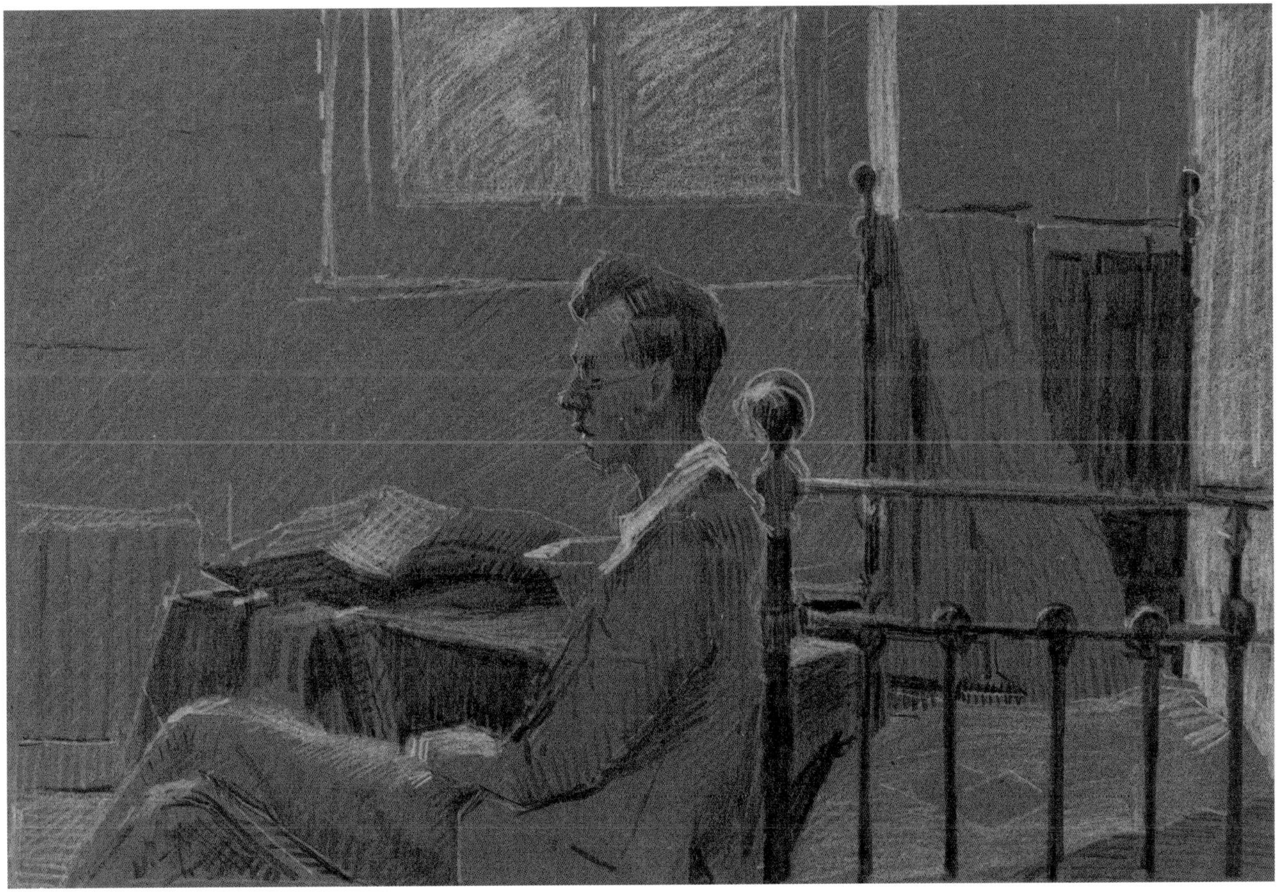

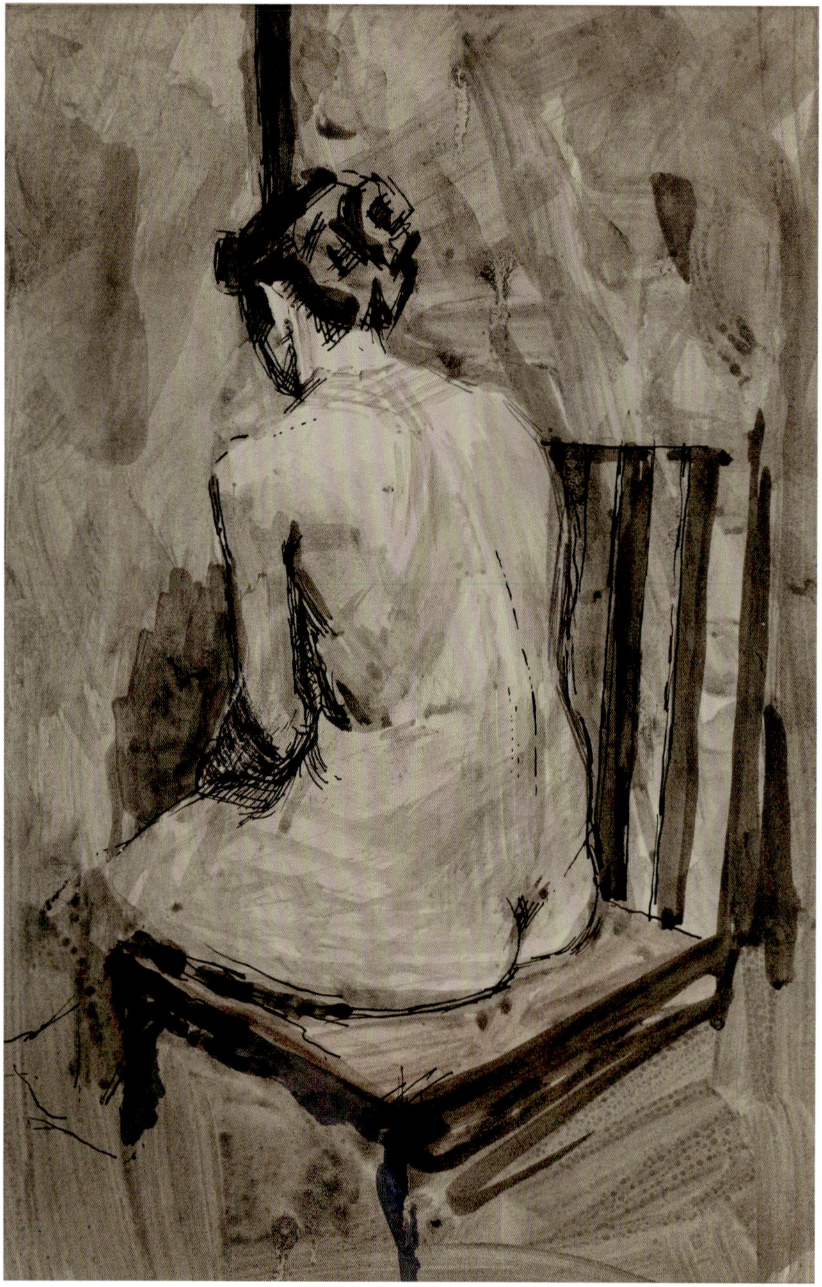

77. Clive Ashwin (b.1937)
Woman Seated on a Chair
1960
Ink and wash, 271 × 181 mm
Collection of the Artist
© The Artist.

78. Michael Twyman (b.1934)
Nude Model in the Life Room
1953-1957
Pencil, 508 × 383 mm
Collection of the Artist
© The Artist.

79. Michael Twyman (b.1934)
Portrait Study of Female Model in a Coat
1953-1957
Conté crayon and ink wash, 385 × 290 mm
Collection of the Artist
© The Artist.

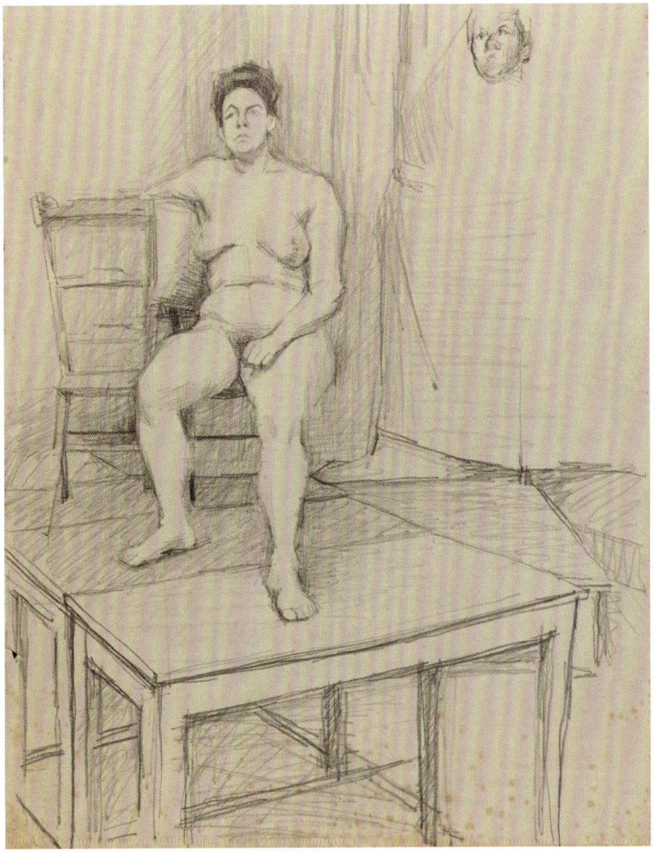

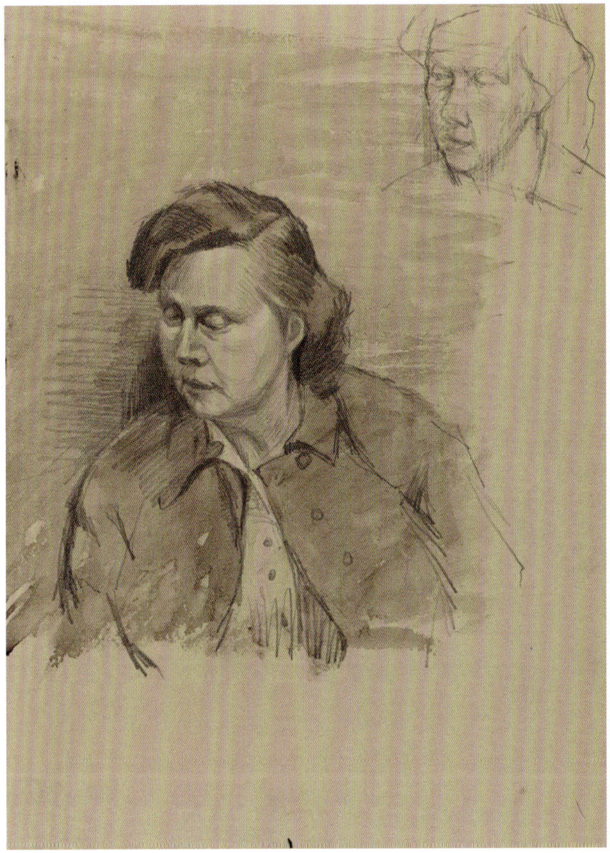

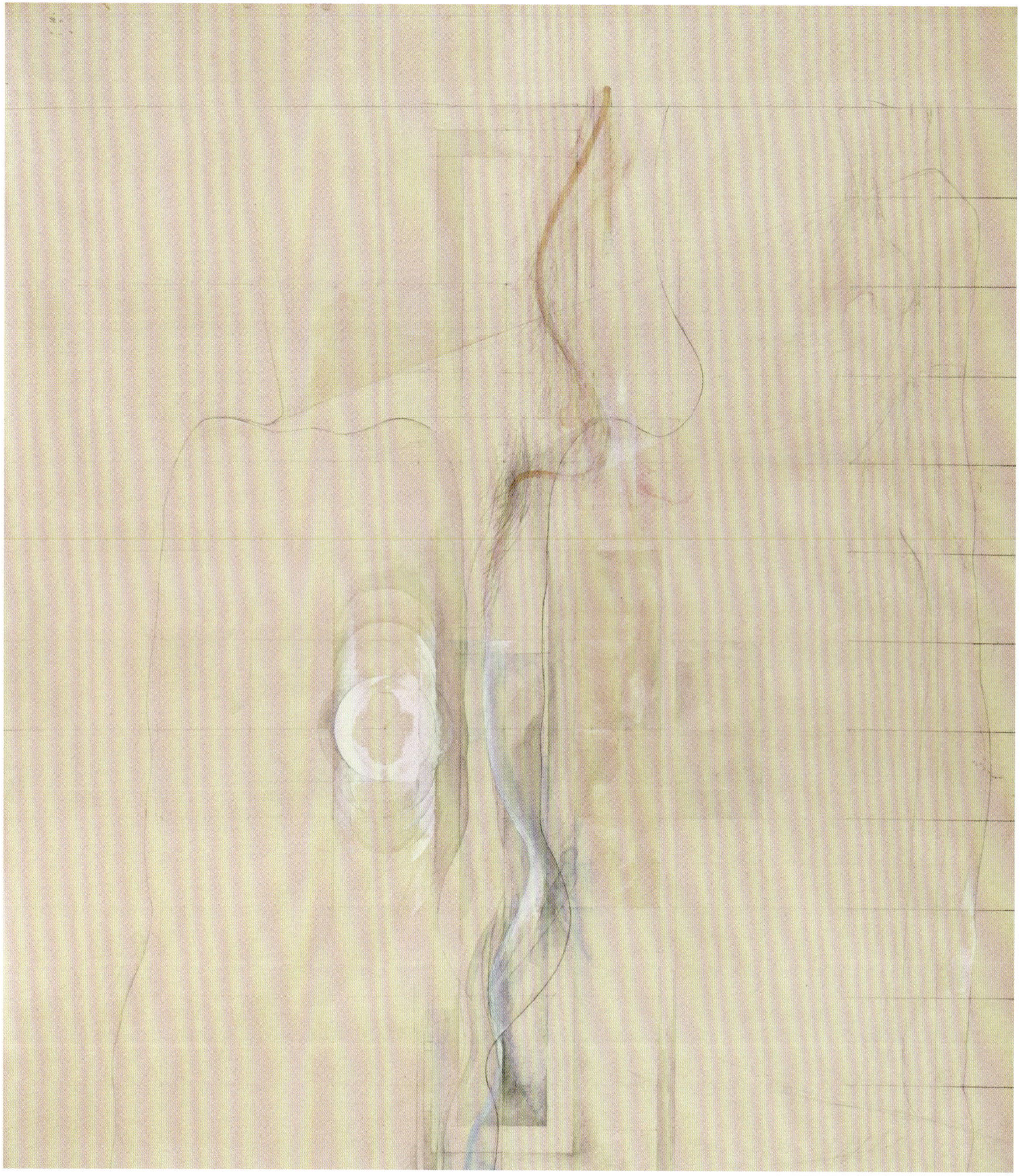

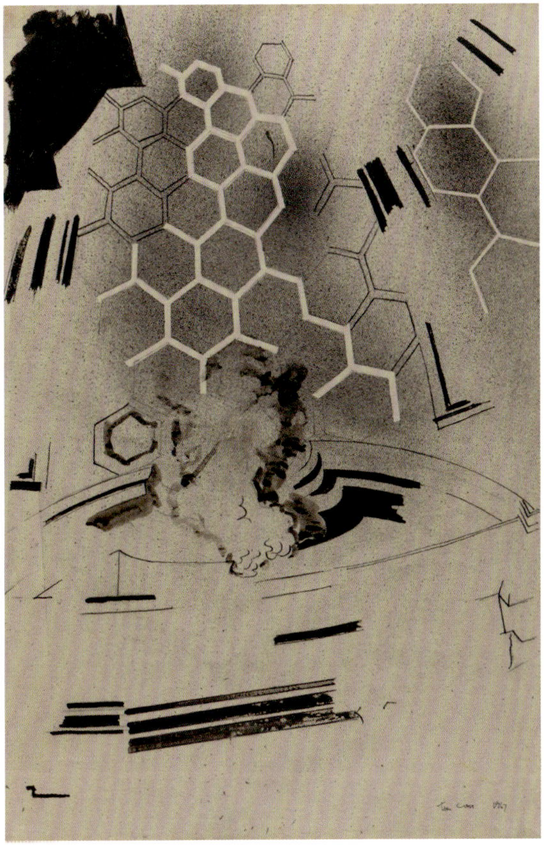

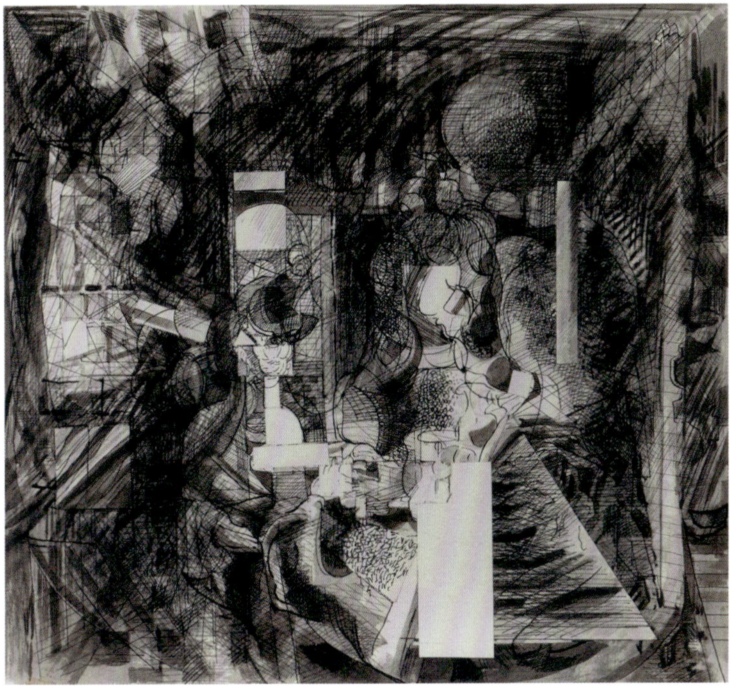

80. Rita Donagh (b. 1939)

Life Size (Transitional Drawing for "Reflection on Three Weeks in May 1970")

1971

Pencil and watercolour, 1720 × 1530 mm

Art Council Collection AC 1385

Provenance: Purchased from Nigel Greenwood Inc Ltd, 5 April 1974.

81. Tom Cross (1931–2009)

San Andreas

1967

Ink on board, 620 × 430 mm

Reading Museum 2001.250.1

Inscription: Tom Cross 1967 *(bottom right, in ink)*; San Andreas 1967 *(verso, bottom centre, in pencil)*

Provenance: Purchased for the Reading Museum Schools Loan Collection, late 1960s.

82. Martin Froy (1926–2017)

At the Table

1982

Ink and collage, 560 × 620 mm

Reading Museum 1986.133.1

Provenance: Purchased by Reading Foundation for Art from the artist, 1982.

Index of Artists